D1015804

REMARKS ON THE USE AND ABUSE OF
SOME POLITICAL TERMS

GEORGE CORNEWALL LEWIS

REMARKS

ON THE USE AND ABUSE OF

SOME POLITICAL TERMS

BY

GEORGE CORNEWALL LEWIS

A Facsimile of the 1832 Text
With Preface and Introductory Essay by

CHARLES FREDERICK MULLETT

UNIVERSITY OF MISSOURI PRESS
COLUMBIA
1970

SBN 8262-0089-3

Library of Congress Catalog Number 72-113816

Printed and bound in the United States of America

PREFACE

THE origins of an historian's interest are seldom easily accounted for; the wind bloweth where it listeth, and so does curiosity. In early investigation of the idea of fundamental law I learned that words play tricks with generalizations. The discovery, always salutary, sometimes humiliating, was exciting; and though often dormant my concern never dried up. A few years ago it revived when I was exploring the ideas of a Scottish political economist, James' Anderson (1739–1808), who among his manifold interests proposed a universal language, criticized the ambiguity of the genitive, and printed installments of a dictionary in his weekly *Bee*. Curious about the prevalence of these and related pursuits and the reasons for them, I looked to his contemporaries and to those who came after, and found among them almost an obsession with various facets of language. Since an historian must seek both antecedents and consequences I pushed my way back through several centuries and forward through several decades, with fruitful results. Here it is enough to say that some of my observations of others' concern with language are presented in the following pages. So austere an explanation is not, of course, the whole story. Historians are stained with the colors of the world about them; what had been historically absorbing became intellectually relevant as the presidential campaign of 1968 illustrated again and again the use and abuse of political terms. Not least among the attractions of Eugene McCarthy was his plea for the honest use of language.

In this present edition of *Remarks on the Use and Abuse of some Political Terms*, an exact reprint of the first, I have not attempted a variorum edition. Such would obscure the emphasis of the Introduction. The second and third editions, both posthumous, contain notes by their editors, bringing readers up to date on some matters of political fact and correcting or enlarging a few of Lewis' citations. Here, as will quickly be apparent, the stress is semantic, the presumption that, whatever the message, the medium has greater influence.

It remains only to declare my indebtedness to the American Philosophical Society, the Newberry Library, and the Research Council of the University of Missouri for enabling me to indulge a curiosity all too indisciplined, proof positive that history is fun.

COLUMBIA, MISSOURI   C.F.M.
FEBRUARY, 1970

Contents

No Intellectual Voluptuary
but a Sagacious Dictionary:

George Cornewall Lewis

1806–1863

I

In 1850 the *Edinburgh Review* pronounced that political speculations had "largely turned from the dramatic,
dynastic, and personal interests of history, to the life of
nations, the destinies of races, and the ultimate prospects of mankind." Why had this change occurred?
Because "our fathers' generation and our own have been
marked by changes so vast and rapid as to strike the
least imaginative minds with an anxious sense of temporal instability, and to fill the most imaginative with . . .
dim visions of a future which no theorems of the schools
and the churches will contain." In such terms did a
sensitive barometer register the reactions of sagacious
minds to the intellectual climate in the middle decades
of the nineteenth century. Although any reader of
George Cornewall Lewis—neither the most nor the least
imaginative of Victorian sages—could have similarly

described the prevailing temper, a precise contemporary diagnosis is worth a dozen post-mortems.[1]

What the *Review* did *not* say was that the sense of instability and the inadequacy of the old theorems intensified the demand for semantic exactitude. The campaign was not new, but its front was expanding. Innovative and far-reaching scientific hypotheses, the rise of social "sciences," the increasing power of the semiliterate, and the concomitant democratization of politics were only the most obvious of the vast and rapid changes. Biological and physical scientists, social scientists even more, complained of inadequate terminology; John Ruskin, lecturing on the reading of books, denounced linguistic debasement, and ecclesiastical as well as political observers deplored the misuse of political terms. Withal, the very concern that issued from this broad range of scholars attests the power of communication, the more powerful because it was inseparable from the creation of opinion. In no contemporary was this concern more evident than in George Cornewall Lewis and the work here introduced.

[1] *Edinburgh Review*, XCII (1850), 340, in a review of Charles Lyell's *Second Visit to the United States of America*. The year before, a journal of the opposite political persuasion, Tory *Blackwood's Edinburgh Magazine*, LXV (1849), 1–2, similarly diagnosed the state of affairs. "The extension of knowledge, the diffusion of education, the art of printing, the increased rapidity of travelling, the long duration of peace . . . have so accelerated the march of events, that what was slowly effected in former times . . . is now at once brought to maturity. . . . Everything now goes at a gallop. There is a railway speed in the stirring of the mind. . . . The social and political passions have acquired such intensity and been so widely diffused, that their inevitable results are almost immediately produced. The period of the seed-time and harvest has become as short in political as it is in agricultural labour. A single year brings its appropriate fruits to maturity in the moral as in the physical world."

Although there is no need here for a biography of Lewis (1806–1863), a sketch of his career will properly preface an account of his legacy.[2] The elder son of Sir Thomas Frankland Lewis, a Poor Law commissioner, George went through Eton, where he excelled in Latin and Greek. At Christ Church, Oxford, he took a first in classics before reading law at Middle Temple, where he attended John Austin's innovating analytical lectures on jurisprudence at University College, London.[3] From study he turned to application, particularly, as one

[2] The following paragraphs are derived principally from *Letters of the Right Hon. Sir George Cornewall Lewis, Bart. to various Friends*, edited by his brother, the Rev. Sir Gilbert Frankland Lewis, Bart. (London, 1870); two essays by Bagehot, "Sir George Cornewall Lewis" and "The Tribute at Hereford to Sir G. C. Lewis," *The Works of Walter Bagehot*, 5 vols., edited by Forest Morgan (Hartford, 1891), III, 222–64, 265–68; the sketch in the *Dictionary of National Biography*; and *Remarks on the Use and Abuse of some Political Terms*, a new edition with notes and introduction by Thomas Raleigh (Oxford, 1898), V–XXIV. Kenneth E. Bock, "History and a Science of Man: An appreciation of George Cornewall Lewis," *Journal of the History of Ideas*, XII (1951), 599–608, is perceptive; and Arnaldo Momigliano, "G. C. Lewis, Niebuhr e la Critica Della Fonti," *Contributo Alla Storia Degli Studi Classici* (Roma, 1955), 249–62, though concentrating on one aspect and that of secondary importance here, characteristically illumines others. He believes that Lewis, as one of the most outstanding and intelligent personalities of the early Victorian age, would merit a long study.

[3] John Austin (1790–1859), the neighbor of Bentham and the Mills in London, became professor of jurisprudence at University College, London, in 1826, whereupon he spent the next two years in Germany preparing his lectures. Lewis, John Stuart Mill, Samuel Romilly, Charles Buller, and several other distinguished intellectuals attended his opening lectures in 1828. Despite this propitious beginning, he attracted few students and so resigned in 1832. In that year he published his acute series of six lectures, *The Province of Jurisprudence Determined*, but the book aroused no response. Two years later he lectured at Inner Temple without success. Meanwhile, in 1833 he had become a member of the

might anticipate from his father's activity, to the Poor Law, becoming in 1833 an assistant commissioner to study the lot of the Irish poor in English cities. This experience produced his essays "Local Disturbances" and the "Church Question" (1836–1837), which, bringing him more prestige than money, inspired the wry observation, "There is no market for books on Irish subjects, unless they are full of religious bigotry." Bigot George Lewis never was.

Even before the publication of these essays he and Austin were appointed commissioners to report on the laws and government of Malta. Here they spent eighteen months in careful observation, noting, among other things, how oppressively the British treated the Maltese upper classes. Lewis and Austin recommended an improved tariff to relieve trade and industry and relaxation of restraints imposed by military governors, and they began the codification of laws for the island, all in a report published in 1838–1839. By this latter date Lewis had succeeded his father as Poor Law Commissioner, just in time to bear the bitter attack on the 1834 Poor Law, including a personal accusation, soon with-

---

Criminal Law Commission but soon resigned in frustration; then, in 1836 he was appointed with Lewis to investigate the law and government of Malta. Although his ideas have been soundly criticized by informed students as rigid, limited in application, and even confused and mistaken, his emphasis on analysis has dominated English jurisprudence since his day; even his "errors" have been fruitful. The essentials of his doctrine and the source of his impact on Lewis can be found in *The Province of Jurisprudence Determined and The Uses of the Study of Jurisprudence*, edited, with an introduction, by H. L. A. Hart (London, 1954). For a more nearly complete assessment, see *Lectures on Jurisprudence or the Philosophy of Law*, 2 vols., 5th ed., revised and edited by Robert Campbell (London, 1885), which contains also a charming and informing memoir by his wife Sarah.

drawn, of conspiracy and falsehood. In 1847 he resigned to enter Parliament where, ever the administrator, he became almost immediately secretary to the Board of Control, the supervisory agency of the Government of India. His Poor Law past survived, however, in *Letters addressed to the Secretary of State respecting the Transaction of the Business of the Commission* (1847) and in a report on parochial assessments (1850).

Meanwhile he had become, first, parliamentary undersecretary to the Home Department, then financial secretary to the Treasury, proving himself in these offices to be an effective though not an eloquent debater. In 1852, after being twice defeated for Parliament, once by a protectionist, once by a local hero, he became editor of the *Edinburgh Review*. Three years later he succeeded to his father's title and seat, at the very time Lord Palmerston, then Prime Minister, was experiencing great difficulty in finding a chancellor of the Exchequer, a post lately held by Gladstone. Two men had already refused the office, but Lewis, always convinced of the responsibility to serve, undertook its duties, despite the enormity of the problems involved. He faced a hard time —the combination of a large deficit and the demands of the budget for the Crimean War. To the horror of Whigs and Radicals, he proposed new taxes and borrowing, but, offsetting their opposition, he found support where he had expected hostility, from Gladstone. In 1857, now vigorously opposed by both Gladstone and Disraeli— the only time they ever agreed—he favored larger expenditures, and won. Two years later, after an election, Palmerston offered reappointment to the chancellorship to Lewis, but he gave way to Gladstone, now willing to take the less problem-fraught office, and became Home Secretary. In 1859 this "homely scholar in spectacles" moved to the War Office. Four years later he died, aged fifty-six.

For all his seeming prosiness and his "student stoop," Lewis had experienced a more rapid political rise than any contemporary. A civil servant for fourteen years before entering Parliament, he reached cabinet rank in eight. Whereas Palmerston sat in Parliament twenty-five years before holding a responsible office, Lewis finished his parliamentary career in half the years it took Pam to become a statesman at all. Though not an attractive speaker, he had great influence on both sides of the House. A man who seemed incapable of losing his head, he was at his best in the cool transaction of intricate business; utterly practical, he brought disparate factors into focus for decisive action and thereby inspired confidence in his reliability as well as ability.[4] Bagehot's assessment, however shrewd, that Lewis was always refuting an hypothesis, cannot stand alone. Penetrating and comprehensive in his thinking, Lewis avoided the prevailing fashion in ideas and scorned men who feared singularity more than error and who accepted numbers of supporters as the index to truth. A Whig-Liberal, he repeatedly warned his fellows against governing too much, forcing actions, and suppressing opinions. The very titles of his many books—essays and inquiries—are antiauthoritarian. Despite the official nature of his career, he had no love of power and turned as easily to his study as to public office.

To appreciate Lewis' character one must turn to that

[4] Connop Thirlwall, historian and bishop (1797–1875), thought that to Lewis "the business of life was all that there was attractive in it" (quoted, Momigliano, 258n.). Such a judgment conveys, at least to us, an unwarranted impression of dullness. Rather let it be said, Lewis combined enormous knowledge, critical acuteness, and good sense with discipline for work.

complete Victorian, Walter Bagehot, who included him in his "fine collection of public animals": One who, despite his activity, never seemed busy, one who was never in the way and never out of it. In the midst of the "Trent Affair" (1861) this Secretary for War found time at 3 P.M. on a busy parliamentary day to discuss with Bagehot for twenty minutes the "comparative certainty (or rather *un*certainty) of the physical and moral sciences." Devoid of vanity, he used his knowledge to amend, not to expose, ignorance; possessed of a mind that was "complication proof," he described himself as merely "equal to business." He took each problem, however complex, in stride, and what he said in explanation of his solution was so credible and sensible his listeners believed they had, from the first, been of the same mind. His conversation was better than his speeches or his books, for, though equally precise, it conveyed a flavor of satire along with its exactitude. A computer in breeches, he was generally right, but even when wrong he was clear; in his exposition of a point there was always the distinct aim, the precise objective, the sense of evidence. He never confused diagnosis with prescription; presented with a plan, he always asked of the planner, What is your object? Because for him issues were simple, he stripped them of befuddling rhetoric and irrelevance. He could not diffuse a mist of vagueness, however useful, over difficulties.

Talking with him, wrote Bagehot, was like reading a chapter in Aristotle's *Politics*, incomplete perhaps, but pregnant. What else indeed could one anticipate from a man who declared intelligibility to be the first, second, and third essentials in a constitutional statesman? What else from a man who believed that "by looking forward to all possible evils we waste the strength that had best be concentrated in curing the *one* evil which happens?" Without being stubborn, he would alter his opinion only when he got new facts; his fellows always knew where they would find his mind, a mind motivated by judgment rather than impulse and hence a sound measure of probability. He did not, to be sure, precisely gauge the unreliability of some "facts." Though always a good learner, and usually a correct reasoner, he did on occasion start from the wrong premises, or from at least constricted ones—those of his class and environment— and so missed points seen by men whose blinkers were set at a different angle. He was unaware that he himself might be drawing, with faultless logic, dubious inferences from dubious premises. No doubt much of this character derived from his role as a refuter of other men's hypotheses. His "factualness" too had its limits: Where some men saw a mirage and reported it as a fact, Lewis dispelled the mirage without assessing the extent to which men had acted upon it.

What then is the evidence for the declaration in *The Times* on April 15, 1863, that he was "unquestionably the most learned Englishman of his generation" and "one of the most learned men of any time"? Was this anything other than obituary rhetoric? The answer to the second question is imbedded in the answer to the first, which must include recognition that all of Lewis' activities constantly intersected one another. He never left his broadly informed brains outside when he entered the House, and he never shelved his wide political experience when he turned historian. For historian he always was, fusing German methodology and practice with eighteenth-century analysis and search for laws and his own political experience, and so verifying Hume's assertion that history is scholarship. Because he saw history as a series of problems he sought meaning, hence the impression that in his official actions and his debates he was always refuting a hypothesis. This impression was particularly evident in his *Inquiry into the Credibility of the Early Roman History* (1855) wherein he faced up to the dilemma that the compulsion to find meaning could readily lead to conjecture, as Barthold Niebuhr had illustrated. Niebuhr, said Lewis, had shelved a "well-authenicated narrative of facts" in the interest of coherence. It was not enough "to claim the possession of retrospective second-sight," which was denied to the rest of the world; historical divination was no substitute for fact-gathering.

So far as concerns Lewis' own reputation for learning, the number and variety of his books is a solid buttress. Their very titles are revealing, not only of his learning but of his temper: *An Examination of some Passages in Dr. Whately's Elements of Logic* (1829), *Remarks on the Use and Abuse of some Political Terms* (1832), *An Essay on the Origin and Formation of the Romance Languages* (1835, 1862), *An Essay on the Government of Dependencies* (1841), *An Essay on the Influence of Authority in Matters of Opinion* (1849), *A Treatise on the Methods of Observation and Reasoning in Politics* (2 vols., 1852), *An Inquiry into the Credibility of the Early Roman History* (2 vols., 1855), and, to go no further here, *Dialogue on the Best Form of Government* (1863). He wrote only one "treatise"; the rest were essays, remarks, inquiries, surveys, whatever the subject.

Although the *Remarks* is the main concern here, several others of his works will properly receive some attention because, whatever the topic, he emphasized correct reasoning, and reasoning cannot be correct if terms are abused and facts disregarded. Whereas his earlier editors concentrated on the public servant and political theorist, I shall stress the semanticist. The public servant is dead and gone, the theorist scarcely less so, owing to the passing of the environment in which his theories were framed. What is still alive—and in varying degrees it penetrated everything that Lewis studied as an administrator or wrote as a philosopher—is the necessity for definition and correct reasoning, a necessity of which the urgency is everywhere apparent.

In the larger sense the significance of Lewis is historical: The good in his ideas has become a commonplace, the outworn is irrelevant. What remains is what a sensitive, thoughtful man regarded as primary in his day. When the *Remarks* appeared, varied tensions—political, religious, socioeconomic—had long dominated public opinion, as the rise of the first industrial society, expanding democracy, increasing literacy, and the greater community of the realm through communication, personal, periodical, and parliamentary, drove the intellectual in politics to inform his fellows of the political and economic facts of life. *Reform, improvement, change* became the prevailing catchwords for the politically aware, with consequent resistance from those who feared the disintegration of values, that is to say, the erosion of their own privileges. After years of repression men now indulged the license as well as the liberty of free speech. Preachers, pamphleteers, politicians, even poets, freely vented their rhetoric on a public that, if quantity be evidence, fully relished the exchange of verbal ordnance of whatsoever caliber. Enjoyment was one thing, however; seduction another. Amid all the rhetorical excitement were some warnings against the wilderness, the absurdity, the fancies of democracy (in this instance not a theory but a crowd).

II

To seize upon a decade as if it possessed a magical completeness is historically ridiculous, yet the 1820's did manifest a confluence of influences that produced specific reforms, not more revolutionary as achievement than as preface. In 1820 Peterloo tarnished Waterloo, and repression led with Newtonian exactitude to equal reaction against its savagery. With mounting vehemence men extended their campaigns against religious penalties, legal inequities, game laws, anticombination laws, the unreformed Parliament, the old colonial system, and such diverse monopolies as trading companies, the College of Physicians, and the Royal Society—the exposed parts of the iceberg of privilege. Despite its force, the vehemence was largely verbal. Whether discussion of public questions of itself accomplished its ends—and the defenders of the *status quo* matched the attackers in strength—it did arouse thoughtful men to the dangers of claptrap, and they sounded their alarms in every medium. Jeremy Bentham's *The Handbook of Political Fallacies* (1824) and Lewis' *Remarks* were only the most precise warnings.

To suggest that those essays sprang full grown from contemporary excitement disregards centuries of concern with language and communication, a concern especially manifest and most fully expressed at the onset of the nineteenth century. Among Lewis' contemporaries, Richard Whately, the Archbishop of Dublin, Hazlitt, Cobbett, Augustus W. and Julius C. Hare, and such economists as Malthus, James Mill, J. R. McCulloch, and Nassau Senior were but the best known of those who shared his concern. That concern, however intellectual in expression, sprang from social urgency, a revolution in the minds as well as the institutions of men. The revolution in language was inseparable from revolution in science, natural as well as social, in politics and society. As De Quincey observed somewhat later, urbanity equates with intellectual culture, and men thrown together in society communicate, communicate about something, something important, at least to them. The taciturnity of country folk is proverbial, if not invariable, and it may at least be allowed that they talk about particulars.

Although a comprehensive account of language as an archive of history would exhaust the reader long before it exhausted the subject, a brief sketch of the persistent campaign to make English a fit vehicle for a nation of a "quick, ingenious, and piercing spirit, acute to invent, subtle and sinewy to discourse," has warrant. The desire to learn generated arguing, writing, and opinions, "for opinion in good men is but knowledge in the making." The campaign involved many sorties, spontaneous and planned, leading to a learned and learnable language. The early efforts to enable Englishmen to preach and pray, to legislate and litigate, to trade and teach in their own tongue were rather the flower than the fruit of nationalism. No sooner did Englishmen achieve some success in their efforts than they realized the handicaps of poverty of terminology, sprawling wordiness, indenture language, extravagant discourse. A man must not be defeated in any enterprise by clumsy tools.

As in many intellectual areas Francis Bacon was England's Aristotle. He described how words were framed and applied according to the conceits and capacities of the vulgar, words that by over-ruling the understanding threw all into confusion and led men to empty controversies and idle fancies. Men, he went on, thought that *they* governed their words, but words, as a Tartar's bow, shot back upon the understanding, even of the wisest, and mightily entangled their judgment. They would do well to set down definitions, because for want of knowing such, they ended where they should have begun. Yet Bacon appreciated the limits of definitions: they consisted of words, which begot words.

Important as was Bacon in stating the problem, many others at different levels were so too—historians, theologians, poets, and, above all, scientists, especially the members of the Royal Society who proclaimed and practiced a plain, natural, naked way of speaking and writing. That words were but appellations of things was the conviction not only of the Boyles and the Lockes but of lesser, almost anonymous men as well, men campaigning for clarity, concision, and grammar. So ardent, even extravagant a campaign at times drew the attention of satirists, none more conspicuous than Swift. At Laputa, Gulliver discovered the inhabitants quite obsessed with language, first, to the extent of shortening discourse by cutting polysyllables into one and leaving out verbs and participles because all things imaginable were nouns, second, to the prospect of abolishing words altogether. Since words were but names for things it would be more convenient to carry things, an expedient that would not only abbreviate conversation but provide a universal language understood by all peoples. Japery though Swift's creation was, it revealed quite as much as the soberest discourse. The latter was more common, however, and often quite as interesting since— Swift apart—much satire wore thin.

Toward the end of the eighteenth century new influences arose to illustrate again that the revolution in language is present at the birth of science, in this instance the birth of social science—political economy, anthropology, and legislation. The revolution immediately found expression in dictionaries, specialized as well as general. Of the first, the legal lexicons are most relevant here, the more that they immediately recall Bentham, who transformed jurisprudence from a philosophy to a science, and pungently exposed the semantics of political persuasion. From him it is a short step to Lewis and his *Remarks on the Use and Abuse of some Political Terms.*

No one can read George Lewis without appreciating his preoccupation with language. For him the argument was inseparable from the words, the message from the medium. Time and again he anticipated the insight voiced a century later by Cook Wilson: "The authority of language is too often forgotten in philosophy, with serious results. Distinctions made or applied in ordinary language are more likely to be right than wrong. Developed, as they have been, in what may be called the natural course of thinking, under the influence of experience and in the apprehensions of truths, whether of everyday life or science, they are not due to any preconceived theory."[5] Nonetheless, Lewis often found ordinary language inappropriate for conveying exact knowledge; it bore too many emotional barnacles. Strongly and variously influenced by Whately, he fought illogic and ambiguity, whatever the topic, as is evidenced not only in the *Remarks* but in everything he wrote.[6] At the same time one must remember that, as

[5] Cook Wilson, *Statement and Inference* (Oxford, 1926), 874–75.

[6] Richard Whately (1787–1863), Professor of Political Economy at Oxford (1829–1831), Archbishop of Dublin (1831–1863), was both prolific and versatile, though a reading of many of his numerous works quickly reveals a continuing preoccupation with the problem of language. The works of particular relevance and the

already noticed, several other contemporaries, diversely motivated, were likewise attacking the same ills.

To assert Whately's influence and separate it from the prevailing temper is immediately to appreciate that of all the epistemological problems facing the historian none requires more caution—and none is more rashly presumed—than *influence*, the quicksand that has engulfed so many fine hypotheses. To avow confidently that Whately influenced the young Lewis more than any other man, even John Austin, is to draw that cold inquiry, How do you know? What can be offered in reply is the title and substance of Lewis' first book, *An Examination of some Passages in Dr. Whately's Elements of Logic*, the title, references, and some substance of the book here introduced, and the steady application of Whately's bidding in many of his other works.

Among the topics in Whately's *Logic* (1826) and *Rhetoric* (1828) language had a prominent place. In the

---

editions used here are *Elements of Logic. Comprising the Substance of the Article in the Encyclopaedia Metropolitana: with Additions etc.* (8th ed., London, 1844); *Elements of Rhetoric comprising an Analysis of the Laws of Moral Evidence and of Persuasion, with Rules for Argumentative Composition and Elocution* (1828; 3d ed., 1830; edition by Douglas Ehninger from the 7th ed. [1846], Carbondale, 1963); *Introductory Lectures on Political Economy* (1832, reprinted New York, 1966); and *The Use and Abuse of Party Feeling in Matters of Religion; Being the Course of the Bampton Lectures for the Year 1822. To which are added; Five Sermons Before the University of Oxford, and a Discourse by Archbishop King, with Notes and Appendix* (4th ed., London, 1859). In the Oxford sermons Whately revealed how deeply political, social, and economic turmoil had penetrated contemporary consciousness. Further testimony of Whately's influence appears in John Stuart Mill's *System of Logic* (1843). Whately, he declared, "has done more than any other person to restore [logic] to the rank from which it had fallen in the estimation of the cultivated class in our own country."

Logic he emphasized that language did not merely supply names, it was a reasoning process, of which the lack accounted for the inability of deaf mutes to reason. Language then had many purposes: to inform, as exemplified by the historian; to please, as exemplified by the poet; to persuade, as exemplified by the orator. It was always liable to abuses, best illustrated by fallacies that were identified by unsound methods, inaccurate terms, question-begging, bad analogies, false assumptions, irrelevant conclusions, elliptical language, ambiguous middles, talking to death, shifting ground, and *ignoratio elenchi*. Such fallacies, said Whately—in alliance, as will be seen, with Jeremy Bentham—were the "stronghold of bigoted anti-innovators who oppose all reforms and alterations indiscriminately." In the *Rhetoric*, though he took a somewhat different tack, scanting language as communication, Whately again stressed his conviction, echoing Locke, that language was primarily an "instrument of thought, a system of general signs, without which the reasoning process could not be conducted." In his opinion no subjectivist could appreciate the full importance of language; rather, it was the nominalist who best understood its character and the need for accurate nomenclature.

He had earlier voiced his belief in this need in the *Logic*, where he pointed out "certain terms peculiarly liable to be used ambiguously," citing among others especially those of political economy—value, wealth, labor, capital, rent, wages, profit. It should come, then, as no surprise that this approach marked his *Introductory Lectures on Political Economy*. The first lecture dilated the disadvantages and inadequacies of *political economy* itself, and the ninth (included in the second but not the first edition, though both appeared the same year, 1832) comprehensively diagnosed the "want of a well constructed and established nomenclature." The terms of the subject, taken from common discourse and "used with great laxity of signification," stood in greater need of accurate definition and rigid application than those of almost any other science. Was this situation, he wondered, the destiny of familiar terms? Many men quite honestly opposed definition as too limiting; others were superficial in their thinking; still others feared precise reasoning: like the thief they rejoiced in a fog. Such opposition could only put a man of well-trained understanding on his guard. Definitions, Whately insisted, were most wanted where terms were in common use, and where, because of their familiarity, it was necessary to use each term in some sense corresponding to that use; otherwise readers would charge innovation. Under the existing circumstances writers should innovate as little as possible. Yet in themselves definitions were not enough; men needed to beware the ambiguity attendant upon employing the same terms in different senses. Dissent excited by definitions was by no means wholly bad; realization of differences was both healthy and essential, many differences resulting only from inattention. Ricardo, for instance, might have got his figures wrong without affecting his general principles, but by using *wages* sometimes as a certain amount and sometimes as a certain proportion he perplexed his readers. Such discrepancies caused denigration of political economy as a field of study. Similarly, elliptical phrases— "out of work" for example—confused readers and, added to other shortcomings, led Whately to assert that "eloquence, in the sense of what is called *fine writing*, is not to be looked for in the treatment of scientific subjects."

Whately's Bampton lectures, *The Use and Abuse of Party Feeling*, preached the same doctrine that permeated the *Logic, Rhetoric*, and *Political Economy*. He warned his audience and readers to attend to their language, to guard against ambiguity and not judge doctrines by their phraseology, to avoid clichés, "the cantlanguage of a party," which engendered strife about words, deadened concern with things, and so led to erroneous theories. It was not the same thing, he emphasized, to be "merely acquainted with the ambiguity of a term, and to be practically aware of it," and to be watchful of its consequences. Unhappily, the name was the last thing people consented to part with.

The same hostility to cant, ambiguity, and sheer negligence, the same awareness of social revolution, appeared time and again in what must be rated among the most perceptive volumes of the time, *Guesses at Truth by Two Brothers* by Augustus W. and Julius C. Hare, who leavened the scholar with the wit.[7] Without for a moment attempting a full account of their reflections and *aperçus*, one cannot refrain from summarizing those judgments most germane to the circumstances that moved Lewis to action. The brothers found that, owing to Scottish influence, a sort of English had of late years become very prevalent—one wherein the sentences had meaning but not the words or, contrarily, owing to Irish influence, one wherein the words meant something, the sentences nothing. English English combined the two influences. Words that lacked precision were useless or, what was worse, corrupting. One should be cautious

---

[7] Augustus (1792–1834) was rector of a small parish in Wiltshire; Julius (1795–1855), schoolfellow of the historians George Grote and Thirlwall, friend of William Whewell, collaborated with Thirlwall in translating Niebuhr.

about abstractions—"mere air propelling words"—that,
liable to be misunderstood and perverted, bred confusion of thought, especially where "a word, used in one
sense in the premises, slips another sense into the conclusion." How many gross blunders might be traced to
mistaking Administration for Government? Scarcely a
man any longer remembered that the business of governors was to govern. Above all, had those who called
themselves *the Government* forgotten this fact, persuad-
ing themselves that their duty was to be servants, or
rather the slaves, of circumstances and public opinion,
the greater the necessity then that language be free of
cant and cliché.

The extent to which these and like sentiments
abounded is further manifest in the opinions of two
contemporaries who inhabited a quite different world
of thought and action from Whately, the Hares, or
Lewis, namely William Cobbett and William Hazlitt.
The first, in his *Grammar of the English Language* (1818),
a series of letters to his son and intended for "soldiers,
sailors, apprentices, and plough-boys," attributed ambiguity and confusion in large part to the overweening
deference to Greek and Latin.[8] As proof he tore up a
passage in Hugh Blair's *Lectures on Rhetoric*, declaring
that a knowledge of Greek and Latin was no defense
against writing bad English and inquiring, therefore,

[8] Cobbett (1763–1835) did not sport the nomdeplume "Peter
Porcupine" without warrant. He boasted "how many false pretenders have I exposed to shame merely by my knowledge of
grammar." He might also have boasted, and no doubt did, how
many pretenders of all sorts he had exposed—at least to his own
satisfaction. His best-known literary legacy is *Rural Rides*. A
relevant excerpt of his *Grammar* is printed in W. F. Bolton, ed.,
*The English Language: Essays by English and American Men of
Letters, 1490–1839* (Cambridge, 1966), 180–84.

with what propriety they were called "learned languages." No less bluntly, Hazlitt in 1829 characterized English grammar as a subject on which the human understanding had played the fool, "hoodwinked" by mere precedent and authority into applying the rules of Greek and Latin "indiscriminately and dogmatically."[9] Their definitions had corrupted a generation, being calculated to mystify and stultify the understanding and inoculate it with credulity and sophistry. Despite sound criticism, said Hazlitt, the same point-blank contradictions and shallow definitions appeared in grammar after grammar, edition after edition: establishments subsisted on "foregone conclusions." The more senseless the absurdity, the more the reluctance to surrender it, for admission of error was pitiful mortification. The greater number of professional laborers sought not truth but a livelihood, and a schoolmaster who chose Horne Tooke's *Diversions of Purley* for a textbook would soon have the village dogs at his heels.[10] So Hazlitt pilloried his contemporaries: the din of quacks drowned out the small pipe of truth. Even the eminent J. R. McCulloch with his *Principles of Political Economy* and James Mill with his *Elements of Political Economy* reminded him of "two barrel-organ grinders in the same street, playing

[9] Hazlitt (1778–1830), an invaluable source for capturing contemporary crosscurrents, can always be counted on to brighten a subject. This essay is printed in Bolton, 185–90.

[10] John Horne (1736–1812), who added the name Tooke from a supporter who owned an estate at Purley, dabbled in law and theology as well as grammar. He defended John Wilkes and a little later was imprisoned for a year for describing the colonial victims at Lexington as "inhumanly murdered." The *Diversions* (1786) stressed the need to seek the meaning of words if "we wish to avoid important error," a plea sharpened by his belief that his conviction owed as much to verbal ambiguity as to his sentiments.

the same tune and contending for precedence and mastery." What was Mozart to any of the four?

This reference to Mill and McCulloch reminds us that political economy, the new queen of the sciences, along with metaphysics a principal export of Scotland and the object of considerable derision, produced many efforts at definition—the response, if the number of volumes and editions be an index, to widespread demand. Mill's *Elements* (1821) had its second edition in 1824, its third in 1826; McCulloch's *Principles* (1825), its second edition in 1830, its third in 1842, its fourth in 1849, its fifth in 1864.[11] More important for present purposes than either was *Definitions in Political Economy* (1827) by Thomas Malthus, the product of the recent harvest as well as contemporary concern.[12] In noting the extensive complaint about differing meanings, he very sensibly emphasized the impossibility of strict definition in a "science" whose spokesmen used common words that were differently understood by different people, a "science" that was constantly adjusting itself to a dynamic society. He fully recognized anomalies and asserted that his only purpose was to draw attention to the problem. The best that men could do was to use terms in the sense they were best understood in ordinary uses; the next

[11] Mill (1773–1836), the most formidable of the Benthamites and, with his son John Stuart Mill, their chief philosophers. His range included not only political economy but history and psychology as well as education, evidenced in the upbringing of his son. John Ramsay McCulloch (1789–1864), a prolific compiler and a constant *Edinburgh* reviewer, was divertingly pilloried by Thomas Love Peacock as "Mr. MacQuedy," son of a demonstration, in *Crotchet Castle*.

[12] Malthus (1766–1834), most quickly remembered for his *Essay on Population* (1798), explored several aspects of political economy, both theory and policy. The *Definitions* had a second edition in 1853.

best was to use them as the best writers had. Alterations were justifiable, but they should be consistent with surviving definitions. More specifically, Malthus criticized French economists for being *too* precise, *too* narrow, Adam Smith for deficiencies in precision and accuracy, Ricardo for shifting meanings of the same term (Whately made the same point), Mill for following Ricardo and either heightening the error or altering without improvement, and McCulloch for finding too readily the resemblances he sought. Whatever else, no writer should run counter to general experience.

Whately's *Introductory Lectures*, already noted, and Nassau Senior's *Outline of the Science of Political Economy* (1836) are equally informing evidence of the appetite for precision.[13] The latter, though it strongly resembles Malthus' *Definitions* in intent and character, goes further afield and clearly owes much to Whately, instanced by the inclusion as appendix, "On certain terms which are peculiarly liable to be used ambiguously in Political Economy," from the *Elements of Logic*. Not only did Senior avow that the great defect of English economists was want of definitions, especially of key words—*wealth, labor, capital, rent*—with consequent ambiguity, but he stressed the practical evil of that lack and, what was equally deplorable, of the varied definitions men had attempted. It were well, he declared, if the ambiguities of *wealth* "had done no more than puzzle philosophers." One, however, had given birth to the mercantile system. In common language, to grow rich was to get *money*, and the terms *wealth* and *money* were

---

[13] Nassau Senior (1790–1864), friend of Lewis and like him much concerned with the Poor Law, was succeeded as Professor of Political Economy at Oxford by Whately and then in after years returned to the post.

in short employed as synonymous. This notion had for centuries done more, "and perhaps for centuries to come will do more, to retard the development of Europe than all other causes put together." Considering that Lewis, though no political economist as Malthus, Mill, McCulloch, or Senior was, never failed to recognize the economic basis of politics, the preoccupation here summarized could not but figure in the *Remarks*.[14]

Before leaving this semantic atmosphere a quick backward glance into the eighteenth century is informing, since both David Hume and Joseph Butler belong among Lewis' educators.[15] Hume's awareness of the signification of words, his recognition that ofttimes

[14] Although William Whewell (1794–1866) contributed his portion to this topic much later, in *Six Lectures on Political Economy* (1862), it can be cited as significant that the historian and philosopher of the inductive sciences—and in time one of the sources of Lewis' opinions—did so, often in terms recalling Whately and Senior. Some questions, he told his Cambridge listeners, "are questions of definition—questions whether this or that is the proper definition of certain words. Other sciences as well as political economy have had such controversies in the course of their history; and you may think perhaps that such questions are of little consequence, since they are questions of words only. You ask, may we not define our terms as we please? No: for we must define our terms so as to be able to assert true propositions. The science of political economy does not rest upon definitions. It rests upon facts. But facts are to be described in a general manner— that is, by means of general terms. And these terms should be well chosen, so as to enable us to assert true propositions. If our definitions do this, they are not bad, merely because the boundary cases are perplexing." Whewell, Master of Trinity College, Cambridge, was one of the most formidable erudits of his day.

[15] T. H. Green and T. H. Grose, *Essays Moral, Political, and Literary*, 2 vols. (London, 1882, 1964), I, 122–26; II, 278. See also Donald F. Henze, "The Linguistic Aspect of Hume's Method," *Journal of the History of Ideas*, XXX (1969), 116–26. For Butler, see Austin Duncan-Jones, *Butler's Moral Philosophy* (Pelican, 1952), 30–35.

opponents disagreed only verbally, found expression in the observation, quoted by Lewis: "Nothing is more usual than for philosophers to encroach upon the province of grammarians and to engage in disputes of words while they imagine they are handling controversies of the deepest importance and concern." In a different area his essay, "Whether the British Government inclines more to Absolute Monarchy, or to a Republic," raised questions that Lewis discussed, seeking to get behind labels—the names that, as Whately would later emphasize, were the last things people consented to part with. Butler, more subtly perhaps, also anticipated Lewis. He shared with Lewis a preference for precision over elegance, appreciation that words—far from remaining unchanged in their meaning, constantly adjusted to their context—awareness of verbal ambiguity and inadequacy, of common words used in an uncommon sense, and of the need for the plain use of plain words. Above all, they valued an intent not to be misunderstood (the negative phrasing is deliberate) and an addiction to a style in which it was impossible to tell lies.

Nevertheless, important as were all these "influences," two other personalities, John Austin and Jeremy Bentham, warrant special assessment, since—Whately apart—they were more closely related to the purpose of the *Remarks* than the rest.[16] First in immediacy of contact was Austin, whose impact was chiefly manifest in substance and outlook. His implicit as well as explicit insistence on definition and analysis of pervading assumptions was identical with Lewis' own. The very title of his first book, *The Province of Juris-*

[16] For Austin, see note 3. Bentham's *Handbook of Political Fallacies* (1824) is available in Harper Torchbooks (1962) with a brief introduction by Crane Brinton.

prudence Determined, published the same year as the *Remarks* and to which Lewis had listened in oral delivery, suggests the same objective. To summarize its content is difficult, first because it is a summary itself, and second because of Austin's anxiety to mark every step of his reasoning by indicating all possible missteps. He not only defined his terms but specified what they did not mean and, in so doing, turned each one inside out.[17] A radical nominalist, he found definition difficult because the elements were unique. He also recapitulated and so put the same terms in different contexts, though this practice did not prevent him from conveying rigidity and absolutism. With Bentham he found Blackstone plausible—and hollow, confused, even absurd, and addicted to jargon and "air-propelling" abstractions—and his attitude probably accounts for Lewis' repeated thrusts at Blackstone—and this at a time when to lawyers, at least, Blackstone and law were synonymous. At the same time, though venerating Bentham for his extraordinary accomplishments, Austin did not hesitate to criticize him for using terms in such a way as to perplex the reader. On the whole, however, the two

[17] No doubt it was this quality that prompted Bagehot to say that Austin's school "underestimated all too obviously the intelligence of readers," and when its disciples saw human beings using inaccurate and vague words they were apt to ascribe all errors to those words and to believe that if human language were put right it would set the world in order. For Bagehot there was no greater mistake. Men, mainly deceived by their passions and interests, cared little for abstract truths but caught hastily at any word that justified what they wished to do, no matter the fallacies and ambiguities. Their language was inaccurate no doubt, but it was the symptom, not the disease, and no one could cure the disease merely by defining words. Characteristically shrewd as this judgment was, it was debatable; moreover, the evidence summarized above indicates that "Mr. Austin's school" had no monopoly on the passion for exact definition, least of all in instigating it.

stood allied in divorcing positive law from precepts of morality and religion, in attacking the assumptions of natural law theorists—nonsense on stilts, in Bentham's phrase—and in promoting law reform. The positivist and analyst in Lewis, however nourished by his own temper and environment, sprang, one is tempted to say, full grown from the head of Austin.

No less closely related to Lewis in substance and outlook was Bentham who, in striking contrast to Austin, gained an attention matched by no other political writer, and who, again in contrast to Austin, was never content to use plain words in a plain way. Consequently, no matter the review, no matter the book, the anvil chorus was in harmony. Even when writers approved his views —which was seldom—they deplored his vocabulary. They ridiculed and denounced his neologisms, his alarming expressions, simple and compound, his application of old words to new constructions. He embarrassed a popular subject with technical nomenclature and perplexed familiar truths with intricate arrangement. He required concentration even when he was obvious; he loved division and subdivision, method more than consequences. Amid all his inventions he had never hit upon a happier one than his adoption of the language of Babel for the doctrine of political confusion; even when correct his classifications were tedious, unimportant verbal distinctions. Discerning the impossibility of giving vent to his doctrines in any language hitherto spoken by men, Bentham coined a new gibberish. He scattered his new Greek words "side by side with his amorphous, tumble-to-pieces English ones, like Columbine dancing with Pantaloon. They want a note to explain what he meant them to mean, and are just such lifeless things as might be expected from a man who grinds them out of his lexicon." When words were brought with a commentary at their heels, it was as if a musician were to stop in the middle of a tune to explain what notes he was playing.[18] His meaning shrank under the hollow armor of big words, a kernel in a huge, tasteless husk, and when found was bitter rottenness. In vulgar scurrility, to be sure, his vocabulary was copious and original; he threw dirt with the hand of a master. Thus, there was nothing to relieve the nausea that arose, chiefly from the constant violence committed on human nature.

More, nature had made a new mold for nonpareil Jeremy, and in the process of breaking it, had cracked him; in consequence his work possessed the peculiar grace to make him "idiosyncratic, democratic, cosmocratic, comicratic Jeremy." Anyone would experience difficulty in adducing from his works, however scientific, any new element of thought or fact; his language darkened knowledge, and his works already translated into French should have been translated into English. His absurdities rendered him almost as harmless as Cobbett, and praise of his work at best "must terminate with cleverness, shrewdness, whimsicality." Even more charitable writers, recalling the ease and elegance of his earlier pieces and allowing that in works generally unreadable one might find felicity, wit, and eloquence as well as worth-while ideas, often mocked his phraseology and related how he fitted himself for his task of codification of laws by taking a "*antejentacular* and *postprandial* circumgyration.*" And his friend Robert Southey characterized him a "metaphysico-critico-politico-patriotico-phoolo-philoso-pher."

Yet, whether because of present-day familiarity with

---

[18] *Guesses at Truth*, 2d ed., 121, 176.

ponderous nomenclature or, more probably, its straight-
forward exposition, the *Handbook of Political Fallacies*
seems totally free of the eccentricities, extravagances,
and neologisms that irritated, baffled, or amused his
contemporaries. Where Lewis sought to define abstract
terms Bentham concentrated on particular obstructions,
summed up under the category of fallacies.[19] Authority,
ancestral wisdom, irrevocable laws, alarm, lack of
precedent, distrust of motives, false consolation, vague
generalities—law and order, the constitution—sham
distinctions, allegorical idols, popular depravity, uto-
pian impracticality, sweeping classification, artful diver-
sion, "the time is not ripe," and a dozen more—often
quite reversible—were defined, illustrated, and exposed,
all without bitterness. Whatever the proposal, such
arguments were voiced, although invariably irrelevant
in view of what laid beneath them—sinister self-interest,
prejudice, self-protection, and adherence to the establishment at all costs or at any price. This devastating
analysis makes it clear that, although the vast majority
of Bentham's critics attacked his vocabulary, what
really distressed them was his exposure of the idols of
the forum, the drawing room, and the market place. His

[19] In addition to agreement on Blackstone's deficiencies, the
two concurred in blasting William Gerard ("Single Speech")
Hamilton's *Maxims of Parliamentary Logic* (1808). Hamilton was
a worshipper of success, whatever the cause, who, invariably op-
posing what was proposed, was quick to cry, "Come unto me all ye
who have a point to gain and I will show you how." Fathers, said
Bentham, should use him as a mirror wherein their sons might see
to what state of corruption a man who was only concerned with
getting the better of his opponent might be reduced. A good sam-
ple of what Bentham and Lewis thought reprehensible is to be
found in the *Maxims*, 29: "The best verbal fallacies are those
which consist not in the ambiguity of a single word, but in the
ambiguous syntaxis of many put together."

vocabulary was the tangible symbol of his intent. As he "rejoiced to see society resolving into its elements," he "seemed desirous to throw back language also into a chaotic state. Unable to understand organic unity and growth, he looked upon a hyphen as the only bond of union."[20]

III

BY contrast, Lewis, interested in communication as well as definition, at no time exposed himself to derision. From his first to his final piece he sought precision. Whereas his substantive opinions and facts need no resurrection, except as they reflect contemporary issues, his persistent concern with getting ideas straight mirrors the transformation of his world. Politics, not merely institutions but what those institutions represented, absorbed him. With his Aristotelian view of man as a political animal, his wish to translate the *Politics* comes as no surprise. Similarly and predictably, he considered an abiding devotion to history as the best foundation for the study of politics and morals, and his view that history dealt with the political community was in no way parochial, for that community encompassed all human activity. To discover why Renan and others saw history as the philosophy of the nineteenth century, a man as central as Lewis is invaluable. His letters, always shrewd, often witty, reveal like his books a tremendous range of interest and mastery. He moved readily from ancient Greece to contemporary England, from India to Canada, from politics to language. The dry-as-dust character that haunts his essays is not there, for all the

[20] *Guesses at Truth,* 123.

seriousness of his judgments. For that matter, to the historian viewing Lewis as an index to social transformation Dry-as-dust was not in the essays either.

Although his letters touched on many topics, here too concern with language in one form or another was never far below the surface. He had no sooner finished the *Remarks* than he turned to the origin and formation of the romance languages, though the work did not appear until three years later.[21] Meanwhile he had begun the study of Sanskrit but was "terrified by the number of letters." During his months in Malta he concluded that Maltese was an Arabic dialect, and on the basis of reports from Wales he wondered how the Welsh intelligence could improve under the handicap of their "villainous" language. No less revealing are his incidental judgments of Macaulay and Carlyle. Macaulay's "Bacon," however sparkling, was shallow and stale in its treatment of philosophy; he would never be anything but a rhetorician, mouthing the commonplaces of the enemies of accurate knowledge. Carlyle also belonged to that class of men who denied all accurate knowledge and induced mankind to accept their own "mysterious dicta." The same sort of oblique evidence popped up in concern with the *meaning* of the Odyssey and the *meaning* of aesthetics. Similarly, as he worked first on the

[21] *An Essay on the Origin and Formation of the Romance Languages; containing an Examination of M. Raynourd's Theory on the Relation of the Italian, Spanish, Provençal, and French to the Latin.* He thought that Henry Hallam, in *View of the State of Europe during the Middle Ages* (1818), had treated the subject superficially. Lewis had published the core of his *Essay* in *The Cambridge Philological Museum* (1832–1833), edited by Julius Hare and Connop Thirlwall, to which he contributed papers on classical subjects. Although there is no warrant for regarding the *Essay* as definitive, it was a pioneer effort.

influence of authority in matters of opinion and then
on methods of political reasoning, Lewis was ever seeking precise statement. He envisaged the second of these
two projects as an organon for political inquirers and
thought that, properly executed, such a work "would
dispose of nearly the whole body of political speculators,
from Plato downwards, without refuting their conclusions separately, by showing that their *methods* were
unsound, and could lead to nothing but error, except by
accident." The apparent arrogance of this pronounce-
ment evaporates under scrutiny of his works wherein,
as in his public career, he was always cautiously but
firmly feeling his way.

Admittedly the primary concern here is the *Remarks*,
but his other pieces warrant attention in the light of his
persisting interest. Prolific he clearly was, fantastically
so when one considers his public career. Neither remark-
ably original, scholarly, nor profound, his works must be
judged by the standards and outlook of his day. To say
that his rhetoric was inseparable from his ideas is to
utter a commonplace, but that union was heightened by
his critique of other men's careless or ignorant abuse of
terms and his own conscious devotion to exactitude.
Even when he criticized the Poor Law Commissioners
for having utterly misconceived the entire subject of
the Poor Law, he declared that what was worse was the
"impudent way in which they beg the question while
professing to argue it." Incomplete, uninformed, even
on occasion ambiguous he might be, but no man ever
tried harder to fit practice to precept.

In his study of romance languages he allowed that
much needed to be done, but he thought his researches
worth publishing as a connected view of the question.
Specifically, he argued that Latin broke up under differ-

ent circumstances with different velocities and modifications in different countries, and he believed that his "tolerably complete solution" could not fail to interest all who considered the intimate connection of the development of languages with the political history of the communities by which they were spoken and with those "refined processes of thought" of which language was at once exponent and evidence. From this standpoint the origin and progress of the modern dialects of Latin had a predominant claim to attention. Having arisen within a purely historical period, they were free from the uncertainty that embarrassed inquiries into the origin of most other languages. The subject presented to the "linguist and metaphysician a clear and full exemplification of the process of a language in discarding its synthetic and introducing analytic forms; of the process by which, at the same time, that its dictionary is enriched, its grammar is impoverished; that while its substance is improved, its form is deteriorated." Such evidence afforded plentiful material for reflection because it supplied the "only certain instance" where the general course of civilization did not tend to "refine and improve all the instruments and appliances of the human intellect." A quarter of a century later he recognized that various studies of German and French had superseded his *Essay* and seemed to have rendered republication superfluous, yet English students wished its reissue, partly at least because not only had intervening works assumed the truth of his position but also because his was still the only English work to treat the problem both fully and compactly.

Characteristically, in this work he was refuting another man's hypothesis; characteristically, he demanded demonstrative proof. Let us, he said, not resort to divination and conjecture. Certainly his own *Glossary of Provincial Words used in Herefordshire* stood on observed practices. He defined provincial words as those not used by educated persons but nonetheless part of the common vocabulary, which he divided into obsolete, poetical, modified, and unused words. He noted the influence of the neighboring Welsh and the extent to which agricultural regions preserved the terms of husbandry and how the manufacturing areas had developed craft terms. He also noted peculiarities owing to local diet, architecture, and amusements. Some words were obviously the relics of a common language, others had limited usage. Throughout, Lewis depended on the evidence of other observers as well as his own observations and on glossaries and the opinions of students of English dialects. He concluded with 132 pages of definitions.

His plea for evidence also permeated his essays, suggestions, and inquiries on ancient astronomy and chronology. Unhappily for his reputation, Homer nodded in his own edition of spurious fables attributed to Babrius, wherein he succumbed to a plausible impostor.[22] Continental scholars, already galled by his critiques, did not miss their chance, and so an historian, were he interested, might produce an essay under that fine seventeenth-century title, *The Refuter Refuted.*

A major stimulus to Continental reaction was Lewis' inquiry into the credibility of early Roman history. This inquiry was no sudden enthusiasm, since early and late he ranged through ancient history. He studied Aristotle

[22] *The Fables of Babrius, in two parts. Translated into English Verse from the text of Sir G. C. Lewis. By the Rev. James Davies* (1860). The translator dedicated his work "To the Right Honourable Sir George Cornewall Lewis . . . blending classical study with the severer duties of life."

critically; in reading Thucydides, the financier of the
Crimean War saw the parallel between the sieges of
Syracuse and Sebastopol. He translated Boeckh's *Public
Economy of Athens*, declaring in the preface to the second edition that a "philologer well skilled in both languages" had compared the text with the original and
that he himself had noticed that Boeckh, in quoting one
inscription, had used an incorrect transcript but that,
since the British Museum held the original, he had si-
lently corrected the text.[23] His translation of K. O.
Müller's *History and Antiquities of the Doric Race* and
*History of the Literature of Ancient Greece, to the Period of
Isocrates* taught him that language was the "earliest
product of the human mind, and the origin of all other
intellectual energies" as well as the "clearest evidence
of the descent of a nation."[24]

Throughout, he kept up with contemporary works on
ancient history, with Thomas Arnold, George Grote,
and Connop Thirlwall.[25] Grote worked like a German

[23] Augustus Boeckh, *The Public Economy of Athens; to which is
added, A Dissertation on the Silver Mines of Laurion*. Boeckh published his work in 1817; Lewis' translation appeared first in 1828
and, in a second edition, in 1842. By the latter date he had begun
serious study of Roman history and regretted that no one had
"attempted to write a work, of similar comprehension and research, upon the interesting subject of the Political Economy of
the Roman State."

[24] The first, translated in conjunction with Henry Tufnell, had
two editions, 1830, 1839; the second, in conjunction with J. W.
Donaldson, also had two editions, 1840, 1850.

[25] These three men, along with Julius Hare, placed the study of
Greek and Roman history on a high and firm plane. Arnold (1795–
1842), Hare, and Thirlwall were disciples of Barthold Niebuhr
(1776–1831). For a penetrating appraisal of their quality, see
Duncan Forbes, *The Liberal Anglican Idea of History* (Cambridge,
1952). Arnold's *History of Rome* (1838–1842) was a "splendid
fragment" in three volumes; Thirlwall, in addition to cooperating

professor but, unlike such, had profited from political experience. German writers on antiquity, "being chiefly professors, and passing their time in learned seclusion," were "infected by the fondness for bold hypotheses and the tendency to go beyond the evidence."[26] The prime example was Niebuhr, with his "wonderful perversions and distortions" of ancient writers, his untenable conclusions and inferences, his vast superstructure on an erroneous foundation, all of which Lewis laid bare, at least to his own satisfaction, in his *Inquiry into the Credibility of the Early Roman History*. In his criticism he demonstrated his familiarity with the seventeenth- and eighteenth-century inquirers into early Roman history, their strengths and weaknesses. He praised Niebuhr for his learning and imagination, for his superiority to his predecessors, for demolishing the old fabric and building a new city. On the other hand, Niebuhr had opened more questions than he had closed; he had supported his hypotheses by analogies, not proof. No wonder that critics had impugned his conclusions. Historical, like judicial, evidence properly stood on the testimony of credible witnesses, not on the "occult faculty of historical divination." Niebuhr illustrated

with Hare in translating Niebuhr, wrote an eight-volume *History of Greece* (1835–1847). Grote, banker and Benthamite, wrote a twelve-volume *History of Greece* (1846–1856). Whereas Thirlwall shone in handling diplomatic affairs, Grote at times seemed primarily concerned with lauding Athenian democracy, yet his was a generally sober account running from 776 B.C. to Alexander the Great. Lewis' own Benthamite leanings led him to rate Grote above Thirlwall.

[26] Lewis also raised an eyebrow at W. E. Gladstone for finding the doctrine of the Trinity in Homer and holding Latona to have been compounded of Eve and the Virgin Mary.

the proposition, the more uncertainty, the more conjecture.[27]

No other of Lewis' books was so widely reviewed, and he was surprised that no one had risen to champion Niebuhr, for he granted that his criticism was purely negative. Yet, though reviewers praised his knowledge, his analysis, his devotion to objective truth, his political insights as opposed to Niebuhr's naïveté, they also emphasized the immense stimulus supplied by Niebuhr. Without him there would have been no Arnold, Grote, or Thirlwall—or even Lewis; he had breathed life into all historical study. Salutary as was Lewis' criticism in emphasizing the need for firm evidence, no historian could go far without a broad latitude of hypothesis.

As one would expect, the stress upon language and logic so evident in his historical ventures was even more weighty in his political ones. Whatever he wrote, even his essays on Ireland (1836), the *Government of Dependencies* (1841), *On Foreign Jurisdiction and the Extradition of Criminals* (1859), he called for precision,

---

[27] The far-ranging historian Edward Freeman (1823–1892), thought Niebuhr's work "wonderful" but admitted that it had been strongly criticized, most extremely by the "party of absolute unbelief." Beneath the "Thor's hammer" of Lewis its edifice had fallen to the ground, for he would accept no evidence except that sufficient "to hang a man." Whereas Niebuhr had given the tragic legend of Virginia, killed by her father to save her from the lust of a decemvir, great political and social significance, Lewis coldly asked, "Who saw her die?" and as nobody was ready to answer he had nothing to say to any of them. Freeman, nonetheless, thought that Lewis had made no impression on Niebuhr's main fortress. For evidence in this matter, see Freeman's *The Methods of Historical Study* (1886), 141; *Life and Letters of Edward A. Freeman* (2 vols., 1895), I, 203; *Historical Essays* (2d ed. 1880), II, 297–300. A century later Momigliano, though regarding Lewis as too skeptical, still found good words for his independence of thought, analysis of sources, and contribution to better methods.

warned against fallacies, and probed the meaning of words. In *The Influence of Authority in Matters of Opinion* (1849) he insisted on the responsibility of every man to examine and define his opinions before pressing them on his neighbors. Here, too, he asserted the value of proverbs as the quintessence of experience—the wit of one but the wisdom of many. More pertinently to the present emphasis, he argued that, just as the stability and success of government hinged on acquiescence, so language depended on usage, the usage of the greatest number, though to argue thus did not deny the importance of the learned few. Although the scientific writer was bound to regard language as a precious depository of established ideas, he must look beyond "mere contemporary usage" in aiming at precision. He must look to the origins and trace the meanings of terms and, not least, examine the works wherein such terms were used.

What Lewis expounded incidentally in this essay he discussed more systematically three years later in the treatise on reasoning in politics, wherein he stressed the unsound methods of political theorists. The character of this work prompted the critical opinion that, by overemphasizing correct reasoning, Lewis might encourage exaggerated expectations from inquiries into the laws of causation in politics. In practice lenient, in theory rigid, he prompted charges of pettifoggery, and one may well surmise that Bagehot, while criticizing "Mr. Austin's school" for magnifying the effect of language, had Lewis in mind. Yet, though no one should disregard Bagehot's salutary "realism," on balance Lewis may have been closer to 1970 than his younger, more brilliant contemporary; the present-day resources of claptrap far exceed anything that Bagehot, incisive observer that he was, could imagine.

Virtually all that Lewis had to say on political rhetoric in *Methods of Reasoning* was contained in the chapter "On the Technical Language of Politics," wherein he testified again and again to the inspiration of Whewell and so made his own contribution to "physics and politics." He began by asserting the need to ascertain the character of the political vocabulary and to inquire how effectively that vocabulary facilitated or impeded the logical processes of which it was the necessary instrument, since in Whewell's words, "every step in the progress of science is marked by the formation or appropriation of a technical term." When knowledge became exact, men required exact language, which would exclude "vagueness and fancy, imperfection and superfluity" and in which each term conveyed a meaning "steadily fixed and vigorously limited." Common language in most cases had a "certain degree of looseness and ambiguity," as common knowledge usually had "something of vagueness and indistinctness," of emotion and imagination. Its "loose and infantine grasp" could not hold objects steadily enough for scientific examination or lift them from one stage of generalization to another. Although Lewis appreciated that science was one thing, politics something else, he saw that in both areas general terms had evolved from particular phenomena.

Recognizing such evolution did not of itself, however, remedy the inadequacy of ordinary language for precise statement, especially in philosophy. The mechanic had instruments for his needs, but the philosopher must depend on crude tools for refined needs, tools acceptable for common communication but unfit for him, tools in

which he must think as well as communicate. The best
he could do was to define his terms, even though he must
still use them in their vague acceptation. With Whewell,
Lewis preferred the appropriation of old words to the
invention of new ones, believing that the user should
retain the original meaning as unambiguously as possible. Pregnant as Whewell's aphorisms were, Lewis
found them salutary rather than applicable. In politics,
exactitude—however desirable—was difficult to attain;
words and definitions were too closely connected with
practice, as even so commonplace a term as *law* illustrated. Moreover, meanings and usages constantly
fluctuated because institutions changed and new
branches of learning came into being, such as Political
Economy, wherein several writers had attempted to
meet current need for definition. How could one attach
the same meaning to many words in the context of
monarchy and of republic, of absolute and of limited
monarchy? Vagueness and inaccuracy often had a
stylistic basis: Fearing inelegance or monotony, anxious
to vary the expression and avoid repetition, men
changed their metaphors. Yet, in the interest of precision there was no safer rule than "always to call the
same thing by the same name"; in science there were no
variations, and politics should at least seek the same
objective. Words adopted into a technical vocabulary
from common use in one language might appear as
original scientific terms; even more confusing was the
use of ancient terms in new situations. What complicated the whole problem was that politics was a condition as well as a theory; not only did it lack a technical
vocabulary but the politician could readily debase its
existing nomenclature by exploiting ambiguity and
emotion.

Although Lewis' final political essay, *Dialogue on the Best Form of Government* (1863) did not explore these same points, it did throughout reflect his continuing concern. Each participant, *Monarchicus*, *Aristocraticus*, and *Democraticus* defined what he was proposing, and *Crito*, the benign moderator—no doubt Lewis himself—sought to ensure adherence to logic and coherence in the use of terms. So it was that, for over thirty years through one outlet after another, he manifested his desire to perfect the use and prevent the abuse of political terms, and hence the abuse of political power, the subject of his first political essay, *Remarks on the Use and Abuse of some Political Terms.*

IV

THOUGH a young man's book, an inexperienced man's book, that essay, with its apt text from *Romeo and Juliet*,

> Seal up the mouth of outrage for a while,
> Till we can clear these ambiguities,
> And know their spring, their head, their true descent,

was no mere prize essay; nor was it a spectral woof of linguistic abstractions. Lewis, a man of *virtù*, skillfully wove empirical weft and theoretical warp. Concerned less with the facts than the rhetoric of politics he concentrated on what political communities *must* be. Every science, he emphasized, should illustrate the various uses of its terms, leaving to logic the responsibility for defining equivocal words that belong to no subject in particular. Such a task fell between a technical dictionary and a scientific treatise, more copious than the first, less so than the second. In achieving it Lewis sought to ascertain usages both in the context of scientific inquiries and the "living Language" of party politics, especially in those works of extensive circulation and established character, which for that very reason were most mischievous. Here he particularly fastened on Blackstone, in whose speculative parts one might find an "epitome of popular fallacies and misconceptions." He also warned readers against passing from one signification of a word to another; even the "most skillful and experienced reasoners" were liable to this fatal error—an observation that might shock persons who had not considered the powerful influence of equivocal language in deceiving the mind. Perhaps in no moral or political treatise of any length had the conclusions escaped the effect of some unperceived ambiguity of language.

Although strictly political, the *Remarks*, in the author's opinion, might influence other areas of reasoning, in contrast to Bentham's *Handbook*, which treated the truth (or falsity) of certain assumptions. The arguments attacked by Bentham were not fallacious, granted certain premises; he disproved the premises but offered no solution to questions that did not involve those premises. For his own part, Lewis attacked the argument where Bentham attacked the propositions. Lest anyone assume that Bentham was getting to the heart of the matter and Lewis only logic-chopping, he should remember the latter's belief that, since the soundness of an inference depended on the use of a term, it was necessary to examine its meaning.

Lewis saw two ways to refute an argument: by exposing the falsity of the premise; by showing that, however true, it did not support the conclusion. Most people could detect falsity more quickly than unsound inference that imperceptibly poisoned the reasoning. Moreover, awareness of ambiguity did not guarantee its defeat. Because of their failure to define terms men wasted time in declamation and invective that they could profitably have used to advance truth—the waste that no doubt Locke had in mind when he speculated on how much more the ill use of words had hindered knowledge than language had promoted it. With that specific opinion Lewis had no sympathy; for him language, whatever its defects and hindrances, alone preserved and communicated knowledge. Nevertheless, men must agree on terms, lest they mistake shadow for substance, interpret statements in a way never intended, and dispute about words when they should be debating premises. In politics a dispute properly turns on the meaning of words, and to avoid confusion men should recognize that dispute as verbal.

Although Lewis tended to assign one meaning to a term, he did not require such limitation, because he realized that most ambiguities resulted from historical associations and translations, and indeed no harm would follow if a misnomer led no one astray.[28] He knew that no one could legislate in matters of language, but he would banish the mischievous ambiguity that confounded things as well as words, and confused, deluded, and even swindled for the sake of victory.[29] In this re-

[28] Cf. the perceptive opinion of R. G. Collingwood, *Speculum Mentis* (Oxford, 1924), 11: "To suppose that one word, in whatever context it appears, ought to mean one thing and no more, argues not an exceptionally high standard of logical accuracy but an exceptional ignorance as to the nature of language."

[29] One of his editors, Sir Roland Knyvet Wilson, disagreed with his opinion that "it is impossible to legislate in matters of language"; the "adoption of a fixed nomenclature and orthography in all laws and legal instruments," said Wilson, "cannot fail to

spect Lewis was also seeking to help persons who needed more than a dictionary to detect flaws in reasoning by which they were not convinced; it was as important to know why some persons were wrong as to know why their opponents were right. Yet, to determine how far party contentions followed the use of certain phrases by interested persons and how far they followed the delusion of language when several terms were crowded together in the same proposition was impossible. Errors clouded the mind, and they were the more difficult to discern when seemingly insignificant and therefore unsuspected. What, therefore, Lewis was pleading for was both accurate knowledge and watchful observance of words. These tools would enable a man to detect fallacies in his own reasoning as well as those in other men's —above all in communicating thoughts—since numerous treatises failed, through neglect of definition and/or inaccurate language, to make a subject intelligible.

Lewis' argument here suggests a new "Malthusian" law: Media increase arithmetically, error geometrically. Everywhere, he said, one met glib nonsense in wellsounding English; critically tested, such flowery declamation shrank to nothing. Shameless impostors should be exposed, although no one could frame infallible rules to undeceive the victims of an ingenious sophist who proved what men wished to believe. How easy to go wrong, how difficult to go right. No statement of truth alone counteracted error, for the latter was manifold,

---

exercise a powerful influence over popular usage; an influence which would have been much more strongly felt in England, had not our laws been expressed for many centuries in a foreign language, and for several more in a verbose jargon almost equally remote from literary English." *Remarks on the Use and Abuse of some Political Terms.* A new edition, with notes and appendix (Oxford, 1877), 7.

full of pervasive inconsistencies. Moreover, in rejecting error men agreed only in rejection; they *affirmed* as many "truths" as there were persons. As regards the terms with which he was specifically dealing, Lewis recognized full well that some readers would find him obvious, others false, yet both groups might also derive value from his statement: Those who found him obvious might be reminded of the connection between their conclusions and their premises, their opinions and their assumptions, even that the positions they condemned sired doctrines they approved; those who found him false should be aware that he was not establishing a theory of government but investigating terms and that he must not be held responsible for erroneous deductions from his own propositions. All should know that many terms were marked rather by differences in phraseology than in opinion; no more than institutions or ideas did terms stand still.

Once Lewis published a book he apparently forgot about it, for though he referred in his letters to what he was doing he seldom referred to what he had done. Apart from the translations of Boeckh and Müller, three of his works came out in second editions only after his death, and one, the essay on romance languages, appeared just the year before he died. The present essay alone had three editions, and although the *Methods of Reasoning* did incorporate some of its matter and although some scholars have preferred that treatise, the earlier work is less dated. During the last quarter of the nineteenth century Oxford teachers were recommending it as a fitting example of the scientific study of law and politics, reason enough for two posthumous editions. Now a different stimulus operates: the parallel rise of linguistics and, what may or may not be a totally independent impulse, mounting awareness of the utter debasement of verbal currency in propaganda and advertising. Definitions may beget a whole genealogy of begats, but, considering the proliferation of cant and claptrap, they deserve a good rating.

The *Remarks* illustrates the refusal to accept a bad argument in support of a good doctrine, on the ground that in theory and practice alike no end is better than the means used to achieve it. Lewis, professing only to seek the "formation of a convenient and consistent terminology," did not belong in the company of those, perceptively described by Sir Thomas Browne, who too rashly charge the "troops of error and remain as trophies unto the enemies of truth." Neither was he a Shelley beating his wings in a void, luminous or murky, but a man committed to a public career in an age of political and social revolution. Throughout, he was addressing his contemporaries in terms particularly applicable to their environment. Nonetheless, it is worth while to disentangle the presumptions of 1832 from those of 1970 as far as may be; in so doing one may discover how universal the particular is. To accomplish this separation, the historian must get behind tangible assertions to the intangible assumptions; he must be at once earthbound and airborne. He must relate what Lewis said to the abiding problems of politics and morals however differently they manifest themselves yesterday, today, and tomorrow.

Throughout, the *Remarks* reveals a positivist who felt that he was going to the heart of the matter for the first time. It also reveals a man alive to the stresses of the time, to the impact of science and political economy as well as politics. The world around was in tension and turmoil, rising and falling elites, scientific revolution, demands for reform in political, religious, economic, educational areas, exchange of ideas through periodicals and societies. To say that in the face of rapid and many-faceted change Lewis registered concern is not to suggest despair or denunciation. Rather than indulge in jeremiads about breakdown and irresponsibility, he sought to bridge the gap between those who held power and those who would hold it in the next generation. After all, 1832 was the year of the Great Reform Act, and on both sides of that year statutes were transforming the structure and function of government alike. In a shifting polity many powerful spokesmen were parroting answers to questions that more thoughtful men had ceased to ask. Lewis' search for stability was no wail of a reactionary but the conviction of a liberal. In dealing with that conviction as voiced in the *Remarks*, the existence and timing of public assertions, in short the relevance—not truth or falsity—is his primary concern. What he cast in particular, empirical terms and has since become commonplace needed to be said, and Lewis said it.

An elaborate commentary on the *Remarks* would in all probability only exemplify the manifest destiny of exegeses, confusing what had once been clear. Yet, though his terms are familiar and his exposition lucid, two points warrant emphasis: first, the reminder that his opinions, which are those of the governing class, are secreted in the interstices of his language as well as explicitly stated; second, his silences. What he talked about was important to his class, and the space he gave to each topic is revealing; what he did not talk about is no less revealing. In assessing this last aspect of his work —almost entirely a matter for conjecture—one must allow for deliberate rejection and total unawareness and even consider whether or not Lewis incorporated some subjects under terms that he used more comprehensively than they are commonly used today. After all he did, in his high Aristotelian way, identify politics with society. His search for political stability embraced the whole community of the realm, as did that of his great contemporary across the Channel, Tocqueville, with whom he occasionally corresponded.

This comprehensive presumption increased his expository difficulties, since, trivial and obvious as the factor seems, he had always to consider his readers. Scholar though he was and administrator though he would be, he was addressing neither professors nor politicians but the public, a changing public too. But changing though it was, it still comprised the governing classes, those in office and those without whose approval office was impossible. His readers apprehended what he was talking about—it was a large part of their experience—and, as the reaction to Bentham indicated, they wanted no terminology on stilts, preferring old words, whether in government or political economy, to neologisms. Yet as Lewis, along with Whately and Whewell, appreciated, this preference produced misunderstandings attendant upon the application of common words to technical subjects, the use of several such words to describe the same thing, and the use of one of them to describe several things—all of which heightened his sensitivity to that problem, historical and contemporaneous: the poverty, hence constriction, of language. When Lewis attacked Blackstone he was attacking vagueness and the acceptance of form for substance; when he was preaching exactitude he was pointing to the social as well as logical evils of ambiguity.

Although he did not compartmentalize those evils it is fitting, in view of his title, to look first at political

terminology. Dealing with terms both abstract and concrete in their usage, he fused his definitions because men
shifted from one use to another without explanation, a
natural consequence of the evolution of the English
polity. In his definitions he steadily reminded his readers how often men used such terms ambiguously, attach-
ing social, economic, and moral connotations, irrelevant
yet decisive in effect. The space that Lewis gave to a
topic varied (in the present edition) from barely more
than a page to nearly thirty, but the specific length in
no way measured his estimate of the importance of the
subject, since he invariably appraised the same terms in
different contexts and took into account their everyday
use as well as their philosophic and historical meanings.

In these respects *constitution* offered an opportunity
which he used to the full and in a fashion relevant to a
different country one hundred and forty years later.
Primarily the arrangement and distribution of power,
the term often signified an imaginary model of excellence
calculated to deceive ignorant persons that a policy was
restoration, not innovation. *Constitutional* and *unconstitutional* conveyed approbation and disapproval, epithets frequently used to denote agreement or disagreement with a subjective standard; the attendant dispute
was often merely verbal, yet to accuse persons of logomachy only excited ill will. *Law*, even more briefly treated
—perhaps because he felt that Austin had said all that
needed to be said—gave Lewis the opportunity to dissent from Bentham's regret that men did not use *right*
when they wished to signify *law* in the sense of the total
body of law, for he believed that *right* had already too
heavy a burden, the more that men often confused *right*
and *power*. He differentiated between law and justice,
citing the proper difference between the treatment of a

depraved criminal and a mad criminal.[30] Law was the command of the sovereign, and disputes concerning it must be decided only by the courts, yet because law often covered moral rules, privately—not publicly—determined, confusion resulted.

Sovereignty not only received a lengthy chapter on its own but, as one might expect, pervaded many others; no term was marked by so many ambiguities, even contradictions, owing in part to the difficulty of reconciling unitary assumptions with a plural society. Although sovereignty was the distinguishing quality of government and although the sovereign had no superior under God, Lewis was wholly empirical in inquiring how long the sovereign had been sovereign and under what circumstances. The sovereign had the "complete disposal of the life, rights, and duties of every member of the community," *but,* who was sovereign? The king was at once the sovereign and not sovereign. If Parliament was sovereign, who was sovereign when Parliament was not in session? Such questions indicate that Lewis, for all his flat assertions, recognized that the problem had long since passed from the simple to the complex.

Although the Austinian emphasis is often apparent, here as in many other topics, Lewis happily avoided the intolerable backing and filling of his teacher. At the same time he showed far more awareness of the intersection of political institutions and social change. Austin defined terms in a vacuum; Lewis, equally anxious to get them straight, recognized that circumambient cur-

---

[30] Many would now question Lewis' assumption that a "depraved" criminal was wholly responsible, though they would applaud his enlightened realization that a madman was not; the majority of his contemporaries, whether educated or not, believed that madness ought to be punished.

rents are as vital to political life and communication as
to physiological. Not only would old theorems not do,
new ones would not either—if they only replaced one
set of dogmas by another. New opinions, new phrases
were everywhere about him. Some men were declaring
that, in the absence of Parliament, sovereignty reverted
to the community or to the electors; others were pro-
nouncing the sovereignty of the people; still others were
accepting "limited sovereignty." Although all these
phrases were, in his opinion, metaphorical, contradictory, meaningless, or even improper, he saw in other
contexts nothing improper in "absolute sovereignty."
The right to vote for the sovereign was not to share in
the sovereignty; representation, "the act of supporting
a vicarious character," though a political right, was no
exercise of sovereignty. Yet such rights increased the
moral influence of the community, and once the representative was elected to the sovereign body and legally
answerable to no one, he was morally bound to promote
the good of the community. In following Lewis on this
topic the reader should bear in mind that he was describing England primarily and that, in addition, his
blanket concession of sovereign power reflected the conviction that without such power lawlessness must triumph and society be overturned. At the same time he
recognized what many declaimers since have not, that
law and order are subjective terms and the *prevailing*
definition is the hypothesis of the ruling class.

Closely related, similarly complicated and reflective
of contemporary circumstances, was *right*. This "question-begging appellative," Bentham called it, being both
substantive and adjective covered many traps. How did
legal rule and moral right mesh? The government had
the *right* to command, subjects the *duty* to obey; what-

ever was to the contrary was a wrong. No claim of authority that could not be enforced was a right. Conversely, said Lewis, a right might be wrong, which was a reason for laws. Did men have a right to do wrong? Was a right right, or a wrong wrong? In every tongue *right* was ambiguity made flesh. Latin had *jus* and *rectus*, but *jus* meant right and law; the French *droit* and German *recht* were equally ambiguous, confusion confounded by translation. The sovereign could not be said to possess rights, since such were enforceable only by a superior authority (which did not exist); nor was the sovereign subject to duties, since the sovereign could not be forced. Sovereigns were morally accountable to God, not legally to their subjects, else government was destroyed. Yet although the sovereign—Parliament in this case—could do no wrong, it must not punish a man for an action not forbidden. All too often men confused a wrong (an injury) with wrong (improper), the legal substantive with the moral adjective.

What caused Lewis to be so exercised about this issue? The broadening sphere of legislation? The rise of new elites? Free and open debate in and out of Parliament? The Benthamite union of morals and legislation? The proliferation of political rhetoric? The proliferation of adjectives? In his consideration of the subjects he found men repeatedly confusing *moral* and *legal*. The notion of right as independent of positive law and institutions directly contravened the truth, and when men referred to *original, inalienable, indefeasible, imprescriptible, natural, inherent* rights they repudiated the sovereign as the source of rights. If ever such rights had existed, the sovereign had long since defeated them. Moreover, such terms were not synonymous, though they were constantly used as such by people who had never heard of the *doctrine* and would reject it if they did. What persons meant was that such rights ought to be sanctioned by positive law, which would immediately prove those rights neither original nor natural nor inherent. To establish such rights, furthermore, would require proof of necessity, and so drive men to question-begging, high-sounding appellatives. *Vested* also required definition. Legally it meant only that the right of the next possessor was ascertained; politically it meant that Parliament had bestowed specific rights on specific people for the time being and that before termination due warning should be given, an obligation especially evident in property rights because they impinged on nearly every aspect of a man's life. Whatever the tack, Lewis worried the issue of parliamentary sovereignty throughout. Parliament could do no wrong because whatever it did was right; it could do no wrong because there was no wrong without a remedy, and against acts of Parliament there was no remedy, except in those instances when, through public opinion, Parliament on its own initiative provided its own remedy.

From these topics Lewis moved to forms of government. England, where sovereignty was one and which had royalty but not monarchy (absolute monarchy that is), was a *commonwealth*; the United States, where government was shared by less than half the community, was an *aristocracy*. *Democracy*, a term of many meanings, was often misapplied in the cases of the United States and Athens, because of the institution of slavery. Mixed government got much more attention, being played off against simple government, though indeed government could not be one and many.

As a political philosopher as well as a political scientist Lewis could not separate forms of government from social classes. Indeed, one could reasonably maintain that he was more concerned with the physiology of society than with the anatomy of politics, a priority explicable in the light of contemporary tension and change. *Aristocracy* meant both a government and a class, sometimes joined as in the Whig Oligarchy. As a class, *aristocracy* might signify gentlemen in the sense conveyed by Chesterfield when he wrote that it was "unbecoming for a gentleman to walk quickly in the streets, because it seemed as if he had some occupation." In this context just as men had often regarded *aristocracy* as government by the rich, so had they interpreted *democracy* as government, not by the majority, but by the poor. In England, he said, it appeared that all measures tending to increase the power of the affluent and educated were "anti-popular," and those tending to increase the power of the poor were "popular," for, according to the *Edinburgh Review*, it was the "immediate interest of the people to plunder the rich." Such conceptions were utterly confusing. As history fully illustrated, these terms were all relative: not one had meaning without the others. Retention of the same label, furthermore, should not imply retention of the same condition. Men must look to the thing as well as the word, since *poor* might embrace those who were not rich, and *rich* might exclude those who were not poor. Today's poor might be tomorrow's middle class; the poor of one country might be the middling sort of people in another. In quoting Brougham's description (1831) of the middle class as the "most numerous, and far the most wealthy order of the community," Lewis properly denied the first assertion and questioned the second, and he insisted that labels should be scrutinized in a caste-ridden country, where to be put below the middle class was to be utterly damned. In England, moreover, men had long differentiated between the deserving (frugal, hard-working, self-sufficient) and the undeserving poor (paupers, beggars, vagabonds), a classification recently extended by Wilmot Horton's definition of the poor as denoting persons who possessed nothing disposable but their labor. Having created an absolute, Horton then proceeded to break it down in four categories—laborers, helpless poor, paupers, beggars—which Lewis criticized as lacking reference to the total environment.[31]

In his opinion, one must consider that the rich and the poor each had an *interest* distinct from the interest of the community, but that the poor and the middle class combined against the rich; consequently their interest was community. Interest, however, meant welfare as well as self-promotion; in the abstract it meant the first, in the concrete the second. When government favored *an* interest it neglected the common good. The common good, Lewis hastened to insist, could not be secured by the uneasy balancing of interests, for out of such could come only tension, competition, and, ultimately, disruption and despotism. What he sought would be achieved by the prudence of the rich, the numbers, wealth, and respectability of the middle class, the diffusion of knowledge among the poor, and, above all by extending the rights of citizenship to everyone. Yet

---

[31] Henry Brougham (1778–1868), enormously energetic and enormously opinionated, was scarcely less versatile than Lewis; he was Lord Chancellor in 1832. Wilmot Horton (1784–1841), chiefly memorable for his concern with colonization, was parliamentary undersecretary for the Colonies, 1812–1827. Lewis also sharply criticized colonial appointments—"briefless barristers, broken-down merchants, ruined debauchees, the offal of every calling and profession."

"sovereignty of the people" was meaningless except insofar as it described a situation in which men exercised moral control. The Revolution of 1688, scarcely to be labeled a revolution, had, without extending sovereignty to more persons than had previously exercised it, increased the moral influence of part of the community. In the United States "sovereignty of the people" was improperly used: The right to vote was no more than the right to express an opinion. Whatever else, men should not confound use with abuse; when they did not distinguish between metaphorical and literal, mischief was bound to ensue.

The same warnings applied to those fine abstractions, *nature, liberty, power*, and even *property*. The first, a term whose bewildering significations made it impossible to decide what was *natural*, could nevertheless be reduced to two applications, one meaning essence or quality, the other excluding human activity. This latter application connoted the corruption of the natural state of virtue and happiness by human activities. Locke's diffuse and indistinct words had furthered this "puerile theory of the progress of society," both untenable and contradictory, a "theory which could only have arisen from the distempered imagination of some day-dreamer, and could only have been tolerated by a blind ignorance or wilful neglect of all history." Historical knowledge had indeed exploded the concept of primitive utopia that, far from being beneficent, was stunted and degraded.

No less than nature did *liberty* have positive and negative connotations, the enjoyment of positive rights and freedom from restraint, the possession of rights and immunity from duties. Liberty was not, however, the ultimate end of government, and to say that men were naturally free was an example of "exsufflicate and blown surmises," an instance where the conclusion supported the premises. As always when Lewis was discussing abstractions, he particularized. Freedom must needs be considered in pragmatic terms: a free government in relation to an arbitrary government. Substantially, that division coincided with the classification of governments into republics and monarchies, though he quickly pointed out that to assume that liberty was possible only under a free government and inevitably impossible in a despotism was mistaken. Free governments might actually be more tyrannical than despotisms, for tyranny was no monopoly of any form of government. Tyranny was not merely irresponsible power, since Parliament, though responsible to no one, was not in fact tyrannical. No man was less free than the head of the house, and men should not confuse the exercise of power with its abuse. *Power* itself was an ambiguous term and lent itself to diverse uses. Authority was power sanctioned by law, but authority and power were not synonymous; moreover, some men exercised power with only moral sanction. Some power admittedly was both legal and tyrannical, but in practice governments, though subsisting by force, applied it rarely. *Anarchy* might follow supinity, but users of the term frequently exploited to the full its resources of vagueness and ambiguity: Whatever was displeasing to the friends of despotism was anarchy.

Many other terms got merely passing attention, for presumably Lewis did not rate their "abusage" significant, though he did again condemn ambiguities. Though he saw no reason to dwell long on *property*, he did, as one must expect, insist upon its rights, particularly that of possession. Such emphasis by no means blinded him to the handicaps of the poor who suffered from the existing distribution of property, above all in times of depression.

What significance has this essay? Originality is no word for publicists: Lewis composed a commentary on a text phrased more than 2300 years earlier, on the other side of the world. "If names are not right, words are misused. When words are misused, affairs go wrong." Then law and justice fail, for "without a knowledge of words there is no understanding men." That Confucius had no monopoly on wisdom is clear from St. Paul's question, "Except ye utter words easy to be understood, how shall it be known what is spoken?" Nor was Lewis the last writer on the subject; the *Use and Abuse* might indeed serve as a matter-of-fact preface to John Ruskin's sermon a generation later. In the first lecture (1864) of *Sesame and Lilies* that eloquent lay preacher first diagnosed the ills to which words are heir, then prescribed the proper regimen. He bade his listeners assure themselves of the meaning of words, for if that were closely watched they would discover that a few words well chosen would do the work that a thousand could not. Words used equivocally did deadly work. Many were skulking about, which everyone used and no one understood, chameleon words, unjust stewards of men's ideas. To use words rightly men should know their origins, descent, and intermarriages, and should ascertain the meanings through which they had passed. Then only would men think and act properly.[32]

[32] Perhaps most active of all who concentrated on the study, the deficiencies, and the importance of words at mid-century was Richard Chenevix Trench (1807–1886) who in 1864 succeeded Lewis' mentor Whately as Archbishop of Dublin. His first major contribution, *On the Study of Words* (1851), went through nineteen

Simultaneously, Lewis Carroll, far less didactically, was ridiculing Jabberwocky, which Alice thought very pretty but hard to understand; it filled her head with ideas, only she didn't know exactly what they were. Historians' English also came in for japery in the exchange that arose when the Mouse was reading how "even Stigand, the patriotic archbishop of Canterbury, found it advisable—Found *what*? said the Duck. Found *it*, the Mouse replied rather crossly: of course you know what it means. I know what *it* means well enough, when I find a thing, said the Duck: it's generally a frog, or a worm. The question is, what did the archbishop find? The Mouse did not notice this question, but hurriedly went on."

Neither so passionate as Ruskin nor so witty as Carroll, Lewis had a value of his own. All political discourses —even the *Republic*, the *Prince*, *Democracy in America* —"date," but they are not for that reason to be cast into outer darkness. However objective their pose they are autobiographies of their time as well as of their authors, reason enough for studying them. Being such, they compel us to ask questions of our time, to examine today's political rhetoric in the light of today's tensions. Lewis analyzed pressing issues and supplied answers, some trivial, some mistaken, many no doubt the mirror of his own political and social bias. But when they are weighed, many still have relevance.

What of the reaction of contemporaries to Lewis' works in this genre? Two examples will suffice, those of John Stuart Mill and Nassau William Senior. The form-

---

editions in thirty-five years, and *English Past and Present* (1855), fourteen editions in thirty-four years. He agreed with Hazlitt in giving high marks to Tooke's *Diversions of Purley*, "an epoch in many a student's intellectual life."

er's lengthy "on the other hand" review of the *Use and Abuse* reveals more of Mill than of Lewis.[33] After brief reference to the translations of Müller and Boeckh and the examination of Whately's logic, Mill described the present essay as a work of no extraordinary merit, but meritorious for a man to have written it. Lewis had undertaken a task for which only a logician was competent, but one of the most important a logician could attempt. Logic did not mean syllogisms but justness of thought and precision of language. In Mill's view Lewis had attacked the confounding of things that, although they were essentially different, happened to bear the same name, and he sought to correct "false and slovenly thinking" in politics. Lewis should also, according to Mill, attend to those "instances in which the confusion of language is the *consequence*, and not the cause, of the erroneous train of thought," which Mill believed to be more generally common. Though possessing an "instructed and intelligent" mind Lewis was not fully conscious of what his subject required: He showed something to be wrong through showing how it might be corrected. Could one, asked Mill, be said to have got at the root of error if he planted no truth in its stead? Was there something he had not seen?

Yet Lewis was entitled to be tried by the highest standard. Because mankind had many ideas but few words, a writer, if he would be understood, was likely to be led into laxity; consequently he needed the cooperation of his readers. Unavoidable ambiguities made it easier for confusion to pass undetected, clarity more

[33] This review, which first appeared in *Tait's Edinburgh Magazine*, I (1832), 164 ff., is reprinted in Charles Street, *Individualism and Individuality in the Philosophy of John Stuart Mill* (Milwaukee, 1926), 121–36.

difficult to achieve, and hence unreason more likely to triumph. Many men teeming with ideas, in Mill's view, could not put them into unobjectionable terms, a view fully as debatable as any put forward by Lewis; others achieved clarity by the poverty of their ideas. More particularly, Mill wondered what Lewis meant by *abuse*. Could not a man employ such terms as he would in order to get his meaning across? Whether Mill missed Lewis' point or simply disagreed with it is not clear. He was in any case denying Lewis his right to use such terms as he would in order to get his meaning across. Mill also questioned Lewis' contention that to call a thing a *right* that could not be enforced by law was an abuse of language, by rejoining that such could be true only if one accepted Lewis' definition of *right*. As to Lewis' disagreement with Locke on *nature*, Mill believed that he should have asked not whether such a state existed but whether there was an advantage in supposing its existence and what morality would be like if no such norm was hypothecated. Such inadequacies did not disqualify Lewis but, rather, prompted Mill to stress the necessity for a treatise on the ambiguities of the moral sciences.

Although Senior did not review the *Use and Abuse*, he adverted to it in his lengthy essay on *The Influence of Authority*, wherein he discoursed on Lewis' concern with public questions as he did also in his scarcely less lengthy review of the *Government of Dependencies*.[34] He noted how Lewis took a small province in philology, politics, or philosophy and produced a more complete and generally more accurate map than he might have achieved

---

[34] *Edinburgh Review*, April, 1846, April, 1850; reprinted in *Historical and Philosophical Essays*, 2 vols. (London, 1865), II, 173–323.

had he chosen a larger area. The *Use and Abuse*, said Senior, had given its subject an importance that no writer in the future could disregard. Similarly, in dealing with *authority*, Lewis brought to bear his wide and diverse experience as well as his broad learning. There were, of course, points to criticize. Senior found the opening portion marked by ambiguity of nomenclature, a fault that often characterized works of an abstract nature. He, like Mill, quarreled with "abuses" of authority, which he felt a misnomer, since the principal subject was the use, not the abuse, of authority. Nonetheless, he could not take leave of the suggestive remarks and acute inferences without admitting his own inadequate treatment of a work that had alluded to so many subjects and opened so many views, often into unexplored regions, and would be studied far more in its own pages than in his.

In addition to the opinions of contemporaries those of succeeding generations warrant mention, specifically as manifest in the two posthumous editions by Sir Roland Knyvet Wilson (1877) and Thomas Raleigh (1898). Their primary concern, as noted earlier, was political theory, and their notes reflect that emphasis, though Wilson, writing when language was still a subject for widespread discussion, did recognize the semantic aspects of the *Remarks*. He also recognized that the essay's value consisted less in the substance than in the method of treating political questions, which would assist the reader when he came to deal with practical politics. (The assumption that the readers were "going into" politics reveals the structure of contemporary society.) Only occasionally did Wilson differ from Lewis; only occasionally did he supplement him. In the latter instances he noted that England had successfully passed through the crisis to which Lewis had adverted in assessing the conflict of interest between classes; the struggle, Wilson thought, was mild, partly because laborers had in some measure become property owners. Similarly, he amplified the discussion of *liberty* by injecting a reference to Joseph Chamberlain's "free land, free labour, free religion, and free schools," of which, he said, the first apparently meant reduction of entail and the second shorter hours; the third in a sense was claptrap, and the fourth contradicted liberty. Here he also remarked what was increasingly disturbing Victorian publicists, the paradox of democracy and liberty. Finally, Wilson included as an appendix, "Some other Political Terms liable to Ambiguity or Misuse," listing words that had little or no relevance in 1832.

Raleigh supplied what Wilson had not attempted, namely, a biographical sketch of Lewis as well as a summary of his opinions.[35] His notes, chiefly modest enlargements of Lewis', require no comment. His estimate, devoid of condescension, excites no dissent, though to be sure it was colored by contemporary issues and outlook, particularly as regards Ireland and the Empire. Raleigh saw a strong believer in the power—and importance—of public opinion, a man who thought that, because of its absence, neither India nor Ireland was ready for self-government. No racist or Protestant, Lewis believed that, had German Protestants undergone the same experiences as Irish Catholics, they would have been equally troublesome; Irish misfortunes were due to the identity of religious, class, and political

[35] Thomas Raleigh, *Remarks on the Use and Abuse of some Political Terms*, a new edition, with notes and introduction (Oxford, 1898).

divisions. Although he opposed the Established Church in Ireland and would have deployed much of its revenue to the benefit of the Catholic clergy, Lewis at the same time was loath to attack property rights. A moderate, neither doctrinaire, intolerant, nor unfair, but austere, so he appeared a third of a century after his death. By then the environment that inspired his books and his policies had largely disappeared, and its problems with it. Yet for all that, he had not dated by 1877 nor by 1898; nor has he dated in 1970. The explanation lies not in his stars but in the man and in his intellectual milieu.

Victorian sages, says a perceptive critic, all sought to "express notions about the world, man's situation, and how he should live."[36] Because of revolutionary changes in knowledge and society they sought to protect, deepen, and unify the culture they knew, and in so doing they became what seems to a later generation unconscionably dogmatic—a corollary, one must suppose, to inner uncertainty. They sought to persuade their readers and listeners of the threats to their culture by quickening perceptiveness as well as by logic, by the right word as much as by the right argument. For them, language was thought, and metaphor an aid to reflection. Lewis, though neither unconscionably dogmatic nor throbbing with inner uncertainty, expressed those aspirations as fully and as clearly as the sages who commonly get firsts in any mapping of the Victorian mind.

Indeed he did so much more happily than the "Gruffian," James Fitzjames Stephen, some decades later, even though he was quite as alive to threats to stability, their sources and possible consequences, and sought

[36] John Holloway, *The Victorian Sage: Studies in Argument* (London, 1953), Chapter 1.

even more persistently to counter them.[37] Stephen, twenty-three years younger but with a similar background, was far more fearful of "democracy" and far more rigid in his response to contemporary turmoil, which was certainly no greater in 1867 than in 1832.[38] Where Lewis believed that if men *thought* precisely, logically, coherently they could and would solve political, that is to say, national problems, Stephen believed that if men *behaved* morally, thriftily, and unselfishly they could and would achieve the same end. Where Stephen was a moralist distrustful of human nature, Lewis was an intellectual, confident of men's ability to achieve, if not heaven here below, at least a reasonably good society. All of which suggests that any appraisal of George Cornewall Lewis must take into account his intent as well as his achievement. He did not, he said, choose his fallacies from any love of detraction, but to assist the progress of political—Aristotelian be it remembered—knowledge, and to do so by calling attention to the questions really at issue, not merely their symptoms. So modest and so salutary a purpose will never lose its relevance in the world of men.

[37] Stephen (1829–1894), the author of *History of the Criminal Law of England,* codifier of Indian criminal law, is chiefly significant in the present context as the author of *Liberty, Equality, Fraternity* (1873), inspired by Mill's essay *On Liberty* (1859) and leveled at the "false and poor" democratic commonplaces of the day. That Lewis recognized the difficulty of curing social pathology by political means is clear, as evidenced by his observation that the "necessity of decision by a majority in a political body, whether its power be legislative, judicial, or administrative, is a defect in the nature of cooperate action." *Essay on the Influence of Authority,* 213.

[38] For brilliant and learned exposition of turbulence in the very years Lewis was writing the *Remarks,* see Eric Hobsbawm and George Rudé, *Captain Swing* (New York, 1969).

Bibliography of
George Cornewall Lewis

Books, Official Reports, Translations

The Public Economy of Athens in four books. To which is added a Dissertation on the Silver Mines of Laurion. Translated from the German of Augustus Boeckh. London, 1828; 2d ed. rev., 1842. 2 vols.

An Examination of Some Passages in Dr. Whately's Elements of Logic. Oxford, 1829.

The History and Antiquities of the Doric Race, by C. O. Müller. [K. O. Müller]. Translated by H. Tufnell and G. C. Lewis. Oxford, 1830; 2d ed., London, 1862. 2 vols.

Remarks on the Use and Abuse of some Political Terms. London, 1832; new ed., with notes and appendix, by Sir R. K. Wilson, Oxford, 1877; new ed., with notes and introduction by T. Raleigh, Oxford, 1898.

An Essay on the Origin and Formation of the Romance Languages: containing an Examination of M. Raynourd's Theory on the Relation of the Italian, Spanish, Provençal, and French, to the Latin. Oxford, 1835; new ed., London, 1839; 2d ed., London, 1862.

On Local Disturbances in Ireland; and on the Irish Church Question. London, 1836.

"First Report of the Irish Poor Inquiry Commissioners. An appendix." *Parliamentary Papers,* 1836, XXXIV, 427–642.

"Remarks on the Third Report of the Irish Poor Inquiry Commissioners, drawn up by the desire of the Chancellor of the Exchequer for the purpose of being submitted to . . . Government. With an appendix and supplementary remarks." *Parliamentary Papers,* 1837, LI, 253–90.

["On Conditions in Malta."] *Parliamentary Papers,* 1838, XXIX; 1839, XVII.

A Glossary of Provincial Words used in Herefordshire and some of the adjoining Counties. London, 1839.

A History of the Literature of Ancient Greece, by K. O. Müller. Translated by G. C. Lewis. London, 1840–1842. 2 vols.

An Essay on the Government of Dependencies. London, 1841; ed., with an Introduction by C. P. Lucas, Oxford, 1891; reprinted, Washington and New York, 1901.

Babrii Fabulae Aesopeae, cum fabularum deperditarum fragmentis, recensuit et breviter illustravit G. C. Lewis. Oxford, 1846. *The Fables of Babrius, in two parts. Translated into English Verse from the text of Sir G. C. Lewis. By the Rev. James Davies.* London, 1860.

An Essay on the Influence of Authority in Matters of Opinion. London, 1849; 2d ed., 1875.

Evidence of G. C. Lewis before a Select Committee of the House of Lords, appointed to consider the laws relating to Parochial Assessments. Parliamentary Papers, 1850, XVI.

A Treatise on the Methods of Observation and Reasoning in Politics. London, 1852. 2 vols.

An Inquiry into the Credibility of the Early Roman History. London, 1855. 2 vols. Translated into German, *Untersuchungen über die Glaubwürdigkeit der altrömischen Geschichte.* Hannover, 1858.

The Financial Statement. 1857. Speech of the Chancellor of the Exchequer in Committee of Supply. London, 1857.

Speech . . . on the Introduction of the Bill for the better Government of India. London, 1858.

On Foreign Jurisdiction and the Extradition of Criminals. London, 1859.

An Historical Survey of the Astronomy of the Ancients. London, 1862.

Speeches . . . on moving the Army Estimates, in Committee of Supply, in the House of Commons, March 3 and 6, 1862. London, 1862.

Suggestions for the Application of Egyptological Method to modern History; illustrated by examples. London, 1862.

Pedigree of the Family of Lewis of Harpton. London, 1862.

A Dialogue on the Best Form of Government. London, 1863; translated into French, Paris, 1867; and Italian, Padua, 1868, 1884.

Essays on the Administrations of Great Britain from 1783 to 1830. Contributed to the Edinburgh Review *by the Right Hon. Sir George Cornewall Lewis.* Edited by Sir Edmund Head. London, 1864.

Letters of the Right Hon. Sir George Cornewall Lewis, Bart. to Various Friends. Edited by his brother, the Rev. Sir Gilbert Frankland Lewis, Bart. London, 1870.

"Characteristics of Federal, National, Provincial, and Municipal Government" [unpublished].

Essays and Reviews

Edinburgh Review

The titles below are the running heads for Lewis' reviews.

Public Schools of England—Eton (a review of classical grammar, texts, and geography), LI (1830), 65–81.
Public Schools of England—Westminster and Eton (a review of a Latin and a Greek grammar), LIII (1831), 64–82.

Legislation for the Working Classes, LXXXIII (1846), 64–99.

Grote's *History of Greece*, Vols. I and II, LXXXIV (1846), 343–77.

Local Taxes of the United Kingdom, LXXXV (1847), 100–115.

The State of the Nation—the Ministry and the New Parliament, LXXXVII (1848), 138–69.

Grote's *History of Greece*, Vols. III–VI, XCI (1850), 118–52.

Lord Derby's Ministry and Protection, XCV (1852), 569–86.

The Late Elections and Free Trade, XCVI (1852), 526–66.

The Fall of the Derby Ministry, XCVII (1853), 240–67.

Lord Grey's Colonial Administration, XCVIII (1853), 62–98.

Marshall on the Representation of Minorities, C (1854), 226–35.

Parliamentary Opposition, CI (1855), 1–22.

The Second Derby Ministry, CVII (1858), 541–82.

The *Celts and Germans*, CVIII (1858), 166–74.

Earl Grey on *Parliamentary Government*, CVIII (1858), 271–97.

The Diaries and Correspondence of George Rose, CXII (1860), 34–58.

The Election of President Lincoln and its Consequences, CXIII (1861), 555–87.

The Military Defence of the Colonies, CXV (1862), 53–65.

Foreign Quarterly Review

Spix and Martius's *Travels in Brazil*, No. 10, art. 3.

Tittman's *History of the Amphictyonic Confederacy*, No. 11, art. 6.

Schaefer's edition of *Plutarch's Lives*, No. 11, art. 11.

On Codification and its Application to the Laws of England, No. 12, art. 12.

The French Revolution of 1830, No. 12, art. 7.

Mythology and Religion of Ancient Greece, No. 13, art. 2.

The Brunswick Revolution, No. 13, art. 9.

Dindorf's *Poetae Scenici Graeci*, No. 13, art. 13.

Raynourd's *Ancient Municipal Institutions of France*, No. 15, art. 6.

Thierry's *History of the Gauls*, No. 19, art. 6.

Philological Museum (Cambridge, 1832–1833)

Vol. I, 122–25, 126–41, 177–87, 280–304, 420–26, 679–86.
Vol. II, 38–71, 243–46, 689–94.

Classical Museum, a Journal of Philology and of
Ancient History and Literature (London, 1844–1850)

Vol. I, 113–24, 389–97; Vol. II, 1–44.

Law Magazine and Review

"Secondary Punishments," VII, 1–44.
"American Penitentiaries," XIV, 31–57.

Fraser's Magazine

"The Roman Book-Trade under the Empire," LXV (1862),
432–38.

Notes and Queries

"Aristotle on Indian Kings," 3 ser. I (1862), 56–57.
"Michael Scot's Writings on Astronomy," 3 ser. I (1862),
131; II (1862), 52–53.
"Centenarians," 3 ser. I (1862), 281–82, 411–12; II (1862),
513.
"Eclipse at the Battle of Crecy," 3 ser. III (1863), 262.
"The Presidency of Deliberative Assemblies," 3 ser. III
(1863), 281–83.

Facsimile Text of the 1832 Edition of
George Cornewall Lewis
Remarks on the Use and Abuse of some Political Terms
First published by B. Fellowes, London, in 1832
New edition, with notes and appendix
by Sir R. K. Wilson,
published at Oxford, in 1877
New edition, with notes and introduction by T. Raleigh,
published at Oxford, 1898

REMARKS

ON

THE USE AND ABUSE

OF SOME

POLITICAL TERMS.

———◆———

BY

GEORGE CORNEWALL LEWIS, ESQ.

STUDENT OF CHRIST CHURCH, OXFORD.

———

" Seal up the mouth of outrage for awhile,
Till we can clear these ambiguities,
And know their spring, their head, their true descent."
Romeo and Juliet, Act 5, Scene 3.

———

LONDON:

PRINTED FOR

B. FELLOWES, LUDGATE STREET.

——

M DCCC XXXII.

LONDON :

R. CLAY, PRINTER, BREAD-STREET-HILL,
CHEAPSIDE.

INTRODUCTION.

THE object of the following work is to illustrate the various uses of the principal terms belonging to political science. It is the duty of every science to perform this office for itself; and those equivocal words which belong to no particular subject might conveniently be assigned to the province of logic. An inquiry of this description may be considered as occupying a middle place between a technical dictionary, and a scientific treatise on the same subject: as being more copious and connected than the one, more meagre and desultory than the other. With the view, then, of affording to political speculation the assistance to be derived from a technical vocabulary, I have attempted to collect from different writers, examples of the principal meanings attached to those terms of political science which seemed of the greatest importance and most frequent occurrence. As it was obviously desirable to ascertain such usages, not only in the set phrase of scientific inquirers, but also in the living language of party discussion, I have purposely selected examples from writers of all opinions, often from modern anonymous publications, having no other care than to represent their statements with fidelity. For the most part, however, I have limited myself to works of extensive circulation and established character, and especially to those employed in this country as elementary treatises in various departments of political knowledge; as their authority has the widest influence, and their errors and confusions are the most mischievous. Hence I have, wherever it was possible, selected instances from the Commentaries of Blackstone, the speculative parts of which work may be considered as an epitome of popular fallacies and misconceptions on most of the fundamental doctrines of jurisprudence and government.

The explanations and distinctions which
accompany and connect the various passages
examined in the following inquiries, are intended to assist in assuring the results or
detecting the fallacies of political reasoning, by
putting the reader on his guard against unconsciously passing from one signification of a word
to another. Of the liability even of the most
skilful and experienced reasoners to this fatal
error, the instances cited in the ensuing pages
furnish examples, which may perhaps surprise
some persons who have not considered and
observed the powerful influence of equivocal
language in deceiving the mind. Perhaps there
is no moral or political treatise of any length,
certainly no considerable argumentative work,
of which the conclusions are not in some degree
affected by an incautious employment, or an
unperceived ambiguity, of language.

The following work is therefore strictly adapted
to the purposes of political *argument;* and even
if the definitions which I have either borrowed
or suggested should be thought incorrect, yet
the investigation of the various senses of each
word, as occurring in popular language, must,

if properly employed, furnish to others the means of detecting fallacy in political discussion. The *Book of Fallacies*, published by Mr. Bentham, was not properly a guide for the detection of sophisms in political argument: it was a treatise on the truth of certain propositions commonly assumed in political reasoning. The arguments which he attacked were not fallacious: like the arguments of a madman, they were correct and conclusive, *if certain premises or principles were granted.* Some of these principles he disproved with great force and ingenuity: but the utility of his book is limited to arguments in which those particular propositions are either stated or implied, and it furnishes no clue for the solution of questions in which those principles are *not* involved.

The following researches, however, relate, not to the truth of any particular propositions, but to the meaning of certain terms used in political reasoning; which being often employed with different senses in the premises and conclusion, have given rise to countless inconclusive arguments, and have thus caused *fallacies of argument* in the proper meaning of the word. The soundness of an inference cannot depend on the truth of a proposition, though it may depend on the use of a term. Hence an inquiry into the meaning of words may furnish an instrumental art for the purposes of argument, applicable to an indefinite extent, which an inquiry into the truth of certain propositions never can.

There are two ways in which an argument may be refuted : viz. 1. By shewing that one of the premises is false; and 2. By shewing that though the premises may be true, the conclusion does not follow from them. In most cases the opponent has his option which of these two courses he shall adopt; for, on account of the mutilated form in which arguments are commonly stated, the entire syllogism may be restored, either by supplying a false premise,—in which case the inference would be good,—or by supplying a true premise,—in which case the inference would be bad. Thus the argument of the ancient Egyptians mentioned by Herodotus, that fire is a living animal because it devours, may be either restored thus,—Fire is an animal, because all things that devour are animals, and fire devours ; when one premise is false, although the inference is correct;—or thus: Fire is an animal, because animals devour, and fire devours; where both premises are true, but the conclusion does not follow from them. So the argument of Mr. Canning, examined below (in p. 220), in its present form, is an unsound inference founded on true premises: it might be converted into a sound argument by assuming one false premise. In most cases, it is advisable to adopt the former course, because the generality of people are better able to comprehend the falsity of a proposition, than the unsoundness of an inference. But out of the whole number of invalid arguments, a very small portion are so palpably inconclusive as those just noticed. In the great majority of instances, the error springs from the hidden and unsuspected source of verbal ambiguity; the effects of which, imperceptibly mingling with the discussion, poison the whole current of the reasoning, and vitiate every part which they touch.

The influence of this cause upon reasoning is the more powerful and extensive, because not even those who *know* the ambiguity of a term are always proof against the confusion which it tends to generate. "It is not the same thing (as has been truly observed) to be merely acquainted with the ambiguity of a term, and to be practically aware of it, and watchful of the consequences connected with it." * For this reason it may be useful, even to the practised political reasoner, to illustrate the various usages of the words with which he is conversant, and to point out the mistakes and confusions to which they have given rise; in order that the impression of their ambiguities, and the conviction of the necessity of attending to them, may be more deeply fixed in his mind.

It is for a want of attending to points which, if ever thought of, would not require half the labour and ingenuity often wasted by disputants in eloquent declamation or personal invective, that (as Lord Bacon has observed) "Magnæ et solennes disputationes hominum doctorum sæpe in controversias circa verba et nomina desinunt: a quibus (ex more et prudentia mathematicorum) incipere consultius foret, easque per definitiones

---

* Whately's Bampton Lectures, p. 413.

in ordinem redigere." *   As the experiment has
never yet been tried, how far, by a close attention to the definitions and meanings of words,
controversies in the moral and political sciences
may be rendered useful in the discovery of truth,
and be relieved from the curse of barrenness
which has hitherto almost constantly been upon
them, it is uncertain how much of the blame
is to be attributed to the insufficiency of the
weapons, and how much to the unfairness and
unskilfulness with which they are used.   So
deep a sense of the imperfections of language
had Locke, that he even goes so far as to affirm
that if any one "shall well consider the errors and
obscurity, the mistakes and confusion, that are
spread in the world by an ill use of words, he will
find some reason to doubt whether language, as
it has been employed, has contributed more to
the improvement or hindrance of knowledge
among mankind." †   Although it is impossible
to agree with this opinion in its whole extent,
as language, whatever may be its defects, is the
only means by which knowledge can be preserved

---

* Novum Organon, lib. 1. aph. 59.
† Essay on the Understanding, b. 3. ch. 11. § 4.

and communicated; yet it is difficult to overrate its influence on reasoning, especially when we remember that language is not only the sign by which we express our thoughts and reasonings, but also the instrument by which we think and reason. The mistake arises not in the expression or communication, but in the conception of the argument. It is an error to suppose that a man cannot be misled by a verbal fallacy, without seeing it formally drawn out in words.

Whether or not the following attempt to unravel some of the chief ambiguities of political language may be found satisfactory, it is obviously desirable that persons about to engage in controversy should be agreed as to the use of certain common signs; otherwise, if they disagree both as to their opinions, and the manner of establishing and expressing them, there is no prospect of any other result from the debate than mutual misunderstanding and misrepresentation. " Quum enim (as Lord Bacon says) nec de principiis consentiamus, nec de demonstrationibus, tollitur omnis argumentatio."* Disputants in this condition are familiarly said to be

---

* Novum Organon, lib. 1. aph. 61.

at cross purposes. Each one is eagerly combating a shadow, which he mistakes for the substance of his adversary's argument. If men are not agreed about their weapons, they cannot engage in controversy. If two duellists go out into the field, the one armed with a sword, the other with a pistol, they cannot settle their dispute.

Unluckily, however, as the difference of weapons is not so obvious in intellectual as in physical conflicts, the disputants proceed to the encounter without further explanation; and as their minds are often too eagerly bent on victory to take a calm survey of the subject, and its real difficulties and obscurities, each one falls upon those statements of his adversary which appear most objectionable, probably because a sense is attributed to them which was never intended; and the controversy commonly ends in the most frivolous verbal questions. "Nothing (says Hume) is more usual than for philosophers to encroach on the province of grammarians, and to engage in disputes of words, while they imagine they are handling controversies of the deepest importance and concern."* As in legal controversy, when

* Essays, Appendix 4. Works, vol. 4. p. 396.

all the facts are admitted by both parties, the point in dispute must be a question of law ; so in political controversy, when all the facts are given, and the question does not relate to some future event, the dispute must turn on the meaning of words. Thus, for example, when it is debated whether an hereditary upper chamber is better than one for life, whether a king is better than a president, &c., the question is real. When it is debated whether the English constitution is a monarchy or an aristocracy, whether it is a pure or a mixed government ; whether the King of England is sovereign ; whether monarchy can be combined with aristocracy or democracy, or both ; these are merely verbal questions. A verbal discussion may be important or unimportant, but it is at least desirable to know that it *is* verbal. For want of attending to this distinction, nearly all controversialists, blinded by the heat and fury of the discussion, treat the merest verbal disputes as questions of vast moment and difficulty, and draw out their arguments to an immeasurable length, until, having fairly bewildered their readers, irritated each other by fruitless wrangling, and embroiled the subject which both undertook to explain, they at last retire from the field for very weariness.

But that verbal questions, if treated *as* verbal questions, and not mistaken for what they are not, may lead to the most useful results, I need not express my conviction, who have compiled the following observations for the sake of explaining the signification of political words. In pointing out their various senses, however, it is not intended to imply, that it is possible, either in scientific or popular discourse, constantly to attribute to each word only one meaning. Many of the ambiguities remarked upon, depend on causes not connected with our own language; and may be traced to historical associations and other circumstances, which have equally influenced the languages of other nations, both in ancient and modern times. Hence many parts of the following pages might be literally translated into French or German, without losing their application or truth. The links which bind together these various shades of meaning, are connected too closely with the general course of our thoughts to be broken at the command of any individual. It is impossible to legislate in matters of language : the evils arising from its imperfections may be eluded, but can never be removed. No mischief however arises from the variable meaning of a word (except sometimes a partial obscurity), unless the argument turns on the double sense. Thus there is no harm in calling the republican government of England and France a monarchy ; there is no harm in calling the aristocratic government of the United States a democracy ; only let it be remembered that they *are* not what they are *called.* There is no objection to a misnomer, so that it does not lead us astray. But if it were argued, that *justice,* not *law,* ought to be administered in courts of *justice ;* that no man can have a *right* to do that which is *wrong ;* that in a *kingdom* the institutions ought to be *monarchical,* &c. ; then the ambiguity is mischievous, because it serves as an inducement to error, and confounds things as well as words.

Such verbal ambiguities generate confusion of thought in those who sincerely seek after truth, and afford an opportunity for delusion to those whose only object is to support a party measure, or a preconceived opinion; who seek an end without caring for the honesty of the means. Still, notwithstanding the vast number of unsound arguments advanced on all great political questions, there are probably few politicians who constantly follow the rules suggested by the author of the work on Parliamentary Logic : they generally share in some degree in the delusions which they propagate, and feel some part of the enthusiasm which they kindle. It is impossible to say how much of the evils of party contention has arisen solely from interested persons making use of certain phrases as a pretext, and how much from honest mischievousness caused by the delusion of language; for it is to be remembered that political terms do not always occur singly in reasoning, and that when several are crowded together in the same proposition or argument, the chances of delusion are infinitely multiplied.*

* " The best verbal fallacies are those which consist not in the ambiguity of a single word, but in the ambiguous syntaxis of many put together," says Mr. Hamilton, in his very acute, though not very honest, maxims of Parliamentary Logic, p. 29. By *best* is here meant, *most calculated to deceive.*

The following researches, however, are chiefly designed for the use of persons engaged in political studies, especially of those beginning such pursuits, who often require some manual, some book of reference, beyond a mere dictionary, which should furnish an explanation of the terms belonging to political science. For want of this assistance, persons not acquainted with the vocabulary of a science, are sometimes unable to detect the flaws in reasoning by which they are not convinced. It often happens that an argument seems inconclusive, without our being able to comprehend *why* it is so : we may be able to disprove the conclusion, but not to refute the argument. It serves, however, greatly to confirm and strengthen our conviction if we can perceive, not only why we are right, but why those who differ from us are wrong.* Now for this purpose

This remark, which refers to ambiguities of construction (as, Aio te, Æacida, Romanos vincere posse), applies with at least equal force to such collections of equivocal words, as " Man has a natural right to his liberty."

* Οὐ μόνον δεῖ τἀληθὲς εἰπεῖν, ἀλλὰ καὶ τὸ αἴτιον τοῦ ψεύδους· τοῦτο γὰρ συμβάλλεται πρὸς τὴν πίστιν· ὅταν γὰρ εὔλογον φανῇ τὸ διὰ τί φαίνεται ἀληθὲς οὐκ ὂν ἀληθὲς, πιστεύειν ποιεῖ τῷ ἀληθεῖ μᾶλλον. Aristotle, Eth. Nic. b. 6. ch. 15.

there is no instrument so powerful as an accurate knowledge, and a watchful observance of the different uses of words. This often affords the master-key which discloses the whole mystery, and at once resolves all difficulties by shewing that they have no existence.

Nor is it only in the detection of the fallacies of others that an attention to the different meanings of words is to be recommended: this test of correctness may be applied with at least as much benefit to our own reasonings as to those of our neighbours. And above all is this attention requisite in *communicating* our thoughts; for it sometimes (though perhaps not often) happens, that a man may clearly understand a subject which, nevertheless, for the want of appropriate language, he may fail to make intelligible to others. To the acute and profound Butler it might, indeed, seem that " confusion and perplexity in writing is indeed without excuse, because any one may, if he pleases, know whether he understands and sees through what he is about;"* but, unhappily, there are few

---

* Preface to Sermons in the Rolls' Chapel.

qualities so rare as a clear perception of the
boundaries of a man's ignorance and knowledge.
The multitude of treatises which discuss a subject without explaining or proving any thing
with distinctness, " darkening counsel by words
without knowledge," owe a great part of their
obscurity and inconclusiveness to a neglect of
definitions, and to an inaccurate use of language.
" They who are accustomed to reflect on
ideas, know well how much ideas depend on
words. Improper terms are the chains which
bind men to unreasonable practices. Error is
never so difficult to be destroyed, as when it
has its root in language. Every improper term
contains the germ of fallacious propositions ; it
forms a cloud, which conceals the nature of
the thing, and presents a frequently invincible
obstacle to the discovery of truth."* Such
errors cloud the minds both of the author and
his readers, of the teacher and his disciples, of
the speaker and his audience ; and from their
very minuteness, and seeming insignificance, are
only the more difficult to discover, and the less

---

* Bentham on Evidence, by Dumont, b. 3. ch. 1.

willingly acknowledged: as people are indig-
nant at being supposed liable to be duped by a
trick apparently so inartificial, or to be eagerly
searching at a distance for that which lies at
their feet.

The number of political arguments now
sent forth into the world by means of news-
papers, magazines, reviews, and other periodical
publications, is so great, that errors arising
from the indistinctness of words are embo-
died in a thousand forms, and multiplied in
a constantly increasing progression.   For this
reason it is the more desirable that, where all
people talk on the same subject, they should be
agreed about the vocabulary with which they
discuss it: or, at any rate, that they should be
aware that they are *not* agreed.   There are,
indeed, too many political discourses, besides
Sir R. Filmer's, of which we may say with
Locke, that " if any one will be at the pains
to strip it of the flourish of doubtful expressions,
and endeavour to reduce the words to direct
positive intelligible propositions, and then compare them one with another, he will quickly
be satisfied that there was never so much glib

nonsense put together in well-sounding English." *
On the application of the tests suggested in the
following inquiries, pages of flowery declamation,
or serious mysticism, shrink into nothing, or
fall to pieces, deprived of their apparent cohe-
rency. Possibly too, the same weapons may
sometimes avail against those shameless impostors, who seek only to produce an immediate
effect without caring for subsequent detection:
like the passers of bad money, to whom it is
indifferent how soon the fraud is discovered,
so that they escape with their dishonest gains.
But let me not be understood to affirm that it
is possible, by any system of rules, however
well framed, to afford an infallible guide for the
perception of fallacious reasoning derived from
the imperfection of language : still less to undeceive those whose minds are under the influence
of arguments, artfully adapted to party feelings,
and urged with confidence and effrontery, by a
practised and ingenious sophist. † When we

---

* Preface to Treatise on Government.

† " Natura cavillationis, quam Græci σόφισμα appellant,
hæc est, ut ab evidenter veris *per brevissimas mutationes* dis-
putatio ad ea quæ evidenter falsa sunt perducatur."—Dig.

think of the difficulty of finding the way when we are most desirous to go right, how easy to mislead those whom we wish to go wrong!

In selecting the words to be included in an explanatory catalogue of the terms of political science, a doubt sometimes arose : as, on account of the imperfect separation between the provinces of government and law, many words of which it seemed desirable to treat, lie on a debatable ground, and owe a divided allegiance to politics and jurisprudence. In these, such as right, sovereignty, &c., I have generally followed the definitions laid down by Mr. Austin in the Outline of his Lectures on General Jurisprudence ;* but although much of what I have

lib. 50. t. 16. c. 177. The method of deceit by a slight variation in the use of a word, is practised in the same manner by the modern, as by the ancient sophist : only instead of displaying his ingenuity by appearing to prove that which his hearers know to be false, he displays it by appearing to prove that which they wish to be true.

* The statements alluded to (which I had, moreover, the advantage of hearing filled up by Mr. Austin, in his oral lectures) are chiefly contained in the following passage:—
" Neither a sovereign one (or a monarch, properly so called) nor a sovereign number (in its collegiate and sovereign capacity) bears a *status* or condition (in the proper acceptation of the term). Conditions are composed of *legal* rights

said under these heads is either stated or implied in the short but comprehensive work referred to, yet the mere statement of the truth, though it implies the correction of error, was not sufficient for the purpose which I had in view. My object was to shew that, although the truth is one, error is manifold; and to point out the inconsistencies, as well as the inaccuracy, of popular views : for it commonly happens that scientific explanations are rejected by a large

and duties, and of capacities and incapacities to take and incur them. But, since such rights and duties are products of positive law, and since positive law is merely the creature of the sovereign, we cannot ascribe a *condition* (which is composed of such rights and duties) to a monarch or sovereign body. We may say that the sovereign has *powers.* We may say that the sovereign has rights conferred by the law of God : that the sovereign has rights (improperly so called) conferred by the law (improperly so called) which I style positive morality : that the sovereign is subject to duties set by the law of God : that the sovereign is subject to duties (improperly so called) which positive morality enjoins. But to say that the sovereign has legal rights, or lies under legal duties, is to say that the sovereign is subject to a sovereign, by whom those rights are conferred, and by whom those duties are imposed. In other words, the proposition amounts to this : that the sovereign is not sovereign."—Outline of a course of Lectures on General Jurisprudence, to be delivered in the University of London, p. 50.

majority, who agree only in that negative opinion; and entertain on the point in dispute
notions just as irreconcilable with one another,
as with the truth which they unanimously
condemn.

When the definition of sovereignty is once
determined, the principle of division for the
different forms of government, and their respective definitions, (as laid down by most
political writers,) flow from it as necessary
consequences. On this important point there
appears to be a difference of phraseology rather
than opinion ; for although the established legal
language of this country gives the title of sovereign to the King alone, yet many eminent
writers, well acquainted with the English Constitution both in its ancient and modern form, and
little inclined to derogate from the authority
and amplitude of the Crown, have considered
the legislative sovereignty as belonging jointly
to the King and the two Houses of Parliament :
nor am I aware that objections have ever been
made to this language. Whether or not the
name of sovereignty is to be given to a power
indispensable to the making of a law, and

subject to no responsibility, is of course a mere question of convenience. But, by whatever *name* this particular kind of power may be distinguished, its *character* is essentially different from power which, though indispensable to the exercise of government, is subject to responsibility. In this respect, however, I have followed the course which seemed to possess the most obvious convenience, and to be sanctioned by the highest authority.

The simple and original method of dividing governments by the number of the governors employed and illustrated in the following pages, may to some persons seem barren and inconvenient; inasmuch as, since the extinction of city communities,—such as those of ancient Greece, or of ancient and modern Italy,—and the general introduction of the system of political representation, there exists no longer such a government as a democracy. Nor can it be denied that according to that phraseology, to say that a state is an aristocracy, conveys very little information as to the character of its institutions, as this name would include governments as different as those of Venice, England,

and the United States of America. But on the other hand, it is to be remembered that the division into monarchies and republics, or into governments where one rules, and where several rule, always marks a mighty distinction in the real character of the respective constitutions; nor can any thing more tend to confusion, both of words and thought, than an attempt to make the names of governments imply more than they rightly denote, by attributing to them subsidiary meanings besides their proper and direct signification. It is thus that the term *republic*, having been distorted from its right sense, and understood to imply particular accidents of some governments designated by that name, has clouded many political discourses, and raised many unfounded prejudices; and the term *monarchy*, by being applied to kingdoms, and confounded with royalty, has induced many persons to transfer to kings the evil impressions justly entertained against arbitrary princes, or *monarchs* properly so called.

In general, I have intentionally avoided all remarks on the meanings of the words examined, which do not fall within the scope of political science. Thus under LIBERTY I have said nothing of freewill and necessity; nor under POWER, have I made any allusion to mechanical powers, powers of the mind, &c. But in the word *Nature*, on account of the difficulty of tracing its numerous and discordant significations, it was necessary to take a wider range than its political applications would include. An attempt was indeed made, many years ago, by Boyle, to lay down the various uses of this word;* but, as his researches are confined to its physical meanings, and although drawn out to a considerable length, they have not exhausted, nor indeed greatly elucidated the subject, it appeared necessary to occupy an independent ground. In the words *Nature* and *Liberty* I have distinguished two senses,—one positive, the other negative; both of which respectively may doubtless be traced to a common head, although it was sufficient for my purpose to indicate without accounting for them. *Liberty*, in its original sense, appears to signify a power of doing what we desire: but as this power may

* Free Inquiry into the received Notion of Nature. Works, vol. 5. p. 158—254. 4to.

be considered in a double light, the word liberty has obtained a double sense, and we sometimes use it in reference to the capacity which enables us to act, and sometimes to the absence of that which disables us from acting. In like manner, Nature seems to have originally expressed a notion of that which any thing is : whence it sometimes means the essence, disposition, &c. of any thing; sometimes that which it was before it was altered.

In a work which contains an examination of so many elementary doctrines, and which incidentally touches on so many debated and debatable questions of political science, it must of course be expected that some persons will find passages which will seem to them obvious truths, not worthy of statement; while others may find assertions which they may think not only false in themselves, but likely to lead to dangerous conclusions:—in short, that many parts may seem to be made up of useless truisms and mischievous paradoxes. To the former I can only say that truths, familiar to them, may possibly not be familiar to all others; that things familiarly known are not always practically observed; and that, moreover, it sometimes happens that people are satisfied of the truth of doctrines to which they were led by steps which they have forgotten;— that they believe the conclusion without remembering the premises. Now to such persons it may, perhaps, be useful if their attention is recalled to the *connexion* between their opinions and the assumptions which these involve; and if they are reminded that the positions which they now at once condemn were the parents of many doctrines to which they still steadfastly adhere.

To the latter class I would submit that the following remarks are not intended to establish a theory of government, but to investigate and explain the use of political words; and that definitions, laid down for the sake of convenience, and sanctioned by the authority of usage, are not to be treated as positions intended to serve as the basis of a system, and established only for the sake of their results. But above all, I would suggest, that, in drawing conclusions from the statements of others, the reader may fancy that there is a real, because there is a verbal connexion; and may think, without reason, that others necessarily draw from certain premises the same inference as himself. There is no objection to a fair use of indirect reasoning; nor can any writer have just cause of complaint, if it be shewn that the doctrines which he establishes necessarily and legitimately lead him to an absurdity. But no man can so far trace the consequences which the greater ingenuity and wider combinations of others may deduce from his statements, as to be justly held responsible for the errors which he may thus be made to seem indirectly to countenance. " There is (says a distinguished writer) among the worst arts of controversy, no fallacy more reprehensible than this, though, unhappily, scarcely any is more frequent. In some minds, the temptation to this unworthy sophistry seems to increase always in proportion to the importance of the subject on which it is employed, and to the extent of public or of private evil which the misrepresentation is likely to produce. It has, in every case, a direct tendency to discourage all freedom of thought and sincerity of speech."*

* Oxford and Locke, by Lord Grenville, p. 75.

But while I guard myself against the cavils of others, it may perhaps be thought that I have myself laboured to disparage the fair fame of many great writers, by minute criticism on insulated passages, without adverting to the general merit of their works, or exhibiting the entire course of their reasonings. To this charge the nature of my inquiries must afford an answer; which did not embrace a view of large treatises or political systems, but were confined to an examination of the usage of certain words by political writers: in which examination, it was necessary to be precise; to be precise, it was necessary to be minute. When, therefore, I may adduce examples of verbal fallacies from the works of celebrated writers, it will not be supposed that they were chosen from a love of detraction, but rather as " exempli documenta in illustri posita monumento," and as being blemishes, rendered more apparent by the excellence of the material by which they are surrounded; still less that I entertained the faintest imagination of imputing any thing that could savour of intentional or deliberate deceit.

If, in the course of these remarks, I have
canvassed with freedom many statements made
by writers of deserved reputation and acknowledged usefulness; and if I have not enlisted
under the banners of any political party or
philosophical sect, let it be remembered that I
have only exercised a privilege without which
no inquiry can possess an independent value,
or bring any sensible contribution to the cause
of science. But I would willingly bear the
blame of needless precision or over-curious
criticism, if the following pages should be
found to afford any, the smallest, assistance to
the progress of political knowledge : or if they
might sometimes help to soften the anger and
direct the efforts of political disputants, by
suggesting an explanation of their differences,
and calling their attention to the question really
at issue.

CONTENTS.

c

I.

GOVERNMENT.

WHEN a body of persons, yielding obedience to no superior, issue their commands to certain other persons to do or forbear from certain acts, and threaten to punish the disobedience of their commands by the infliction of pain, they are said to establish or exercise *political* or *civil government.**

The persons who issue and enforce these commands, or the sovereign body, are said to possess the governing power, and their acts are called the acts of government. Government, in this sense, is a certain exercise of the highest power over a whole community.

Government is likewise used as synonymous with *form of government,* or *constitution,* to signify the arrangement or disposition of the ruling

* " The annexing pleasure to some actions, and pain to others, in our power to do or forbear, and giving notice of this appointment beforehand to those whom it concerns, is the proper formal notion of government."—Butler's Analogy, part 1. ch. 2.

B

power in the members of the community ; thus we speak of a free government, a monarchical government, a republican government.

It is moreover used to express the *persons* in whom the ruling power, or some part of the ruling power, resides. Thus we say that the people rose against the government ; that the government was overthrown by rebels; that it maintained its ground against them, &c. In such expressions as these we mean the whole body in whom the sovereignty is vested : sometimes, however, the word has a narrower sense, being applied only to those who have the administrative power, or (as they are commonly called) the ministers ; as, a tory government, a whig government, a strong government.

The primary and derived meanings of the word *government* are marked with sufficient clearness, and do not seem likely to afford occasion for fallacy or confusion. Sometimes, however, this word and its conjugates are employed to denote neither the exercise of the sovereign power, nor the members of the sovereign body, nor persons deriving their authority from the sovereign : but persons having only a vote for the election of members of the sovereign body, who themselves can never, in that capacity, possess any portion of the ruling power. It is by attributing this double sense to the terms government, governing power, governing

body, &c., that those constitutions are represented as democratical, in which the right of
suffrage is widely extended, although the governing power resides in a small minority of
the whole nation. On this subject more will
be said in another place.*

* See in DEMOCRACY, PEOPLE, and REPRESENTATION.

II.

CONSTITUTION.—CONSTITUTIONAL.

CONSTITUTION signifies the arrangement and distribution of the sovereign power in the community, or the *form* of the government. This is the meaning of such expressions as a free constitution, a democratic constitution, the British constitution,* &c.

Constitution therefore, properly, expresses something which either has, or has had, a real existence : it is however frequently used to signify something ideal; an imaginary model of excellence which the government has never, in fact, attained, though in the writer's or speaker's opinion it has constantly been tending to it. Hence people speak of the maxims of the constitution, the theory of the constitution, the spirit of the constitution, meaning some supposed rules to which, in their judgment, the

---

* Sir J. Mackintosh, in his Discourse on the Law of Nature and Nations, defines the constitution of a state to be "the body of those written and unwritten fundamental laws which regulate the most important rights of the higher magistrates, and the most essential privileges of the subjects," (p. 65 ;) but this explanation does not agree with the common usage, the *jus et norma loquendi.*

constitution ought to conform, though, in fact, they have never been observed. Constitution, in this sense, is little more than a vague term of praise, though it is calculated to deceive ignorant persons into a belief that a measure or law recommended to them is only a recurrence to ancient institutions, and that the change is restoration, and not innovation.

Hence is derived the common use of *constitutional*, and its opposite, *unconstitutional*. When certain practices or usages, though not legally binding on any part of the community, have been constantly observed both by the governors and governed, they are properly styled constitutional; and any measure or practice contrary to them, is styled unconstitutional. But more usually these terms are used with a very indefinite meaning, and convey little more than a general sentiment of approbation or dislike. If persons are agreed as to the history of any country, there can be no doubt whether a measure is to be characterized as constitutional or unconstitutional; but often, in controversy or debate, these epithets are applied to a measure without any regard to reality, and merely denote agreement or disagreement with some imaginary standard of propriety which each man sets up for himself. Generally, therefore, when discussions arise, whether any thing is or is not constitutional, the dispute is merely verbal, and can only be terminated by mutual explanation; yet, unfortunately, men " regard it as so high an affront to be suspected of being unconsciously engaged in a logomachy, that he who proposes to terminate a contest by proving that it turns on the ambiguity of words, must prepare himself to incur, from the eager controversialists of both parties, even more ill-will than they feel towards their opponents." *

* Whately's Bampton Lectures, p. 196.

III.

RIGHT. — DUTY. — WRONG. — RIGHTFUL. — WRONGFUL. — JUSTICE.

WHEN the sovereign power commands its subjects to do or forbear from certain acts, the claim* for such performances or forbearances which one person thereby has upon another, is called a *right;* the liability to such performances or forbearances is called a *duty;* and the omission of an act commanded to be done, or the doing of an act commanded to be forborne, is called a *wrong.*

All rights therefore must be subsequent to the establishment of government, and are the creatures of the sovereign power; no claim upon another, which may not be enforced by process of law, *i. e.* by calling in the assistance of the sovereign, however recommended by moral justice, can, without an abuse of language, be termed a right. The existence of a *moral claim* may often be a matter of doubt when the facts are ascertained, and one party may demand what

* There does not appear to be any reason why *claim* or *requisition* should not be considered as the genus of *right;* though Mr. Bentham (Principles of Morals and Legislation, vol. 2. p. 24, n.) says, that right has no superior genus.

the other may not think himself bound in conscience to yield; but, the facts being given, the existence of a *right*, or a *legal claim*, can never admit of dispute, as it is defined and conferred by a third party, who will, if required, step in to enforce it.

Properly, therefore, *right* signifies a claim conferred or sanctioned by the sovereign power, *i. e.* a *legal* right. Sometimes, however, it is used to mean a claim recommended by the practice, analogy, or doctrines of the constitution, *i.e.* a *constitutional* right; and, sometimes, a claim recommended by views of justice or public policy, *i. e.* a *moral* right.

By the first and proper sense, is meant a claim which may be enforced in a court of law, or by the proper authorities, and which actually exists: by the two last, a claim which *cannot* be enforced by any public authority, and which does *not* exist. Thus, in the first sense, it is said that a man has a right to his own property, reputation, &c., meaning that he has an available claim which can be enforced by process of law. It is also said that, constitutionally, every British subject who pays taxes has a right to vote for a member of the House of Commons; meaning that such a claim is supported by the practice or doctrines of our constitution. It is also said that all the people have a right to be represented; that they have a right to choose

their own governors, to cashier their governors
for misconduct, and to frame a government for
themselves; that the poor have a right to be
maintained by the rich; that the poor have a
right to spoil the land-owners, and divide their
lands; that the poor have a right to spoil the
rich, and divide their property, &c. In the
latter cases, the persons who use these expressions mean that, in their opinion, there is a
claim founded in justice and expediency, which
they call a right; though, in truth, what they
mean to express is, that it ought, by the sanction of the legislature, to be *made* a right.

Burke's explanation of rights, in fact, amounts
to no more than that last stated, though he appears to have intended something very different;
as his definition is perfectly consistent with the
doctrines which he is professedly combating,
and which he held in utter abhorrence. The
following passage from his work on the French
Revolution, is in answer to those who maintained the doctrine of the natural rights of men.
" The pretended rights of these theorists are all
extremes; and, in proportion as they are meta-
physically true, they are morally and politically
false. The rights of men are in a sort of middle,
incapable of definition, but not impossible to be
discerned. *The rights of men in government are
their advantages;* and these are often in balances
between differences of good, in compromises

sometimes between good and evil, and sometimes between evil and evil." If this doctrine
were admitted, a man would have a right to
every thing which might appear advantageous to
him, and private opinion would be the only rule
of law.*

No objection, even on the score of inconvenience, can be made to the use of an equivocal
word when its different senses are plain and
palpable ; as, for example, the word *light,* which
sometimes means the contrary of *heavy,*—sometimes the contrary of *dark;* or the word *duty,*
which sometimes means a legal or moral obli-

---

* " When I went into the house first, (says one of the
witnesses examined on the trial of Watson for high treason,)
I went in company with a nobleman's servant who wore a
livery ; they seemed discoursing among themselves for a
little while, and then turned round and observed that the
crest upon his button was the crest of a lord, and they asked
him who made his master a lord.   He could make no answer,
not readily, to this question that was put to him.   After a
little while they turned to me, upon which I explained it as
well as I knew how: and after my explanation, they asked
me how this nobleman came to be possessed of so much
landed property as he was possessed of; and they turned
round to the servant, and told him he had a *right* to as much
land as his master, and that the time was now fast approach-
ing when he would be as good a man as his master, and possess as much property ; and also asked *by what right* he
held this property."—2 Watson's Trial, 65.   This passage
affords a striking example of the effect which may be produced on ignorant persons by the ambiguity of imposing
terms, and the employment of (what Mr. Bentham has
termed) *question-begging appellatives.*

gation,—sometimes a tax on a commodity. By such ambiguous terms as these, no one could be misled. But when the two significations lie on each other's confines, the one being perhaps a metaphorical or derivative use of the same word, there is great difficulty in marking the boundaries which the ambiguity always tends to confound ; though the distinction is the more important, because, even if the names were different, such near neighbours would be likely to encroach on each other's territories. In the present case, the confusion of legal and moral rules, to which, at all times, mankind are sufficiently prone, is heightened by an *additional* meaning of the word in question.

Right is sometimes a substantive, sometimes an adjective. When used as a substantive, it properly signifies a legal claim, and answers to *duty*. Where the law confers a right on one person, it creates a corresponding duty in another. *Wrong*, the substantive, signifies the violation of a right. But, when used as an adjective, *right* expresses agreement with the standard of morality (whatever that may be), and is opposed to *wrong*, the adjective, that which disagrees with this standard. Thus *a* right may be *right* or *wrong*, (*i. e.* a claim given by law may be just or unjust, politic or impolitic,) in the judgment of different persons. The necessity of a legislative sovereignty, or of a power of altering old and enacting new laws, is entirely founded on the supposition that *rights* may be *wrong*,—a truism which has sometimes been treated as a paradox and an antithesis. If the different senses of *right*, just pointed out, really coincided; that is, if all claims founded on justice and sound policy were legal rights, and all legal rights were founded on justice and sound policy, there would be no necessity for deliberative assemblies or legislative enactments, and the whole business of government might be confined to the administration of existing laws.

This ambiguity, so manifest when pointed out, and so easily detected by a translation into Latin (which has different terms for the substantive and adjective)* has yet misled many unreflecting

* *Jus* means *a right*, the substantive; *honestus* or *rectus*, right, the adjective. On the other hand, the Latin language has an ambiguity of *jus*, from which the English is free, viz. that it means both *law* and *right*, an ambiguity which has led Blackstone into the most fearful errors.—See Mill's British India, vol. 1. p. 195; and Austin's admirable Outline of a Course of Lectures on Jurisprudence in the London University, p. 48. (London, 1831.) The French *droit*, and the German *recht*, have the ambiguities both of the Latin and English words, for they signify *lex*, *jus*, and *rectus*. Ambiguities of words are often brought out in translation; for instance, *lingua* in Latin and Italian, in English is sometimes rendered by *tongue*, sometimes by *language*. The most perplexing ambiguities, however, run through all the commonly known languages of civilized nations. It may be remarked as a singular circumstance, that the Greek language should possess no term for right, or *jus*. The treatise of Aristotle

persons, and even some writers of high authority, who might have been expected to keep
clear of so obvious a fallacy. Thus Paley,
in his Moral and Political Philosophy, b. 1,
chap. 9, says that " right is a quality of persons
or of actions;—of persons, as when we say,
Such a one *has a right* to this estate, &c. ;—of
actions, as in such expressions as the following :
It is right to punish murder with death, &c."
The argument by which Blackstone proves the
latter part of his definition of municipal law,
that it is " a rule of civil conduct prescribed by
the supreme power in a state, *commanding what
is right, and prohibiting what is wrong*,"* proceeds entirely on this uncertainty of meaning.
" In order to do this completely (he says), it
is first of all necessary that the boundaries of
right and *wrong* be established and ascertained
by law. And when this is once done, it will
follow of course that it is likewise the business
of the law, considered as a rule of civil conduct,
to enforce *these rights*, and to restrain or redress *these wrongs*."† If, in defence of Blackstone, it should be said that by *right* and *wrong*

entitled δικαιώματα πόλεων, appears to have been upon the
rights, or privileges, of different states (see Neumann, Aris-
totelis πολιτειῶν fragmenta, p. 43) : but the word δικαίωμα
never came into general use in the sense of *jus*. Sir J.
Mackintosh, misled by a false reading πολέμων for πόλεων,
represents this as a treatise on the *laws of war*.—On the Law
of Nature and Nations, p. 16.

* 1 Com. 44.   † 1 Com. 53.

he only means that which the law enjoins or
forbids, then the latter part of his definition is
superfluous, and to say that *a law is right* would
be an identical proposition.* Hence also Crabb,
in his Dictionary of English Synonyms, says,
that "*right* (the substantive) signifies what *it is
right* for one to possess." The same confusion
of the two very different senses of *right* is well
shewn in the following passage, where the argument turns upon the double sense. "If it be
right that the property of men should be protected, and if this can only be done by means
of government, then it must be *right* that some
person or persons should possess political power.
That is to say, some person or persons must
have a right to political power."† The apparent
force of this argument rests on a mere verbal
fallacy. So the author of the Dictionary of English
Synonyms, just cited, states, that a certain conclusion cannot be received, "unless we admit
the contradiction that men have a *right* to do
what is *wrong*."‡ This instance is perhaps the
more worthy of notice, because it occurs in the
work of a writer whose *professed* object was to
point out and illustrate the different meanings

---

* It is however obvious, that he uses right and wrong in
the former sense, as he quotes the words of Cicero, repeated
by Bracton, that a law is " sanctio justa, jubens *honesta*,
et prohibens *contraria*."—1 Com. 122.

† Edinburgh Review, vol. 52. p. 364.

‡ Crabb's English Synonyms, in *Right*.

of words.* In the celebrated verse which would represent as a paradox " The right divine of kings to govern wrong," the antithesis is only in sound and not in sense : if a sovereign has not the power to enforce his commands, whether right or wrong, that is, whether the subject thinks them right or wrong, he is not sovereign. " When governors shall be so perfect, as never to propose a measure that is not faultless, and when subjects shall be so infallible in their judgments, and so candid in their dispositions, as universally to perceive and acknowledge this perfection, — then, and not till then, may a peaceable and permanent government be established on such principles." †

It may moreover be observed, that if all rights are the creatures of the sovereign power, and can only be enforced by calling in the assistance of a superior authority ; no absolute monarchs or sovereign governors can be said to

---

* Mr. Bentham, in his Principles of Morals and Legislation, vol. 2. p. 257, n., points out an ambiguity of the English word *law*, which signifies both a single law, and the whole body of laws, or (as we say) *the* law ; and appears to lament that we have not, like the Germans, appropriated the word *right* to the entire *corpus juris*, i. e. to *law* in its collective sense. Doubtless it would be desirable to have two different words to express the two ideas distinguished by Mr. Bentham ; but it cannot be wished that any additional burden should be laid on the term *right*, which has already a sufficient weight of meanings to sustain.

† Whately's Sermon on Obedience to Rulers, p. 292.

possess *rights*, or to be subject to *duties*, except
in a moral sense.   A claim which a man gives
himself, of which he is alone judge, and which
he can alone enforce, may undoubtedly be called
a *right*, though it seems much more precise and
simple, in such cases, merely to speak of power ;
but a sovereign, whether one or many, can
never be liable to any legal duties, because a
legal duty implies the legal means of enforcing
it ; and if a sovereign power could be legally
forced to any act, it would not be sovereign.
That governors have not, as governors, any legal
duties, is distinctly stated by Dr. Whately, in a
sermon preached before the University of Oxford,
although he too speaks of the *rights* of a governor.*   " The governor," he says, " is bound to
make a good use of his power, no less than his
subjects are to obey him ; and he is accountable
to God for so doing ; but not to *them;* for if this
merely conditional right to obedience be once
admitted, it must destroy all government whatever." †   The attributing of rights to governors
appears to have arisen from a confusion of the
effects produced by the exercise of the power of
a sovereign, and of the right of a subject.   A
man by hiring a servant acquires a right to his
services and obedience ; a sovereign issues its
commands, and thereby has a claim on the

* Bampton Lectures, p. 292.
† Ibid. p. 296.   And see p. 297.

submission of its subjects : whence it is inferred that the claim of the sovereign is of the same nature as the claim of the master; *i. e.* that they both have a right to the performance of the respective duties. But in the one case, the claim is given by a third party ; in the other, it is obtained by an exercise of individual volition : three parties are necessary to the existence of a legal right, as two parties are necessary to the existence of moral justice. A man cannot be just towards himself, nor can that be a right which A gives himself against B, and A alone can enforce.

In this country, a mistaken notion as to the rights of subjects has arisen, from confounding the powers of the King and those of the Parliament. The people have rights as against the *King;* and hence it is correct to say, that Charles the First and James the Second violated the rights of their subjects : without having the legislative sovereignty, they commanded acts to be done which were contrary to law. But the people have no rights as against the *Parliament,* or the whole sovereign body ; and hence such expressions as the Parliament withholding or refusing the rights of the people, are not only unmeaning and absurd, but also mischievous, as they tend to encourage the idea that members of that body are legally, as well as morally, answerable for their acts.

In a like manner, the rule of the English constitution that *the King can do no wrong*, appears to be an absurdity, and startles some who hear it, only because a breach of legal right is confounded with a breach of moral duty. Neither the whole sovereign body, nor any part of the sovereign body, so far as it is sovereign, can do a wrong, that is, infringe a right; as that implies a superior power to redress the wrong or enforce the right, which, by the supposition, does not exist. All orders issued by a competent authority are necessarily dispunishable; but this immunity does not extend to those who execute them, if contrary to law. For example, the king may order his ministers to do an illegal act, but they will obey at their peril. The House of Commons may order their serjeant-at-arms to arrest a man for an act not falling within their jurisdiction, but their officer will obey at his peril. If the House of Lords, or House of Commons, were to go in a body and kill a man, they would be guilty of murder, because this would not be an act done in virtue of the sovereign power which in their collective capacity they severally possess for certain purposes. This is stated in substance by Blackstone,* though

* 1 Com. 244. Boswell, in his Life of Johnson, vol. 1. p. 388, reports a conversation on this point, between Goldsmith and Johnson. Goldsmith argued, that "as the king might, in the exercise of his regal power, command and

his expressions are not strictly accurate. " The supposition of law is," he says, " that neither the King nor either house of Parliament (collectively taken) is capable of doing any wrong; since, in such cases, the law *feels itself* incapable of furnishing any adequate remedy ; for which reason, all oppressions which may happen to spring from any branch of the sovereign power, must necessarily be out of the reach of any stated rule or express legal provision." He afterwards states, that the maxim that " the King can do no wrong," means two things : 1. " That whatever is exceptionable in the conduct of public affairs, is not to be imputed to the King, nor is he answerable for it, personally, to his people ;" and, 2. " That the prerogative of the crown extends not to do any injury."* As to the first of these rules, it is clear that the King cannot be

cause the doing of what was wrong, it certainly might be said, in sense and reason, that he could do wrong." (This is what the logicians call an *ignoratio elenchi ;* the question was, whether the king could do *a* wrong.) Johnson in answer, among other things, said, " We hold the king can *do no wrong,* that whatever may happen *to be wrong* in government may not be above our reach by being ascribed to majesty. Redress is always to be had against oppression by punishing the immediate agents. The king, though he should command, cannot force a judge to condemn a man unjustly; therefore it is the judge whom we prosecute and punish." Johnson's sentiments are quite accurate ; though he too falls into the common error of confounding wrong, *an injury,* with wrong, *improper.*

* 1 Com. 246. And see 3 Com. 254, 255.

answerable for any act done by him in his capacity
of sovereign ; as this immunity is implied in the
idea of supreme power : while the second is
merely a statement, in different terms, of the
proposition that " The King can do no wrong ; "
for *King*, putting *prerogative of the crown ;* and
for *wrong, injury*. By *injury*, a *breach of law*
can only be meant ; as all political parties think
that the King does that which is hurtful to the
nation, when he chooses his ministers from their
opponents.* The statement of this rule by
Hume, in his Essay on Passive Obedience, is
very precise, and seems framed for the express
purpose of cautioning persons against the superficial error, so often committed, of confounding
a legal injury with a moral impropriety. The

---

* The Attorney-General, in his speech in Hardy's trial,
cites a passage from an American work communicated to an
English political society, where it is said, that " in government, the maxim being that *a King can do no wrong*, the
maxim ought to be that *he can do no good.*"—See Erskine's
Speeches, vol. 3. p. 199. If the author of this passage had
understood the maxim which he objects to, so far from thinking that his remark was pointed and antithetical, he would
have seen that it is absolutely unmeaning. Mr. Hallam, in
his History of the Middle Ages, vol. 2. p. 243, 4to ed.,
says, that " In the prudent fiction of the English law, no
wrong is supposed to proceed from the source of right."
This statement is not correct ; it is not a legal fiction, but a
plain truth, that the King can do no wrong. It is another
maxim of English law, that there is no wrong without its
remedy : and against the acts of the King, no remedy is, or
can be, provided by law.

King of England, he says, " though limited by
the laws, is, in a manner, so far as regards his
own person, above the laws, and *can neither be
questioned nor punished for any injury or wrong
which may be committed by him.*"*

Before the word *right* is dismissed, it may be
useful to notice some of the epithets applied to
it; the number, variety, and discordancy of
which, are almost past belief: though, when
they come to be examined, most of them will be
found to be either unmeaning or inapplicable.
The following passage occurs, as spoken by
Dr. Johnson, in a conversation preserved by
Boswell :† " Every man has a right to liberty
of conscience, and with that the magistrate
cannot interfere. People confound liberty of
thinking with liberty of talking; nay, with liberty
of preaching. Every man has a *physical right*
to think as he pleases; for it cannot be discovered how he thinks : he has not a *moral right,*
for he ought to inform himself, and think justly."
Here *physical right* must mean *power; moral
right* appears to mean *legal right,* for Johnson
never could have intended to say that a man
is, in conscience, bound to conceal opinions
which he thinks true: the doubt would rather be
the other way, whether a man is *justified* in

---

* Part 2. Essay 13.
† Life of Johnson, vol. 2. p. 111.

concealing what he thinks true. On another occasion, he said that " there seems to be in authors a stronger right of property than that by occupancy ; a *metaphysical right,* a right, as it were, of creation, which should, from its nature, be perpetual."* This expression is manifestly founded on the erroneous supposition, that a right to a tangible is more corporeal than a right to an intangible object : but elsewhere he uses a more common epithet, when, speaking of government, he says that, " if the abuse be enormous, Nature will rise up, and, claiming her *original rights,* overturn a corrupt political system."† It is, however, a contradiction to speak of *original rights,* if by original is meant anterior to government ; for, as has been shewn above, the notion that " right is altogether an abstract thing, which is independent of human laws and institutions,"‡ is not only not true, but is the direct contrary of the truth. The verse of Dryden, in the Wife of Bath's Tale, that

" Sovereign monarchs are the source of right,"

expresses the truth, but not the whole truth ; as not only sovereign monarchs, but all sovereign

* Vol. 2. p. 122.   Burke, in his Thoughts on the French Revolution, also speaks of metaphysical rights ; where, by *metaphysical,* he appears to mean *imaginary,* or *unreal.*

† Vol. 1. p. 389.

‡ Crabb's English Synonyms, in Right.

legislatures, whether of one or many, are, and are alone, the sources from which all rights flow. Yet we hear of original rights, natural rights, indefeasible rights, inalienable rights, imprescriptible rights, hereditary rights, indestructible rights, inherent rights, &c., where there is no pretence of legislative sanction: indeed the only object of using these names is to induce the legislature to convert these supposed rights into real rights, by giving them the sanction of law. The phrase, *natural right*, takes its origin from the doctrine of a state of nature, which will be more fully explained below.* It appears to signify a claim recommended by natural law, or by those rules which were recognised by common consent, when mankind were in a state of nature. An *indefeasible right* is a right which man enjoyed in a state of nature, and which he only surrendered conditionally at the making of the social compact; so that nothing has since been able to defeat or destroy it, and it is ready to be revived at any time. An *imprescriptible right* is a right which was prior to the social compact, and which continues to exist without being subject to prescription or failure by lapse of time. An *inalienable right* is a right which cannot be alienated from a man. Indestructible rights,

* In the word NATURE.

inherent rights, hereditary rights, birthrights of liberty, &c., appear to have nearly the same meaning: viz. that they are dormant rights, never exercised by the possessors, and not extinguishable by any law. In fact, however, these imprescriptible, inalienable, indefeasible rights, in most cases never have been rights, or, if they have, long since were alienated and defeated by the sovereign power. These various expressions have all taken their origin from the theory of the state of nature and the social compact; but they are frequently used by persons who have never heard of this absurd and mischievous doctrine, and would perhaps reject it if they knew it. All that those persons mean is, that, in their opinion, the claims which they call *rights* ought, in sound policy, to be sanctioned by law. It is the duty of such persons to shew that sound policy requires what *they* require; but as this would require a process of reasoning, and as reasoning is often both hard to invent and to understand, they prefer begging the question at issue by employing some of the high-sounding phrases just mentioned.

Rights are, moreover, divided into *political* or *civil* rights, and *private* rights: the meaning of which division will be explained elsewhere.*

Vested rights is another expression which has

---

* In the word POLITICAL.

been much used of late years. In its *legal*
sense, *vested* is opposed to *contingent*, and expresses a right of which the next possessor is
ascertained, whenever the prior right to the
same object may determine; as opposed to a
right of which the next possessor is not so
ascertained. But its *political* sense (with which
alone we are now concerned) is widely different
from its legal acceptation, and appears to have
no connexion with it whatever. When a legislature passes a law, not for any temporary purposes, nor limited as to the time of its operation,
and which therefore may be reasonably expected
to be permanent,—and persons, confiding in its
permanency, embark their capital, bestow their
labour, or shape the course of their life, so that
their only hope of success is founded on the
existence of the law,—the rights which they have
acquired in the reliance upon its continuance
are termed *vested rights;* and persons in this
situation are considered as having a moral
claim on the legislature for the maintenance of
the law, or at least for the allowance of a sufficient time to withdraw their investments, and
to take the measures necessary for guarding
against the loss consequent on so large a change.
When duties are imposed for the purpose of
excluding a cheap foreign commodity, in order
to enable it to be produced at a higher price
at home, the persons who carry into effect the

intentions of the legislature, by engaging in the
favoured manufacture, are considered as having
a vested right in their undertakings, and possessing a claim to notice of a reasonable length,
before the duties are removed; for although
their profit is not larger than it would have
been in any other unprotected branch of trade,
and although the public lose the difference between the prices of the foreign and native commodity; yet having, in consequence of the
encouragement of the legislature, once engaged
in the protected trade, they cannot, at a moment's warning, withdraw their capital and invest
it elsewhere, without incurring a certain loss.
In consequence of the high duties on French,
Portuguese, and Spanish wines, many persons
were induced to invest their capital in the making
of wine at the Cape of Good Hope. They produced an inferior commodity at a higher price :
but when it was proposed to equalize the import
duties on wines, it was allowed that the *vested
rights* of these persons ought to be respected,
and that they were fairly entitled to have a
sufficient time to engage in new speculations.
All preferences given to particular classes of
traders create vested rights of this description ;
and it is for this reason that, although the existence of such preferences is an unmixed evil,
their abolition is very far from being an unmixed
good.

A *vested right* may therefore be described as a *right of investment;* giving to its possessor a moral claim upon the legislature, for the permanency or tardy abolition of a law, which he has gained by employing his capital or labour in adventures only compatible with the existence of the law. Being founded on the principle of not disappointing expectations, it is founded on a principle of the wisest and most enlarged policy; but the doctrine of vested rights must not be stretched too far, as there is scarcely a right on which some expectations are not founded, and which does not, in some degree, serve as a guide of conduct: it can only be admitted where the loss would be great, and the probability of the law being repealed or modified was inconsiderable.

Of vested rights, that on which the greatest number of calculations and expectations is founded, and which, in most states, offers the fairest hope of permanency, is the *right of property.* There is scarcely a step in a man's life, if it has any prospective view, which is not taken in reference to his property. His bodily and mental habits, his connexions, whether of friendship or marriage, are all formed with reference to the rank of society in which his property places him. A man is brought up by his parents, and insensibly adapts himself, to the situation which he is likely to fill. A poor man suddenly made rich is not more likely to be happy, and is much less likely to do good to others, than a rich man suddenly made poor. There is no change in the condition of human life, except the change from freedom to slavery or imprisonment,—no deprivation of rank, honours, dignity, political power, military power, or sovereign dominion,—which blights so many prospects, which chills so many hopes, which brings such bitter disappointments, and such painful humiliations,* which offers such violence to a man's familiar habits and thoughts, and forces him into courses for which he is so little fitted, as the change from affluence to beggary. The interruption of this right takes a man from a station where he is contented, and which he is fitted to fill, to put him in a station where he will be discontented and dangerous, and which he is not fitted to fill. The effect on the person who is supposed to be benefited by his loss, need not be considered ; as, at times when this right is interrupted, the resistance is usually so great, that although the plundered are impo-

---

* It is to this that Juvenal probably refers, when he so feelingly says, that

> " Nil habet *infelix* paupertas durius in se
> Quam quod ridiculos homines facit."

Men are not ridiculous simply by *being* poor ; it is when they *become* poor, that the shifts and expedients to which they are driven, in order to conceal their poverty and keep up a semblance of their former wealth, too frequently make them ridiculous.

verished, the plunderers are seldom enriched.
It is for these, among many other reasons, that
the right of property is one of those vested
rights which should be most sparingly and
tenderly interfered with by a wise legislature;
but, like all other rights, it is the mere creature
of the sovereign power, which can at any
moment destroy what it created : and to deny
the power of the legislature to dispose of it at
pleasure, is to confound expediency and justice
with fact, and to conclude that what *ought not*
to be done, *cannot* be done.

Wrongful and rightful are the adjectives of
wrong and right the substantives; and differ
from wrong and right the adjectives, inasmuch
as the former signify that which agrees or disagrees with the rule of *law*, the latter that
which agrees or disagrees with the rule of
morality.

Justice is commonly used by political writers
in the sense of moral justice. In this sense
alone it is applicable to acts of the legislature.
Sometimes, however, it is used as identical with
law, as when we speak of the *administration of
justice*, of *courts of justice*, &c.*

---

* "The legal criminal intention necessary in criminal law
is not identical in strictness with the evil intention imputable
in morals. It is enough, that there exists an intention to do the
act. It is not necessary that the party should know that the
act is morally wrong. It makes no difference even if the

party believe that the act is morally virtuous. . . . . . A case like that of Martin the incendiary will illustrate the distinctions. There could be no pretence for his acquittal, supposing the jury of opinion that he believed that it was morally or religiously right to burn York Minster, but knew, at the same time, that it was legally wrong. If they meant by their verdict to express that his understanding was too disturbed to be capable of knowing that it was legally wrong, the acquittal was correct."—Edinburgh Review, No. 107, p. 221, 222. There could be no doubt that Martin was aware that the burning of York Minster was a criminal act, as his contrivances for escaping observation in committing the deed evinced considerable forethought ; and the same remark applies to nearly all cases of crimes committed by madmen. If madmen were acquitted only when proved to be ignorant of the law, they would be acquitted, not on the ground of their madness, but on quite a different plea, of which others, besides madmen, might avail themselves. The true state of the question seems rather to be, whether, when a man's mind is so diseased that he believes himself to be driven by an overwhelming duty, whether moral or religious, to the commission of an act which he knows to be illegal, he is to be considered as a person whose punishment can be useful to society, and whom society can hold as responsible for his acts. A merely depraved man may think murder or robbery indifferent acts; he may deny the existence of right and wrong, or of all moral rules whatever : but if he commits murder or robbery, he is properly amenable to punishment. But a madman is not *indifferent* to a moral duty ; he is hurried on to a violation of law by the suggestions of a deranged understanding and a heated imagination, which seem to him far to outweigh all other considerations. A man in this state of mind is no more an accountable political agent, and a fit subject for the animadversion of the law, than he is an accountable moral agent, and a subject for moral disapprobation : as a moral agent, his errors can only be pitied ; as a political agent, he must only be prevented from doing further mischief.

IV.

LAW.—LAWFUL.—UNLAWFUL.

A FULL investigation of the different meanings of the word *law* would of itself furnish matter for a long treatise ; but as it is a subject which belongs properly to the province of jurisprudence, and could not be satisfactorily explained without diverging into questions unconnected with political science, I shall limit myself to one remark on an ambiguity which has a very extensive influence on political reasoning.

Law properly signifies a general command of the sovereign, whether conveyed by the way of *direct* legislation, as in the case of statutes, or of *permissive* legislation, as in the case of legal rules established by courts of justice. The only proper mode of determining a dispute as to the existence or construction of a law, is by application to a competent tribunal, which alone has authority to decide it.

Law, however, is often used to denote, not the commands of a sovereign, but certain moral rules, the existence of which can only be determined by the arguments of private individuals, and not by the authority of public officers. It is in this sense that we speak of the law of God, the law of nature, the laws of honour, &c.

The same confusion of legal and moral rules is likewise transferred to the adjectives derived from this term: for, as Archbishop Whately has observed, " The words lawful and unlawful are sometimes employed with reference to the law of the land, and sometimes to the law of God and the dictates of a sound conscience: so that the same thing may be lawful in one sense, which is unlawful in another."*

* Bampton Lectures, p. 337.

V.

SOVEREIGN.—SOVEREIGNTY.

" For a state to be entirely sovereign (says Martens, in his Treatise on the Law of Nations,*) it must govern itself, and acknowledge no legislative superior but God." That is to say, some person or persons in a state are said to be sovereign, or to possess the sovereign power, when they yield no obedience to any person on earth, and when they receive obedience from the community which they govern. The independence of a state, or the non-obedience of its sovereign to any foreign power,—and the existence of a government, or the obedience of a community to a sovereign power,—are both questions of degree, to be decided by the length of time during which obedience has been yielded or withheld, as well as by other circumstances; and thus can only be determined according to the facts of each particular case.

As long as a government exists, the power of the person or persons in whom the sovereignty

* P. 23, Engl. transl.

D

resides, over the whole community, is absolute and unlimited. The sovereign has the complete disposal of the life, rights, and duties of every member of the community. It has also power to modify or change the existing form of government. There is no law which it has not power to alter, repeal, or enact.

When the sovereign acts as sovereign in a legislative capacity, it cannot be said to possess rights, or to be subject to duties. By legislating, it confers rights and imposes duties; but its legislative power is not founded on any right, or restrained by any duty.

Not only cannot a sovereign be limited by any power residing in the community which it governs; but it cannot limit itself, so far as its own subjects are concerned. It can limit itself, *i. e.* bind itself and its successors, by agreements with foreign powers, as then it is party to a contract, which it is not when it makes laws. A law excludes the idea of a compact; "for a compact is a promise proceeding *from* us, law is a command directed *to* us. The language of a compact is, ' I will, or will not, do this;' that of a law is, ' Thou shalt, or shalt not, do it.'"* No agreement can exist, except in a moral sense, between a sovereign and its subjects,—between a government and

* Blackstone, 1 Com. 45.

people,—as there is no legitimate means of enforcing it. A sovereign can only be liable to duties towards another sovereign, in which relation it becomes, as it were, an individual in the great community of nations.

The sovereign power may be exercised in two ways; viz. in making laws, and in administering them or carrying them into execution. Of these two functions, the latter must, for the suppression of crime, and the maintenance of civil rights, be kept in constant activity.* A day's interregnum of lawlessness—during which the sovereign slept, no protection was allowed to persons and property, and there was a complete impunity of crime—would be sufficient to overturn the most flourishing society. The existence of the executive sovereignty is therefore uninterrupted. But when a state has once been founded, and laws established, the legislative sovereignty is often in abeyance for long periods of time; nor, in modern times, is it ever kept in constant existence, except in absolute monarchies. Thus, in Great Britain, the legislative sovereignty is only alive during the session of Parliament: during a prorogation, or after a dissolution, it is in abeyance, and does not

* In this country, the prosecution of a civil suit, or of a criminal, cannot at all times be carried to its last stage: but the preliminary steps, such as arresting a debtor, or committing an offender for trial, may be always taken.

revive until it vests in the whole Parliament at its next meeting. It has been sometimes imagined that, during such intervals, the legislative sovereignty resides in the community at large, or in those who have votes for the election of members of the House of Commons : but this opinion, if taken in its plain and direct sense, has evidently no foundation in truth; and it is difficult to understand what benefit can be derived from giving metaphorical or figurative meanings to expressions of such importance as that now in question.

Such is essentially the nature of sovereign power, whether it be possessed by one person or by several; and if by several, whether by a minority or majority of the state. There is no difference in the *nature* of the power belonging to an arbitrary monarch, to a supreme council of nobles, or to a democratic assembly; the difference lies in the manner of exercising it.

Nevertheless there may not unfrequently be traced, in the speculations of political writers, a vague notion that the sovereign power is less absolute in free governments than in despotisms; that is, in governments where the sovereignty resides in many, than where it resides in one; and that a limitation of the *King's* power is also a limitation of the *sovereign* power. Whereas, in fact, a King's power is limited, not by destroying it, but either by taking it from him and giving it to others, or by compelling him to share it with others. On the other hand, some writers, thinking that the discretion of the sovereign body is, in limited monarchies, subject to a regular check and control, have mistaken the exercise of sovereign power in republics for arbitrary or tyrannical power ; confounding the use of sovereign power with the abuse of it,—an error which may be observed in the following passage in Mr. Hallam's Constitutional History of England : — "Numerous bodies (he says) are always prone to excess, both from the reciprocal influences of their passions, and the consciousness of irresponsibility; for which reasons a democracy, *that is, the absolute government of the majority,* is the most tyrannical of any." (ch. 16.) In a democracy, the government of the majority is absolute, for the same reason that the government of one is absolute in a monarchy, and the government of a minority absolute in an aristocracy ; viz. that the majority are sovereign. The same confusion is discernible in the following extract from one of Mr. Canning's speeches, who appears, at the moment, not to have adverted to the fact, that the *royal,* not the *sovereign* power, is limited in a limited monarchy :—"Now to this view of the matter I have no other objection than this,—that the British constitution is a limited monarchy ; that a *limited monarchy* is,

in the nature of things, a mixed government;
but that such a House of Commons as the
radical reformer requires would, in effect, constitute a pure democracy,—a power, as it appears
to me, inconsistent with every monarchy, and
unsusceptible of any limitation." *   Mr. Mitford,
also, in his History of Greece, frequently confounds the tyrannical acts of the Athenian democracy with the sovereign power possessed by
the body of citizens; which, he seems to think,
ought to have been legally checked or balanced,
in order to prevent misgovernment.   Thus in
one place he says, that " despotic governments,
whether the power be in the hands of one or
of a multitude, will have a near resemblance of
character."†   Again, he remarks, that " the
balances of Solon's constitution were no sooner
overthrown, and *sovereign power became absolute*
in the hands of those without property, &c., than
the interest of all who had property placed
them necessarily in the situation of conspirators
against the existing government." ‡   In another
place, professing to translate Aristotle, he says,
that "absolute democracy is tyranny;"§ meaning,

* Speeches, vol. 6. p. 383.

† History of Greece, vol. 5. p. 22.

‡ Ibid. p. 34.

§ Ibid. p. 37.   The words of Aristotle are ἡ δημοκρατία
ἡ τελευταία τυραννίς ἐστι, i. e. " the extreme or worst form
of democracy is a tyranny;" for instance, such a government as existed at several periods during the great French

as it appears, that a democracy in which
there is an absolute or sovereign power, is
necessarily tyrannical. This confusion is easily
cleared up by remarking that all checks and
balances in governments arise from the construction and internal arrangement of the sovereign body, and the manner in which it is formed,
and not from any outward authority controlling
its actions; and that the sovereign is equally
absolute in all forms of government. This
obvious truth has long since been stated and
explained by writers of high authority. Thus
Sir William Temple observes, that " all government is a restraint upon liberty ; and, under all,
the dominion is equally absolute where it is in
the last resort."*   So likewise Blackstone says,
that " however the several forms of government
began, or by what right soever they subsist,
there is, and must be, in all of them, a supreme,
irresistible, uncontrolled authority, in which the
jura summi imperii, or the rights of sovereignty,
reside."†   Paley, moreover, lays it down, that
"there necessarily exists in every government a
power from which the constitution has provided

---

revolution, which may assuredly be with justice called tyrannical. But Aristotle never meant to imply, that the *Athenian*
government, even at its worst periods, was a tyranny.

* *On the Original and Nature of Government,* Works,
vol. 2. p. 34. 8vo. ed.

† 1 Com. 48.

no appeal; and which power, for that reason, may be termed absolute, omnipotent, uncontrollable, arbitrary, despotic, *and is alike so in all countries.*"* These remarks, which are implied in the very notion of sovereignty, may serve to explain an expression which some have found mysterious, unintelligible, and even profane; viz. the phrase *omnipotence of Parliament*, as applied to the English constitution. In fact, however, it is nothing more than a hyperbolical or exaggerated method of signifying the legislative sovereignty of Parliament, which necessarily overrules all other powers, even the executive sovereignty,—which alone can alter the established constitution, and can cause any act to be done which it is in the power of the state to effect.

From the above remarks, it sufficiently appears that, in its proper sense, the word *sovereignty* means the supreme power of the person or persons who are sovereign in the state, and are legally uncontrolled both from within and without; frequently, however, it is used in an improper and metaphorical sense, to signify the moral influence of a whole or a part of the community, upon the acts of the sovereign. It

---

* Moral and Political Philosophy, b. 6, ch. 6. at the beginning. See likewise Bentham, Fragment on Government, p. 112.

is in this sense that we must understand those persons who speak of " *the sovereignty of the people*" in states where the people, in any sense of that word, is not sovereign. The phrase, *sovereignty of the people*, unlike most of the political terms, is of a very recent origin; as no expression corresponding to it occurs in the ancient writers, although they wrote on all forms of government, and although in many ancient states the people really were sovereign : nor is it very easy to give it any determinate meaning; but, as some have laid great stress on the principle of popular sovereignty, in states where the sovereign power is clearly defined, and does *not* reside in the people, we may presume that they meant to express the moral control and influence exercised by the community at large upon the acts of the legislature.

In the same sense we are to understand the difference between constitutions imposed upon and accepted by the head of the state, and constitutions granted by him, to which so much importance has been attributed. If, in an arbitrary monarchy, the King were voluntarily to divide the sovereign power with a representative chamber on certain terms, or if he were compelled to divide it on the very same terms by the complaints or rebellion of his subjects, the sovereignty would belong to identically the same persons ; but the moral influence exercised on the sovereign legislature, by the rest of the community, would be widely different. Thus, at the Revolution of 1688, by which the principle of the sovereignty of the people is said to have been established in England, the sovereign power was not extended to more persons than had enjoyed it in the reign of James the Second. But the moral influence of a part of the community, and particularly of the members of the legislative body, on the head of the state, was greatly increased.* So likewise, if, at the late revolution of France, the very same charter had been *accepted* by Louis Philippe which was *granted* by Louis the Eighteenth, the moral influence of public opinion on the two kings and their ministers, and on the whole legislative body, would have been very different, though the sovereign power would have been possessed by the same persons, standing mutually in the

---

* " It could not be held, (says Mr. Hallam, speaking of the effects of the Revolution,) without breaking up all the foundations of our polity, that the monarchy emanated from the Parliament, or even from the people. But by the Revolution and by the act of settlement, the rights of the actual monarch, and of the reigning family, were made to emanate from the Parliament and the people. In technical language, in the grave and respectful theory of our constitution, the crown is still the fountain from which law and justice spring forth. Its prerogatives are, in the main, the same as under the Tudors and the Stuarts ; but the right of the house of Brunswick to exercise them, can only be deduced from the convention of 1688."—Constit. Hist. of England, ch. 14.

same relations to one another. In one case it would have been said that the principle of the sovereignty of the people had been asserted; in the other, that it had not.

Sometimes the phrase, *sovereignty of the people,* means the admission of all the members of the community, or all the free adult males, to the election of representatives or magistrates. In this sense, it appears to be applied to the government of the United States of America: but this usage is not less improper and figurative than the other just mentioned; as the right of voting for the election of one who is to possess a share of the sovereignty, is itself no more a share of the sovereignty, than the right of publishing a political treatise or a political newspaper. The exercise of the one right may influence the decision, as the exercise of the other may influence the formation, of the sovereign body.

When the difference between the literal and metaphorical meanings of the sovereignty, — between legal power and moral influence,—is clearly perceived, there is no danger in speaking of the sovereignty of the people in states where the people is not sovereign: we may indeed avoid it, as a clumsy and inaccurate mode of expressing an idea which may be conveyed by precise and convenient terms, but not from any fear of its producing a worse result than obscurity.

This phrase, however, is often presented to persons little acquainted with political reasoning, who may easily confound real with figurative sovereignty, and thus be led to suppose that the people truly possess the sovereign power, and therefore are not subject to it. On the mischievous tendency of such notions, which are incompatible with the existence of government, it is unnecessary to make any comment.

The strict and scientific meaning of sovereignty appears to be so well ascertained, and to admit of so little doubt, that political writers might have been expected to agree on this point, if they agreed on no other. Nevertheless, explanations of sovereignty have been proposed, which sin both in excess and defect, by including what ought to be excluded, and excluding what ought to be included. Thus Heeren, in his Discourse on the History of Political Science,* after laying it down that the distinction between monarchies and republics depends on the possession of the sovereign power, says that, in a monarchy, if the prince is hereditary and inviolable, and nothing can be done in the affairs of state against his will, he is sovereign. This definition would be satisfied, if a tribune of

* Historische Werke, vol. 1. p. 436—440. Heeren's definition is framed with considerable ingenuity, to account for the common practice of calling limited Kings sovereigns: on which see in MONARCHY.

Rome, or a member of the Polish diet, was termed a prince; and the office of the one was hereditary, and the person of the other inviolable. It is not, therefore, sufficiently comprehensive; as there are some parts of the sovereign power which it omits.

According to Blackstone, "by the sovereign power, is meant the making of laws; for wherever that power resides, all others must conform to, and be directed by it."* It is, no doubt, true, that the executive is so far subordinate to the legislative sovereignty, that the legislature may model the form of the administration at its will and pleasure : but both branches of the sovereign power are equally necessary to the existence of a state, and each is dependent on the other; for although laws could not be administered if they were not made, it would be useless to make them if they could not be administered. The inquiry, therefore, as to their comparative importance, is not more profitable than the question, which is the worst, he who plots a crime, or he who carries it into execution. If, on the one hand, it is said that a crime would not be contrived if there were no one to effect it; on the other it may be answered, that if the crime had never been planned, it never would have been committed.

* 1 Com. 49.

The fact is, that in all such cases, where both parts are indispensable, one is as important as the other. With regard to its *exercise*, the executive is of greater moment than the legislative sovereignty: for the latter may be dormant for long intervals of time, while the former must necessarily be kept in constant watchfulness.

On the other hand, Rousseau has given to the term sovereignty, an unwarrantable extension; and it is from his doctrines on this point that the modern phrase of *sovereignty of the people,* and the opinions connected with it, have chiefly been derived. According to the theory explained in his *Contrat Social,* governments are formed by all the members of the community agreeing to a certain compact, by which each places his person and his power under the supreme direction of the general will. When this compact has been formed, the whole community becomes sovereign; the sovereignty is the exercise of the general will, and is inalienable and indivisible. This account is given by Rousseau, not as a sketch of a perfect state, of the manner in which a new society *ought* to be founded; but as a general theory of government, to which all states, whatever their constitution, *must* necessarily conform. All, therefore, that need be said in refutation of it, is, that in no state has any such surrender or compact

been made : in no state is the *general will,* or
the whole community, sovereign : nor in any
state is the sovereignty inalienable or indivisible.
It is, indeed, possible that all the members of
a community might make the compact which
Rousseau describes, or, without entering into this
compact, (which proceeds on the false assumption that persons before the existence of a government have rights to surrender,) might make the
whole community sovereign; and such was really
the case in the Athenian and other Grecian
states, if by community we understand the adult
freemen without the free women and children
and without the slaves : but that the sovereign
power in any state should be inalienable or
indivisible, is a simple impossibility ; and no
compact or contrivance of any kind could prevent a sovereign body from surrendering the
sovereignty, as the Romans did to their dic-
tators, as the Syracusans did to Dionysius, and
the Danes to Frederick the Third,—or dividing
it, as the Albans are said to have done with
the Sabines in the infancy of Rome, and as the
English did with the Scotch and Irish at the
two Unions.

The origin of Rousseau's error appears to have
been, that he saw that the whole community
so far virtually possesses the sovereign power,
that if all, or a large part, of the members of
it agree to destroy the existing government, and

substitute another, they can carry their agreement into effect, as all government is ultimately a question of superior force.*   But because the community holds in its hands the issues of sovereignty, it is not to be called sovereign, any more than the Earl of Warwick is to be called *King*, because he was called *King-maker*.

According to the above observations, the two marks of sovereignty are : 1. Necessity of consent ; and 2. Irresponsibility.   When there is any person or body in a state, whose consent is necessary to the doing of a public act, and who cannot be called to account for his or their conduct in the exercise of such power, then (if the definition just proposed is correct) this person or body has a part of the sovereign power.   Thus the consent of the Houses of Lords and Commons being, in England, necessary to the passing of a law, and the members of these two bodies not being answerable for the votes given in their legislative capacity, the Houses of Lords and Commons severally possess a part of the legislative sovereignty.*   But,

---

* This is what Aristotle means, when he says, that ἐν ταῖς ὀλιγαρχίαις καὶ πανταχοῦ τὸ πλέον μέρος κύριον.   Pol. b. 4. ch. 4.   Elsewhere he uses κύριος for *sovereign*, in its strict sense.

† " Parliament (says Blackstone) hath sovereign and uncontrollable authority in the making, confirming, enlarging, restraining, abrogating, repealing, reviving, and expounding of laws, concerning matters of all possible denominations,

although the King cannot issue a proclamation without the advice of his privy council, yet the members of the privy council, being answerable for their advice so given, in case a royal proclamation should command a breach of the law, have not a share of the executive sovereignty. In like manner, although pleas of the crown and civil actions cannot be tried by the King in person, but must be tried by the King's justices, whose consent is therefore necessary to the exercise of the judicial sovereignty; yet as these officers are responsible for their acts, and may be impeached before the proper tribunal, they cannot be said to have any portion of the judicial sovereignty, the whole of which resides in the crown. The same remark applies to all the other officers intrusted with the administration of the laws; whence it is apparent (as Blackstone has laid it down) that the whole executive power of the English nation is vested in the King.*

The King of England is usually called *sovereign* (and such is his legal and constitutional title), because he is in all things *supreme*. The

ecclesiastical or temporal, civil, military, maritime, or criminal: this being the place where that absolute despotic power, which must in all governments reside somewhere, is intrusted by the constitution of these kingdoms." 1 Com. 160.

* 1 Com. 190. 242.

court of Parliament is called the King's court, in which he presides, which is held by his authority, which is assembled and dissolved by his command. All laws are enacted " by the King's most excellent Majesty, by and with the advice and consent of the Lords spiritual and temporal, and Commons, in Parliament assembled, and by the authority of the same." These laws, when in activity, are administered by the King; and all executive officers derive their authority from him. Proclamations to enforce laws are issued by the King, with the advice of his privy council. In the King's courts, and by the King's justices, all laws are administered; the King being " in all causes, as well ecclesiastical as civil, supreme."* He is likewise head of the army and navy, and of the church as by law established. He is the fountain of all honours and dignities, and every inhabitant of the United Kingdom is his subject, and inferior to him. Nevertheless, according to the scientific definition of sovereignty, the King of England cannot be considered as sovereign, *i. e.* as possessing the entire sovereign power; as he is not able to make laws by his sole authority, and it is necessary that the advice and consent of two bodies, irresponsible in a corporate capacity for

---

* A subject can only obtain redress from the King for a civil injury by *petition.*—See Blackstone, 3 Com. 256.

such advice and consent, should previously be offered and obtained. Hence it is that the King of England is termed a limited monarch, and the government of England is called a limited monarchy; because the power of the King in enacting laws is limited by the necessity of obtaining the consent of the two Houses of Parliament to their enactment. And thus the King of England cannot properly be said to possess the entire sovereign power, because all sovereign power is unlimited and uncontrolled; and a *limited sovereign* is a contradiction in terms. The difference between an absolute and limited monarchy is, that in one the entire legislative sovereignty belongs to the prince, in the other it is shared with several. It is indeed generally admitted, that all sovereign power is uncontrolled: and it is expressly laid down by Blackstone that " the sovereignty of the British constitution is lodged in the three branches of the Parliament ;"* and in another place he calls the King " one of the constituent parts of the sovereign legislative power:"† so that, although, according to our legal language, and the written doctrines of our constitution, the King is our sovereign lord, yet in a general sense he cannot properly be called sovereign, or be said to possess the entire sovereign power : sovereignty, in this

---

* 1 Com. 51.   † 1 Com. 243.

peculiar acceptation, being only equivalent to preeminence,* or supremacy, and not signifying unlimited and absolute authority.

Division of Forms of Government.

When the whole sovereign power over a community belongs to one person, the government is called a *monarchy :* when it belongs to several, it is called a *republic* or *commonwealth.* In a commonwealth, if the sovereign power belongs to a minority of the nation, the government is called an *aristocracy,* if to a majority, a *democracy.*

Such appears to be the division of governments most consistent with the received phraseology, formed on the *number of the persons who possess the sovereign power.* This was the basis of the division into monarchy, aristocracy, and democracy, when the respective merits of those three forms of government were discussed by the Persian conspirators after the death of Smerdis the magician; which debate, as reported by Herodotus,† contains the earliest use of the

* " The law ascribes to the King the attribute of sovereignty, or preeminence."—Blackstone, 1 Com. 241.

† B. 3. ch. 80 — 82. The terms used are δῆμος, ὀλιγαρχία, and μούναρχος· and they are employed in their strict sense; monarchy to signify the sole government of one,

triple division of governments with which we are acquainted. It is partially adopted by Plato,* and also by Aristotle † (who, however, proposes another principle of division for republics

and democracy to signify the government of the majority. Pindar, however, had previously described the forms of government thus: παρὰ τυραννίδι, χὥποταν ὁ λάβρος στρατός, χὥταν πόλιν οἱ σοφοὶ τηρέωντι (Pyth. 2. 160.) *i. e.* absolute monarchy; aristocracy, or the government of the educated; and democracy, or the government of the multitude.

* Plato's division of governments, contained in his Republic, b. 8, p. 544, 545, ed. Steph. is as follows:—1. His own perfect state, or aristocracy, that is, the government of the ἄριστοι, or most virtuous. 2. The Cretan and Lacedæmonian form of government, in which the love of distinction or emulation is the prevailing motive. 3. Oligarchy, in which the prevailing motive is a love of wealth. 4. Democracy, in which the prevailing motive is a love of liberty and equality. 5. *Tyranny*, or Despotism, in which the prevailing motive is the personal gratification of the prince. This, in fact, is not a logical division, but rather an enumeration of governments, as they follow one another in a constant cycle. Plato's doctrine as to this regular succession of governments is, however, completely demolished by Aristotle, Politics, b. 5. ch. 12.

† Aristotle's division of governments (Politics, b. 3, ch. 5. Ethics, b. 8, ch. 8) may be best understood by means of the following scheme :—

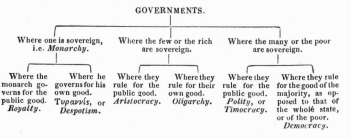

GOVERNMENTS.

Where one is sovereign, i.e. *Monarchy*.		Where the few or the rich are sovereign.		Where the many or the poor are sovereign.	
Where the monarch governs for the public good. *Royalty.*	Where he governs for his own good. *Τυραννίς*, or *Despotism.*	Where they rule for the public good. *Aristocracy.*	Where they rule for their own good. *Oligarchy.*	Where they rule for the public good. *Polity*, or *Timocracy.*	Where they rule for the good of the majority, as opposed to that of the whole state, or of the poor. *Democracy.*

which will be presently noticed), is fully explained by Polybius,* and is briefly stated by Cicero.† By these writers, (though they likewise admitted the doctrine of mixed governments,) the words were understood in their strict and proper sense : that is to say, in communities where an absolute majority of the whole number of citizens or freemen shared in the sovereign power, the government was considered as democratic; in communities where a minority of the whole number of citizens or

* Polybius (b. 6, ch. 3) objects to the triple division of governments into royalty, aristocracy, and democracy, which, he says, was employed by most political authorities in his time ; and substitutes a classification of his own into six kinds (ch. 4), which nearly resembles that of Aristotle ; *i. e.* each member of the triple division is subdivided according to the mode in which the government is administered. 1. Monarchy. This government Polybius appears to consider as the starting - point of society, and therefore excludes it from his sum total of governments. 2. Royalty. 3. Τυραννίς, or Despotism. 4. Aristocracy. 5. Oligarchy. 6. Democracy. 7. Ochlocracy, or mob government. Polybius considers that these governments follow one another in regular order. Plutarch's explanation, with regard to the three chief forms of government, and their corruptions or deviations, is nearly similar. De Monarchia, c. 3.

† Cicero's definitions are contained in the following sentence. " Cum penes unum est omnium summa rerum, regem illum unum vocamus, et regnum ejus rei publicæ statum. Cum autem est penes delectos, tum illa civitas optimatium arbitrio regi dicitur. Illa autem est civitas popularis, sic enim appellant, in qua in populo sunt omnia." De Rep. b. 1. ch. 26.

freemen shared in the sovereign power, the government was considered as aristocratic : it being understood that slaves were left out of the account, as not being members of the state (πολῖται, or *cives*.) The same principle of division has been adopted, since the revival of learning, by many writers on various subjects, whether moral, political, or historical, and indeed has usually been taken for admitted and understood. Amidst such a multitude of examples, it will be sufficient to select four of the clearest explanations given by professed political inquirers. " The difference of commonwealths (says Hobbes) consisteth in the difference of the sovereign, or the person representative of all and every one of the multitude. And because the sovereignty is either in one man, or in an assembly of more than one ; and into that assembly either every man hath right to enter, or not every one, but certain men distinguished from the rest, it is manifest there can be but three kinds of commonwealth. For the representative must needs be one man, or more ; and if more, then it is the assembly of all, or but a part. When the representative is one man, then is the commonwealth a monarchy ; when an assembly of all that will come together, then it is a democracy or popular commonwealth ; when an assembly of a part only, then it is called an aristocracy. Other

kind of commonwealth there can be none : for
either one or more or all must have the sovereign
power entire." *   According to Montesquieu,†
governments are divided into those where one
rules, and those where several rule, or republics.
In a republic, if the people in a body has the
sovereign power, it is a democracy ; if the sovereign power is in the hands of a part of the
people, it is an aristocracy.   Rousseau says, that
" the sovereign (that is, in his vocabulary, the
whole nation,) may give the government to the
whole people, or to the majority of the people,
which form of government is a *democracy ;* or
it may confine the government to a minority,
which form is an *aristocracy ;* or it may con-
centrate all the government in the hands of a
single magistrate, from whom all the other
magistrates derive their power ; which form is
called a *monarchy,* or *royal government."* ‡   The
same triple division is adopted by Mr. Mill, in his
Treatise on Government.   " There are (he says)
three modes in which it may be supposed that
the powers of protecting the community are
capable of being exercised.   The community
may undertake the protection of itself, and of

---

* Leviathan, part 2. ch. 19.

† Esprit des Lois, liv. 2. ch. 1, 2.   His subdivision of
the government of one is examined below, in the word
DESPOTISM.

‡ Contrat Social, liv. 3. ch. 3.

its members. The powers of protection may be placed in the hands of a few. And, lastly, they may be placed in the hands of an individual. The many, the few, the one, these varieties appear to exhaust the subject . . . . And these varieties correspond to the three forms of government, the democratical, the aristocratical, and the monarchical."* The *government*, in the language of Rousseau, and the *powers of protection* in that of Mr. Mill, appear to have the same meaning, and to signify the sovereign power. The common usage of the three terms in question, in modern times, does not, however, at all agree with these definitions, as will be explained elsewhere.

It is quite evident that the division of governments just explained, must be exhaustive ; and that in every possible state, whether real or imaginary, the sovereign power must reside in one, or in a minority, or in a majority of the whole people. Nevertheless, most political writers, both of ancient and modern times,

---

* Supplement to the Encyclopædia Britannica, vol. 4, p. 492. See likewise p. 497, where Mr. Mill says, that " if the powers of government are intrusted to one man, or a few men, and a monarchy, or governing aristocracy, is formed, the results are fatal." Here, too, monarchy and aristocracy are clearly used to signify governments, in which one man or a few men possess the sovereign power. This writer, however, is not consistent in his language. See below in PEOPLE, and REPRESENTATION.

have made a fourth form of government, compounded either of any two or of all three of these forms, and different from all; which is known by the name of a *mixed government.* On this variety of government, which is commonly considered as different from either monarchy, aristocracy, or democracy, though in fact it is not opposed to them, more will be said in its proper place.

VI.

MONARCHY.—ROYALTY.—KING.

Monarchy, in its proper sense, signifies the government of one; that is, when the whole sovereignty belongs to one person. "When the sovereign power (says Blackstone) is intrusted in the hands of a single person, the government takes the name of a monarchy."* Examples of this are afforded by the government of France under Louis the Fourteenth, who used to say, "L'état c'est moi;"† and by the actual governments of Russia, Austria, Prussia, Spain, Portugal, Turkey, &c. It is in this sense that Machiavelli understands the word in his treatise on the art of monarchical government, his *Principe*. The same definition of monarchy is also given in the passages quoted above from Hobbes, Montesquieu, Mill, and

---

* 1 Com. 49.

† The same expression, applied to a monarch, occurs in Æschylus, Suppl. 370.

> σύ τοι πόλις, σὺ δὲ τὸ δήμιον,
> πρύτανις ἄκριτος ὢν,
> κρατύνεις βωμὸν ἑστίαν χθονός.

Rousseau; the latter of which writers has enlarged upon the subject in another place, always restricting it to the supremacy of one person.*
So likewise Mr. Crabb, in his Dictionary of English Synonyms, says, that "Monarch signifies one having sole authority;" and again, "The term monarch does not define the extent of the power, but simply that it is undivided, as opposed to that species of power which is lodged in the hands of the many."† In this sense the *kingly* office is taken by a late writer on the history of England:—"If by the royal dignity (says Mr. Palgrave ‡) we are to understand a permanent authority, enabling the sovereign to give laws to his subjects in time of peace, to command them to follow him in time of war, and to impose taxes or tributes upon the nation at all times, such an authority was wholly unknown to the Jutes, Angles, and Saxons, before they settled in Britain." The same definition of monarchy is also given by Martens; who says, that "when the rights of sovereignty, and consequently the majesty of a state, are lodged in the hands of one person, the government is monarchical; when they are lodged in the hands of several persons, it is republican." He proceeds, however, to modify this definition

---

* Contrat Social, liv. 3, ch. 6.
† In the word *Prince.*
‡ History of England, vol. 1. p. 73.

by adding, that "when we say that the rights of sovereignty are intrusted to some one, we do not always mean that he possesses them all without exception; it is understood that he possesses the greatest part, or the most essential of them."* And he further states, that "in applying these principles to the states of Europe, it is easy to perceive that every state in it which has a *King* for its chief, is *monarchical.*"† Such undoubtedly is the common use of the term *monarchy*, although it does not result from the principles laid down by Martens. For, at the time when his book was written, neither the greatest part,· nor the most essential, of the powers of sovereignty belonged to the King of England, although the English government was then, and ever since has been, called a monarchy; and the same is now the case with the King of France. The fact is, that, by common agreement, we call all governments of which a King is chief, monarchies; which agreement is solely derived from historical recollections, and is not founded on the actual state of things. There was a time when the Kings of France were truly monarchs, or absolute princes: there was a time when the Kings of England were, in practice, nearly absolute, and when the crown was by far the most important part of the constitution.

* Law of Nations, p. 34.   † Ibid. p. 35.

The King of England is always, in solemn language, styled "our sovereign lord."* Yet the King of England possesses only a part, and that the least important part, of the sovereign power. With regard to the administration of the laws, and the declaration of peace and war, he is sovereign; but the entire legislative sovereignty he shares with two deliberative bodies, altogether forming a Parliament, which alone possesses the power of making laws. To this arrangement of the supreme power Gibbon has adapted his account of monarchy, when he says, that " the obvious definition of a monarchy seems to be that of a state in which a single person, by whatsoever name he may be distinguished, is intrusted with the execution of the laws, the management of the revenue, and the command of the army."†

According to this usage, therefore, monarchy would signify, not only a government in which the whole sovereign power is possessed by one, but all governments in which the head of the state

* This, however, (as was above remarked,) does not prevent us from calling our government a limited monarchy, and our King a limited King : although a *limited sovereign* is an impossibility.

† Decline and Fall of the Roman Empire, ch. 3. at the beginning. Under the *army*, he probably means to include the *navy;* but it is to be observed, that he studiously excepts the making of laws, in which, according to Blackstone, all sovereign power is centered. Above, p. 45.

is called King, Prince, or Emperor, although
he may only be part of the sovereign body.
Another method of distinguishing monarchies
from republics, different both from the scientific
and the popular mode, is adopted by Mr. Millar,
in his Historical View of the English Government, according to whom a republic is " a
government in which there is no king or hereditary chief magistrate."* Although, on the
other hand, Mr. Millar appears to consider
monarchy as a government in which the King
alone is sovereign ; yet we may assume that the
point on which he intended to rest the distinction between monarchies and republics, was the
mode of nominating the chief magistrate: if the
first place in the state is elective, the government is a republic; if hereditary, the government
is a monarchy.† This method of division is
perfectly accurate ; but it does not agree with
common usage more than the method of
division according to the numbers of the sovereign body. For if we deny the name of

* Vol. 3. p. 326.

† Millar's words, " no King or hereditary chief magistrate," I have taken to mean, " no King, or, *in other words*,
no hereditary chief magistrate :" the particle *or* being used
in its explanatory sense. If it was meant to have its disjunc-
tive sense, so that the words import " *neither* a King *nor* an
hereditary chief magistrate," Mr. Millar adopts the common
distinction, adding, at the same time, another distinction of
his own.

monarchies to governments where the King is elected, the kingdom of Hungary will be a republic, the kingdom of Sweden will be a republic; Rome, before the expulsion of the Tarquins, would be a republic or commonwealth, because the kings were elective. To speak, with Lord Bacon, of an elective monarchy, would be to make a contradiction in terms : and to compare, as Paley* has done, the advantages of an hereditary monarchy with those of an elective monarchy, would in fact be to compare the advantages of a monarchy and a republic. If therefore we are to depart from the received usage, it would perhaps be more convenient to take for the basis of the division, the numbers of the sovereign body, than the mode of nominating the head of the state, as being a more characteristic and important point of disagreement.†

---

* Moral and Political Philosophy, b. 6. ch. 6.

† As a set-off to the common practice of calling kingly republics by the name of monarchies, we have the following passage of Rousseau, according to which some pure monarchies are to be called republics. "By the word *republic* (he says) I understand not only an aristocracy or a democracy, but in general every government guided by the general will, which is the law. For a government to be legitimate, it must not be confounded with the sovereign, but be its minister : then monarchy itself is a republic."—Contrat Social, liv. 2. ch. 6. n. This division into monarchies and republics appears to coincide with Montesquieu's division into republics, monarchies, and despotisms : the republic of Rousseau, comprising both the republic and monarchy of

All attempts of this kind to reconcile the common usage of monarchy with any general principle must be unsuccessful, as it is only determined by the accidental circumstance of the style and title of the chief magistrate ; whether he is, or is not, called a *King* or *Prince*. If, instead of the numbers of the sovereign body, the election of the chief magistrate is taken as the touchstone of monarchies and republics, then the governments of Sweden, and Hungary, and of Rome before the expulsion of the Kings, cannot be called monarchical, and an elective monarchy is a contradiction in terms; if the election of the chief magistrate only *for a term of years*, then the Pope of Rome, the Doge of Venice, the Stadtholder of the Netherlands, are to have the name of monarchs. The common phraseology is too capricious and arbitrary to be explained on any rational ground.* So far

Montesquieu, and the monarchy of Rousseau being equivalent to the despotism of Montesquieu. See below in the word DESPOTISM.

* " In qua re publica (says Cicero) est unus aliquis perpetua potestate, præsertim regia, quamvis in ea sit et senatus, ut tum fuit Romæ, quum erant reges, ut Spartæ Lycurgi legibus ; et ut sit aliquod etiam populi jus, ut fuit apud nostros reges ; tamen illud excellit regium nomen, neque potest ejusmodi res publica non regnum et esse et vocari." De Rep. 2, 23. Undoubtedly, states in which there are Kings may properly be called *kingdoms*, but they are not therefore to be called *monarchies*. It does not follow that, because some monarchs are Kings, all Kings are monarchs.

indeed has the doctrine of attending to the mere name of King been carried, that a most accurate writer has called the government of Sparta a monarchy, although there were *two* Kings at the head of it.*

It is perhaps unfortunate that usage has sanctioned the extension of the term monarchy to all states in which a King is chief; in other words, has identified *monarchy* with *royalty*. For as the mind, even of the most careful, is insensibly influenced by words, the idea is naturally suggested that there is a greater affinity between a commonwealth with a King, and a genuine monarchy, than between a commonwealth with a King, and a commonwealth with a chief elected for a term of years. The difference between a state in which one person has the whole sovereignty, and a state in which the legislative sovereignty is shared among a large number, of whom many are chosen by popular election, is immense. The maxims and acts of the two governments, and their influence on the community, must be most dissimilar. But when we compare a royal commonwealth with a

---

* "A monarchy under a double race of Kings."—Clinton, Fasti Hellenici, part 1. pref. p. 6. This is the only inconsistency in the received use of monarchy and republic that I am aware of, as the government of Sparta is generally called a *republic;* an irregularity which Mr. Clinton has most consistently, according to the common usage, corrected.

commonwealth not royal (or, in common language, a limited monarchy with a republic), the principal difference is, that in one the chief is hereditary, and for life; in the other elective, either for life or for a term of years. It is not that the forms of government differ greatly; or the powers of a King, and of a President, Doge, or Stadtholder; but the manner in which those powers are acquired, and the time for which they endure. For instance, the government of England resembles that of the United States of America (barring the differences caused by the nature of a federal union) far more nearly than that of Austria or Russia. The representative franchise may be more extended, property may be more equally divided, in one state than in the other: but the principal difference in the construction of the sovereign power is, that in one state the chief is determined by election, in the other by inheritance; that in one state the office lasts for life, in the other only for a limited time. Yet Austria, Russia, and England, are generally classed together as monarchies, and together opposed to the United States as a republic. Monarchical institutions, in a limited monarchy, are also frequently opposed to republican institutions, and the two are considered as incompatible. If, at the Revolution, the *name* of the King of England, as well as his *power*, had been changed, but he had nevertheless exercised precisely the same influence in the constitution as the crown has exercised since that time, the government would have been called republican, instead of monarchical; although the only difference would have been in the name of the first person in the state.

The influence of ambiguities of this kind upon the course of our thoughts is in most cases so subtle, that the fallacies produced by them can seldom be detected and presented to readers in a tangible form. The transition from the strict to the popular sense of monarchy may, however, be traced in the following argument of a celebrated institutional writer, whose work unfortunately abounds in similar errors. In speaking of the several advantages and disadvantages of the three simple forms of government, Blackstone lays it down that " a monarchy is the most powerful of any; all the sinews of government being knit together, and united in the hands of the prince."* In another place, he says that " the great end of society is to protect the weakness of individuals by the united strength of the community; and the principal use of government is to direct that united strength in the best and most effectual manner, to answer the end proposed. Monarchical government (meaning *absolute* monarchy) is allowed to be

* 1 Com. 50.

the fittest of any for this purpose : it follows
therefore, from the very end of its institution,
that in a monarchy (meaning a *limited* monarchy)
the military power must be trusted in the hands
of the prince."*

One of the chief mischiefs of this confusion
both of words and thought, has been that, in
comparing the advantages of a limited monarchy
and a republic (to use the common expressions),
it has not been perceived that the principal
question is, whether it is more advantageous
that the headship of the state should be determined by election or succession, and whether it
should last for life, or for a term of years? All the
other advantages actually possessed by limited
monarchies seem communicable to republics,
and *vice versâ*. The real difference by which
their respective merits should be tried, is the
mode of determining the first person in the
state. The objections to an hereditary succession are (as Gibbon† and Paley have remarked)
obvious to all the world. To confer on a man

---

* 1 Com. 262. The well-known and often-quoted passage
of Claudian,

"Nunquam libertas gratior extat
Quam sub rege pio,"—

'the sentence,' according to Gibbon, (ch. 29. note 54,) 'so
familiar to the friends of despotism,'—is not more applicable
to absolute than to limited Kings, although it is always applied to the former.

† Decline and Fall, ch. 7, at the beginning.

the largest political powers in a state, not because he is the wisest or the best, but because
he is the son of a particular person, seems at first
sight the very height of absurdity.　It would
appear more reasonable to imitate the ancient
Æthiopians, and make the tallest or the fairest
man King.　But the real, and not less obvious
benefits, of hereditary succession, are that it puts
an end to all questions of supremacy; that it
prevents the constant existence of intrigues,
cabals, factions, and party measures, for the
sake of attaining to the first place in the state;
and saves the community from ever being disturbed by a contest for the possession of its
highest honours.　It is not because a King is
wiser or better, or more versed in political
affairs, or more skilled in the art of governing,
than any of his subjects, that he is King.　He is
King that no one else may be King: to make it
certain, that, as long as the established government lasts, all attempts to obtain the chief rank
in the state will be fruitless.　In the republics
of Athens and Syracuse, if a man by his political
talents, or from any other cause, obtained great
influence over his fellow-citizens, he might be
banished by ostracism or petalism, lest he should
make himself prince over his fellow-citizens.
Under a King, such a person could never be first
in the state, and must always acknowledge a
superior.　Whatever his ambition, or wealth, or

station, or eloquence,—whether he be a victorious general, a noble formidable from his opu-
lence and connexions, or a statesman backed by
a large and powerful party,—he must still be
content constantly to shew at least an outward
respect to the royal name and person; and
gratefully himself receive, and see all others
receive from the King, the highest marks of
honour, and the chief places of power. The
station and the hereditary succession of the
King render his possession of great political
ability and influence both improbable and hurtful; while the impossibility that a subject can
become king, prevents his political talents being
wholly perverted by ambition.*   In this manner,

---

* "The advantages which seem to us to be peculiar to
this arrangement are, first, to disarm the ambition of dangerous and turbulent individuals, by removing the great
prize of supreme authority, at all times and entirely, from
competition; and secondly, to render this authority more
manageable and less hazardous, by delivering it over,
peaceably, and upon understood conditions, to an hereditary
prince, instead of letting it be seized upon by a fortunate
conqueror, who would think himself entitled to use it, as
conquerors commonly use their booty, for his own exclusive
gratification."—Edinburgh Review, vol. 20. p. 333.   "The
chief advantage of monarchy consists in its taking away the
occasions of contention for the first place in the state, and, in
a manner, neutralizing that place by separating it entirely
from any notion of merit or popularity in the possessor." —
Ibid. p. 324.   The force of the argument with regard to
conquerors, in the first of these passages, is not very apparent.

the greatest and most useful talents are safely brought into the service of the public, and the good of the individual is reconciled with the good of the community. We may reverse the maxims of Æschylus,* and say, that it is both desirable to breed a lion in the state, and easy to curb it when grown into vigour.

Even if the evils caused by a perpetual competition for the chief magistracy, and the danger of uniting the greatest legal authority with the possession of the greatest personal influence, are left out of the question, it is to be observed that persons, who have made great sacrifices to obtain an object, sometimes think that they are at liberty to abuse their acquired power in order to indemnify themselves for the toils which it has cost them to acquire it; as the French judges, who bought their offices, reimbursed themselves by taking bribes. Elective chiefs may likewise come to the head of affairs, loaded with a debt of gratitude to their friends and supporters, which they must at all rates pay, and which they cannot pay consistently with the public good.

The argument of those who prefer an elective to an hereditary chief, on the ground of

---

* Οὐ χρὴ λέοντος σκυμνὸν ἐν πόλει τρέφειν.
ἢν δ' ἐκτραφῇ τις, τοῖς τρόποις ὑπηρετεῖν.

Aristoph. Ran.

economy, is as old as the reign of Charles the Second, when, according to Dryden,

> " Others thought kings an useless heavy load,
> Who cost too much, and did too little good.
> These were for laying honest David by,
> On principles of pure good husbandry."*

But this is a motive completely inadequate for the change of an existing government, and would only turn the scale at the creation of a new state, if the other benefits were equally balanced.

Whatever may be the merits or demerits of hereditary royalty, it stands on a perfectly different footing from hereditary nobility or title. The arguments for or against each, do not apply to the other; nor does the one necessarily require the presence of the other.

* Absalom and Achitophel.

VII.

COMMONWEALTH.—REPUBLIC.— REPUBLICAN.

COMMONWEALTH, or republic, is a general name for all governments in which the sovereign power resides in several persons, whether they be few or many. Thus we speak of the commonwealths or republics of Rome in early times, Venice, &c., which were aristocracies; of Athens, of Rome in later times, &c., which were democracies. A few instances of this usage will be sufficient to exemplify it. Thus Machiavelli, at the beginning of his Principe, says, "Tutti li stati, tutti i dominii che hanno havuto e hanno imperio sopra gli uomini sono stati e sono o republiche o principati." Dryden, in the following couplet, opposes commonwealths generally to kingly governments (*i. e.* monarchies):

> " Plots, true or false, are necessary things
> To raise up commonwealths and ruin kings."*

Hume, in his Essay on the Populousness of Ancient Nations, remarks, that " at present

***

* Absalom and Achitophel.

there is not one *republic* in Europe, from one extremity of it to the other, that is not remarkable for justice, lenity, and stability, equal to, or even beyond Marseilles, Rhodes, or the most celebrated in antiquity. Almost all of them are well-tempered *aristocracies.*"* In this passage Hume makes aristocracy a species of republic ; on the other hand, so many writers have included democracy under it, that some have been led to confine the term republic to democracies. Thus Crabb, in his Dictionary of Synonyms, says, that " governments are divided by political writers into three classes,—monarchical, aristocratic, and republican." Here he makes a republic equivalent to a democracy.† He does not, however, adhere to this usage ; for afterwards he says, that " most of the constitutions of Europe, whether republican or monarchical, are indebted to time and the natural course of events for their establishment :" ‡ where his republic includes all governments not monarchies.

According to the custom already noticed of identifying royalty with monarchy, or of calling all states in which a King rules, monarchical, it

* Works, vol. 3. p. 461.

† This use of *republic* appears to be of very frequent occurrence, though it is difficult to discover what is commonly signified by this word.

‡ In *Government, Constitution.*

is usual to class England and France with monarchies, and not with commonwealths or republics, to which, in strictness, they belong. * The
interval in English history, between the death of
Charles the First and the Restoration, is commonly known by the name of the Commonwealth : although, during part of that time, the
state was more absolutely under the rule of one
individual than it has ever been since the
Restoration, or, at any rate, since the Revolution.
By the writers, indeed, of the age which preceded the Civil War, the English government
(as Mr. Mitford has remarked †) is often called
a commonwealth : but they appear to use this
term as nearly synonymous with state, or
res publica. This is the sense in which Locke
uses the word in his treatises on government :
and such he considers to be its genuine signification.‡ Unquestionably, however, since the

* Thus Hume notices " the common opinion that no large
state, such as France or Great Britain, could ever be mo-
delled into a commonwealth ; but that such a form of government can only take place in a city or small territory."—
Essays, part 2. essay 16.

† History of Greece, vol. 9. p. 53. However, in the
following passage from Lord Bacon's Essay on the True
Greatness of Kingdoms and Estates, *commonwealth* appears
to be opposed to *kingdom :*—" In the great game of kingdoms and commonwealths, it is in the power of princes or
estates to add amplitude and greatness to their kingdoms."

‡ " By commonwealth I must be understood all along to
mean, not a democracy, or any form of government, but any

end of Charles the First's reign, it has received the narrower meaning of a republic; (thus, at the end of the seventeenth century, a *commonwealth's-man* signified what a *republican* does now;) although, even now, it occasionally obtains its wider acceptation. And hence, in such passages as that where Mr. Hallam calls the Kings of England, " the chiefs of the English commonwealth," * it is uncertain in what way the term should be understood. Probably, however, no one would call an absolute monarchy by this name ; would speak, for example, of the Turkish commonwealth, or the French commonwealth under Louis the Fourteenth.†

Commonwealth and commonweal are synonymous, and mean a society formed for the

___

independent community, which the Latins signified by the word *civitas;* to which the word which best answers in our language is commonwealth, and most properly expresses such a society of men, which community or city in English does not : for there may be subordinate communities in a government ; and city, amongst us, has a quite different notion from commonwealth : and therefore, to avoid ambiguity, I crave leave to use the word commonwealth in that sense in which I find it used by King James the First: and I take it to be its genuine signification ; which, if any body dislike, I consent with him to change it for a better."—On Government, b. 2. § 134.

* Constitutional Hist. of England, c. 14.

† " Commonwealth, although not appropriately (query not *in*appropriately) applied to any nation, is most fitted for republics."—Crabb's English Synonyms, in *State.*

common good ; *wealth* and *weal* being originally
the same word, and signifying welfare or happiness.

Res publica is used by the Romans in rather
a wider acceptation, as it included all governments except a violent despotism : thus Cicero,
in his dialogue *De re publica,* says, " When all
are subject to the rule of one tyrant, the state
cannot be called a *res publica.**

A republican is defined by Johnson to be
" one who thinks a commonwealth without
monarchy the best government." More precisely, " one who thinks a commonwealth
without *royalty* the best government." A commonwealth with royalty is usually called a
monarchy. *Republican,* however, seems to
have obtained a narrower sense than *republic.*
For *republic* is applied to all aristocracies and
democracies of which a King is not the head;
whereas a *republican* generally signifies a de-
mocrat, as opposed either to an aristocrat, or
to a favourer of kingly government.

---

* " Ergo illam rem populi, id est rem publicam, quis diceret
tum cum crudelitate unius oppressi essent universi; neque
esset vinculum juris, nec consensus ac societas cœtus, quod est
populus? . . . Ergo ubi tyrannus est ibi non vitiosam, ut
heri dicebam, sed ut ratio cogit, dicendum est plane nullam
esse rem publicam."—De Rep. 3. 31.

VIII.

ARISTOCRACY.—OLIGARCHY.—NOBILITY.

ARISTOCRACY signifies a government in which the sovereignty is shared by several persons, being less in number than half the community. Such are the governments of England, France, Bavaria, the United States of America, &c.

It also signifies a certain class in a state, whatever may be the form of its government. Thus we speak of the French aristocracy, when the government was a monarchy; of the aristocracy of Rome, when the government was democratic: and many writers have called the English government an aristocracy; and a class of persons in England, the aristocracy.

Aristocracy, as the name of an order or class of persons, is applied variously to the following classes:

1. To the class of *nobles:* as when we speak of the French aristocracy before 1789, meaning the clergy and the *noblesse;* and the English aristocracy, meaning the members of the House of Lords and their families.

2. To the class of *wealthy land-owners*. In this sense the members of the House of Lords, together with most members of the House of Commons, and a considerable portion of the rest of the community, would, in England, form the aristocracy. Thus, in a recent pamphlet, it is said, that " For all England there are eighty-two county members. These, if any, are supposed to be chosen by the landed interest,—the aristocracy."*

3. To the class of *rich men* generally, from whatever source their wealth is derived, or that class which, in England, is known by the name of *gentlemen*.† Thus, Mr. Mill says, in his

---

* Friendly Advice to the Lords, (London, 1831,) p. 12.

† In England, whenever *gentlemen* are spoken of as a class, the rich are signified, as opposed to the middle ranks and the poor. In a narrower sense, and as applied to individuals, the word *gentleman* is used to denote persons remarkable for the qualities and attainments which ought to distinguish those who have had the advantage of a liberal education, and, from their birth upwards, have associated with persons of refined and cultivated minds. It is likewise employed, in a restricted sense, to mean those who, by their wealth, are enabled, and by their disposition are induced, to live in entire idleness, engaged only in the pursuit of pleasure. In this latter sense, Lord Chesterfield (if I am not mistaken) remarked, that it was unbecoming for a gentleman to walk quickly in the streets, because it seemed as if he had some business or occupation. So Aristotle, in his Rhetoric, defining the popular acceptations of words, says, that "things useful are those which bring a profit ; gentlemanlike, (ἐλευθέρια,) those which are for the sake of enjoyment."

Essay on Government, that "the class which is universally described as both the most wise and the most virtuous part of the community, the middle rank, are wholly included in that part of the community which is not the aristocratical:"* plainly identifying the aristocracy with the rich.

The ambiguity of this word has been turned to great account by modern writers and speakers, who shift from one sense of it to another, as it suits their purpose, and having succeeded in raising a prejudice against one class, transfer and direct it against another, by merely confounding them under one name. Substantially, however, aristocracy, as the name of a class in England, is synonymous with the rich in the widest sense: and any measure tending to increase the power of the rich is considered aristocratic; and any measure tending to increase the power of the poor, is considered anti-aristocratic.

Oligarchy, as well as aristocracy, signifies both a form of government, and a class of

(Rhet. b. 1. ch. 5. § 7.) Nevertheless, this latter meaning is commonly given to the word in question by those who scarcely belong to the class which they describe,—the vulgar in mind,—who seek to obtain admiration by insisting on the casual eccentricities of a few, or at least to the unimportant accidents of the class, without adverting to its genuine characteristics, which they are unable to appreciate.

* Supp. to Encycl. Brit. vol. 4. p. 505. See below in RICH and POOR.

persons in a state. It is generally used as an opprobrious term by those who think either that the government is in the hands of too few, or that in an aristocracy the rulers govern oppressively.

Nobility is a narrower term than either aristocracy or oligarchy; and signifies only those who have titles of honour or dignity, accompanied with political privileges.*

In the republics of Ancient Greece, where there were no titled orders, or hereditary marks of distinction conferred by the state, the nobles were not distinguished from the rest of the community by any precise line; but nobility was a moral rather than a legal distinction, and consisted in the ancient wealth and respectability of a man's family.† It appears that the distinction between persons of high and low birth (εὐγενεῖς, δυσγενεῖς) existed down to the latest times of the Greek states, even when it received not the slightest countenance from the law.‡

---

* See Lord Bacon's Essay on Nobility.

† See Welcker's Prolegomena to Theognis, p. 58.

‡ The universally prevailing opinion in favour of noble or gentle descent, *i. e.* of a descent from a wealthy and respectable family, is founded on truth, so far as one generation is concerned: for a person brought up by parents in the same rank of life to which he himself belongs, is more likely to have early formed the habits and imbibed the notions suitable to his station, than one who has been the cause either

of his own rise or fall in society. Beyond this point, the feeling of pride in an illustrious ancestry is akin to that which makes us glory in the renown and great deeds of our countrymen: the national pride which an Englishman feels in being the countryman of Bacon and Shakspeare, is exactly analogous to the family pride of an individual in the ancient exploits of his forefathers.

IX.

DEMOCRACY.

DEMOCRACY properly signifies a government in which a majority of the whole nation or community partake of the sovereign power. Such were, at one time, the governments of Athens, Rome, and many other Grecian and Italian states, as well as of some of the Italian and German cities in the middle ages, in which all the male adult citizens had a voice in the supreme legislative assembly.

It is also used to signify a government in which either a majority or a large portion of the people have, by means of the right of election, an influence on the appointment of members of the supreme power. In this sense the federal government of the United States, as well as the governments of the several states, are called democracies; although, both in the one and in the others, the sovereign power resides in a very small minority of the whole people. Even during the rule of the multitude in the French revolution, at the worst periods of the reign of terror, the sovereignty was never shared by a large part of the population of France. The government was really in the hands of the lower orders of Paris, and hence it was termed a democracy. This agrees with the definition of Aristotle, who says that democracy is not, according to the common opinion, a government in which the *many* govern, but a government in which the *poor* govern. It so happens (he adds) that the rich are always the minority, the poor the majority of the people; and hence accidentally a democracy is a government where the many rule.*

In the following passage, Mr. Millar extends the term democracy to those governments where the right of voting for the election of members of the sovereign body belongs to a majority of the nation. " Many politicians (he says) have asserted that a republican constitution is peculiarly adapted to a small state, and cannot be maintained in a large community. This doctrine seems to have arisen from a view of the ancient republics, in which the whole people composed the legislative assembly; and is evidently inapplicable to those modern systems of democracy, in which the legislative power is committed to national representatives. Nothing is more common than for philosophers to be imposed upon

* Politics, b. 3. ch. 8; b. 4. ch. 4; b. 5. ch. 1; b. 6. ch. 2. See below in RICH and POOR.

by the different acceptation of words."* It is, however, very questionable whether Mr. Millar and other philosophers, who have given the name of democracy to governments in which the sovereignty belongs to a small minority, have not themselves been imposed upon by the doubtful acceptation of words; or, even if they have advisedly employed this phraseology, whether it is not likely to impose upon others less wary and keen-sighted than themselves, less familiar with political reasoning, and less aware of the fallacies likely to arise from the use of equivocal terms.

In states where there is a slave population, the form of government is commonly decided by the arrangement of the sovereign power among the freemen or citizens : thus it has been above remarked that the government of Athens was, and is always called, a democracy, although the whole number of the freemen, men, women and children, was not, in the times of which we have any accounts, above a fifth part of the number of slaves. In like manner, some of the southern states of the American Union are said to possess a democratic government, notwithstanding the large slave population which they contain. This phraseology has been objected to by Mr. Bentham, who in his Fragment on Government

* Hist. View of English Government, vol. 3. p. 325.

has the following remarks : " What is curious (he says) is, that the same persons who tell you that democracy is a form of government under which the supreme power is vested in all the members of a state, will also tell you that the Athenian commonwealth was a democracy. Now the truth is, that in the Athenian commonwealth, upon the most moderate computation, it is not one tenth part of the inhabitants of the Athenian state that ever at a time partook of the supreme power; women, children, and slaves being taken into the account."* If, in computing the numbers of a community in respect of its government, women and children are not taken into the account, not only has there never been, but probably there never will be a democracy, in whatever sense that word is taken. As to slaves, the constant usage has unquestionably been to exclude their numbers in determining the question of aristocracy or democracy; and to attend solely to the distribution of the sovereign power among the citizens, freemen, or body politic (πολίτευμα). Nevertheless, Mr. Bentham's remark should never be neglected; and in comparing two governments, it should always be borne in mind, that although they may be the same in name, their true characters may be widely different, if in the one state all manual labour, whether in

---

* P. 68. note.

manufactures or husbandry, was performed by slaves, in the other by free men.

Mr. Mill, in his Essay on Government, appears to follow the common use of this word, not assenting to Mr. Bentham's remark; for he says that " in Greece, notwithstanding the defects of democracy, human nature ran a more brilliant career than it has ever done in any other age or country."* Now if we take from the rolls of democracy the illustrious name of Athens, and give to the cause of aristocracy the splendid achievements of her sons in every department of literature, science, and art, there will be little ground for extolling the renown of Grecian democracy. Indeed there was no republic in Greece which, according to this phraseology, would not have had an aristocratic government.

* Suppl. to Encyclopædia Brit. p. 494.

X.

MIXED GOVERNMENT. — BALANCE OF POWERS.

A MIXED government is opposed to a *pure* or *simple* government, and belongs to a classification of governments upon a different principle from any hitherto examined; though what that principle may be, or in what manner it is connected with the theory of the *balance of powers* in a state, to which it is always linked, cannot be very readily or satisfactorily determined. The common notion appears to be, that there are three pure forms of government, viz., monarchy, aristocracy, and democracy, in which there is no balance of powers: but that by combining any two of these forms of government, or all three together, a mixed government is formed in which a balance of powers exists; that is to say, in which the elementary parts of the compounded constitution mutually check and counterpoise one another. This notion is subject to the obvious difficulty, that as the triple division of governments is strictly accurate and logical, it must be exhaustive, and its members

must be opposed to one another; whence it
follows, that there can be no form of government
which is not one of these three, and that a combination of any two of them, much more of all
three, is as inconceivable as that a number should
be odd and even at the same time; inasmuch as
the notion of one excludes that of any other. For
example: monarchy is the government of one,
aristocracy of more than one: therefore, as a state
cannot be governed both by one person and by
several persons, it cannot, at the same time,
be both a monarchy and an aristocracy.
Aristocracy is a government of less than half,
democracy of more than half the community:
therefore, as a state cannot, at the same time,
be governed by more and less than half its
members, it cannot be, at the same time, a
democracy and an aristocracy. Still less can
it be governed by one, by a minority, and a
majority of its members, all at once. On whatever principle the division of governments into
monarchies, aristocracies, and democracies is
taken,—whether on the numbers of the sovereign
body, on the presence of a King in the state,
on the inheritance of the chief magistracy, on
the wealth or poverty of the governors, or any
other circumstance,—the difficulty still remains
the same: for by whatever test monarchy,
aristocracy, and democracy, are distinguished
from one another, by the very hypothesis there

is a distinction between them, and, therefore, no two can be united in the same state. This irreconcilable hostility between the three forms of government, may be illustrated by the three numbers in the Greek language, the singular, dual, and plural; each of which represents something distinct from the others, and incompatible with either or both of them. A noun can no more be at once of the singular, dual, and plural numbers, than a state can be at the same time a monarchy, an aristocracy, and a democracy.*

---

* D'Alembert, in his Analysis of Montesquieu's Esprit des Lois, disposes of this difficulty in the following easy manner; that is, he states the inconsistency, and thinks that by the *statement he accounts for it.* " Three sorts of government (he says) may be distinguished,—the republican, the monarchical, and the despotic. In the republican, the people in a body has the sovereign power. In the monarchical, one person governs by the fundamental laws. In the despotic, no other law is known than the will of the master, or rather of the tyrant. *This does not mean that there are not in the world any but these three kinds of states; it does not even mean that there are states which belong, wholly and strictly, to some one of these forms :* most states, are, as it were, mixed or shaded with one another. In one, the monarchy inclines to despotism ; *in another, monarchical is combined with republican government;* in a third, not the whole, but only a part of the people, have the power of making laws. But the preceding division is not less accurate or less just. *The three kinds of government which it includes are so distinguished, that properly they have nothing in common ;* and, moreover, all the states which we know partake of one or the other of them." D'Alembert here

As the use of the term in question is quite familiar and established in language, and yet there appears no way of escaping from the perplexity to which it gives occasion, it will be desirable to examine the principal passages in the works of political writers, where the doctrine of mixed governments is laid down.

Plato, in his Treatise on Laws, introduces the Lacedæmonian interlocutor in the dialogue, speaking thus : " When I consider the constitution of Lacedæmon, I cannot readily say by what name it should be called. In the first place, it appears to resemble a *despotism,* for the power of the Ephors has a marvellously despotic character : and yet it sometimes seems to be more *democratic* than the government of any other state. On the other hand, not to call it an *aristocracy,* appears altogether absurd. Moreover, it has *Kings* who hold their dignity for life, belonging to a lineage confessedly more ancient than any other in Greece. So that being thus suddenly called on for my opinion, I must acknowledge myself unable to define the constitution of my native country." The Cretan then adds, " It appears that I am in the same difficulty myself : for I cannot say positively that the constitution of Cnosus (in Crete) can be distinguished by any one of these names."

proposes to remove the difficulty by the very considerations which give rise to it.

Upon which the Athenian remarks, " The truth is, my friends, that the governments of your two countries are severally made up of all these different forms."*

Aristotle, after speaking of the mode of establishing a government between an oligarchy and a democracy, by taking some of the peculiarities of each, and combining them in the same state, proceeds as follows :—" The test by which to try whether democracy and oligarchy have been well mixed, is that the same government may be called either by one name or the other. The perfection of the mixture is evidently the cause of this doubt; and the same is the case with regard to any thing placed between two extremes, as it seems to partake of both. An instance of this uncertainty is afforded by the Lacedæmonian constitution, which some call a democracy, some an oligarchy : a democracy, because there are in it many democratic institutions, † such as the equal treatment of the rich and poor, both as regards education and the public tables; and of the two chief offices, the one (the Gerusia) is conferred by the people,

* Leg. l. 4. p. 712. ed. Steph. The final remark of the Athenian stands thus in the original : ὄντως γὰρ, ὦ ἄριστοι, πολιτειῶν μετέχετε.

† In the original, we should, as it appears, read διὰ τὸ δημοκρατικὴν πολλὰ τὴν τάξιν ἔχειν, for διὰ τὸ δημοκρατικὰ πολλὰ τὴν τάξιν ἔχειν.

and to the other (the Ephoralty) they are
eligible : an oligarchy, because many of its
institutions are oligarchical; such as that all
the offices are conferred by election, and none
by lot,—that a few persons have the power of
inflicting sentence of death and banishment,
and many more regulations of a like kind.
A constitution which is well mixed ought to
appear to be both, and neither, of the governments of which it is composed : and it should
preserve itself without foreign aid; that is, both
parties in the state, the rich and the poor, should
be contented with the existing order of things."*

The next writer to be noticed, in reference
to this question, is Polybius, who, when about to
prove that the Roman government was mixed,
introduces his subject by speaking of the Lacedæmonian constitution in the following terms.

" Lycurgus, instead of adopting either of the
single forms of government, collected what was
excellent in them all, and so joined together
the principles that were peculiar to each several
form, that no one of them might be extended
beyond proper bounds and slide into the evil
to which it was inclined by nature; but that
each separate power, being still counteracted
by the rest, might be retained in due position,

* Politics, b. 4. ch. 9. Compare what is said on the
mixed nature of the Lacedæmonian government, in b. 2.
ch. 6. (p. 321. C. ed. Duval.)

and the whole government be evenly poised and balanced,—on the principle by which a vessel is steadied by being impelled against the wind." After exemplifying the manner in which the different powers in the Lacedæmonian government mutually checked one another, and making some further remarks, he proceeds to say that " the three kinds of government of which we have been speaking were all found united in the commonwealth of Rome. And so even was the balance between them all, and so regular the administration that resulted from their union, that it was no easy thing, even for the Romans themselves, to determine with assurance whether the entire state was to be esteemed an aristocracy, a democracy, or a monarchy. For if they turned their view upon the power of the *consuls*, the government appeared to be purely *monarchical* and *regal*. If, again, the authority of the *senate* was considered, it then seemed to wear the form of *aristocracy*. And, lastly, if regard was had to the share which the *people* possessed in the administration of affairs, it then appeared plainly to be a *democracy*."* Hence Cicero, doubtless adopting the opinions of Polybius, laid it down in his Dialogue *De Republica*, that " the best form of government is a

* Polybius, b. 6. ch. 10, 11. Hampton's translation has been followed, except in some places, where he seemed to depart unnecessarily from the original.

moderate mixture of royalty, nobility, and democracy."*　In the same treatise he says, that
" he does not know whether royalty (*i. e.* monarchy) is not far preferable to any other simple
form of government,—if indeed he could approve
of *any* simple form."†

Some years afterwards, Tacitus, following
only the course of his own vigorous and original
mind, remarked that " all states are governed
either by the people, the nobles, or a single
person; but a form of government, selected
and combined from all these kinds, is more easily
praised than put in practice, or, if put in practice, is not likely to prove lasting." ‡

* Statu esse optimo constitutam rem publicam quæ ex
tribus generibus illis, regali et optimati et populari, confusa
modice, nec puniendo irritet animum immanem ac ferum . . . .
De Rep. b. 2. ch. 23.　In this passage, which is preserved
by a grammarian, and does not form part of the fragments
discovered by Mai, the last words are either corrupt or
mutilated.

† Ibid.　In another place, he says, that a simple form
is " non perfectum neque optimum, sed tolerabile tamen,"
b. 1. ch. 26.

‡ Annals, b. 4. ch. 33.　Tacitus was probably led to
this remark, by considering the political changes of his own
country, in which a despotism had been submitted to, as a
less evil than the anarchy which it had superseded.　Otherwise it is not easy to understand by what course of thought
he arrived at this opinion : for the Spartan constitution,
which had a longer duration than that of any other Greek
or Italian state with which we are acquainted, was, by all
the ancient politicians, considered to be a mixed government.

Having extracted these detailed passages from the ancient political writers, I will now subjoin some of the doctrines of modern philosophers on this subject, with whom the theory of mixed governments is sometimes supposed to have originated;* although the foregoing extracts prove, that not only the notion of combining the simple forms of government was current in antiquity, but that the doctrine of the *balance of powers* was likewise known. Indeed, this very expression is employed by Polybius to signify the reciprocal action of the different parts of the sovereign body.

Blackstone's account of the mixture of the three forms of government in the British constitution, is so strongly marked with the vagueness and obscurity which characterize his method of treating political subjects, that his opinions on this point cannot be very satisfactorily ascertained. His doctrine on this question is, however, chiefly contained in the following passage. After having described the partition of the sovereign power among the King, the Lords, and the Commons, he proceeds to say, that "in no other shape could we be so certain of finding

---

* " The political writers of antiquity will not allow more than three regular forms of government (viz. democracy, aristocracy, and monarchy). All other species of government, they say, are either corruptions of, or reducible to, these three."—Blackstone, 1 Com. 49.

H

the three great qualities of government so well and so happily united. If the supreme power were lodged in any one of the three branches separately, we must be exposed to the inconveniences of either absolute monarchy, aristocracy, or democracy; and so want two of the three principal ingredients of good polity,—either virtue, wisdom, or power. If it were lodged in any two of the branches,—for instance, in the King and House of Lords,—our laws might be providently made, and well executed ; but they might not always have the good of the people in view : if lodged in the King and Commons, we should want that circumspection and mediatory caution which the wisdom of the peers is to afford : if the supreme rights of legislature were lodged in the two Houses only, and the King had no negative upon their proceedings, they might be tempted to encroach upon the royal prerogative, or perhaps abolish the kingly office, and thereby weaken (if not totally destroy) the strength of the executive power."* Rousseau says, that " properly speaking, there is not such a thing as a simple form of government. A single prince must have subordinate magistrates ; a popular government must have a head."† The same extraordinary

---

* 1 Com. 51, and compare Bentham's Fragment on Government, ch. 3.

† Contrat Social, liv. 3. ch. 7.

doctrine is likewise maintained by Paley, though not on the same grounds:—" Political writers (he observes) enumerate three principal forms of government, which, however, are to be regarded rather as the simple forms, by some combination and intermixture of which all actual governments are composed, than as anywhere existing in a pure and elementary state." Then, after treating of monarchy, aristocracy, and democracy, he adds, that "A mixed government is composed by the combination of two or more of the simple forms of government above described."* It may be observed that, in all these passages, either one or each of the kinds of republic, *i. e.* aristocracy or democracy, is supposed to enter into the composition of a mixed government; but in the following extract from Mandeville's Fable of the Bees, it is assumed that a combination may be formed of a monarchy and a republic generally.—" These are the arts which tend to worldly greatness: what sovereign power soever makes a good use of them, that has any considerable nation to govern,—whether it be a monarchy, a commonwealth, or a mixture of both,—can never fail of making it flourish."†

Although there are some prevailing ideas which seem to run through all the above passages, yet there are no less obvious differences

* Moral and Political Philosophy, b. 6. ch. 6.
† Fable of the Bees, vol. 1. p. 116.

in the sentiments of the various writers. For instance, Plato, Aristotle, Cicero, Tacitus, and Blackstone, conceive that there may be both simple and mixed governments,—and such is probably the common opinion. Rousseau and Paley, however, maintain that no government can be simple; while, on the other hand, Mr. Mill has proved, by a long and laboured argument, that no government can be mixed.* These contradictions and inconsistencies may, however, as it appears, be explained by the aid of the following considerations, although they cannot be reconciled either with reason or with one another.

1. When a government is called mixed, on account of certain institutions established in it by the sovereign power, the origin of the appellation may be explained on the following principles. In a monarchy, where one rules,—in an aristocracy or oligarchy, where the few rule,—or in a democracy, where the many rule,—certain practices and institutions are generally found to prevail, and to be in harmony with (what is termed) the spirit of the constitution. Such, for example, in an aristocracy, is any measure tending to lessen the number and increase the power of the ruling few; in a democracy, to increase both the number and the power of the ruling many. These several usages and insti-

* On Government, p. 496.

tutions thus acquire the name of monarchical, aristocratic, and democratic. If, then, there is a state in which several of the institutions thought characteristic of either government co-exist; the original principle of division, viz. the number of the governing body, is lost sight of, and the government is said to be mixed of monarchy, aristocracy, and democracy. It is on this principle that Plato represents the Lace-dæmonian as a mixed government. It has certain institutions which resemble those of the simple states. Thus the Ephors have a power resembling that exercised by an arbitrary mo-narch; the people have likewise a power resembling that which they enjoy in a demo-cracy; the nobles have a power resembling that which they possess in an aristocracy: and hence, neglecting the principle on which these governments are called monarchies, aristocra-cies, and democracies, Plato doubts whether a state, containing institutions similar to those caused by these various arrangements of the sovereign power, is to be named by one appel-lation or the other; and ends by determining that it has an equal right to all. So, again, Polybius, because the Roman consuls had, on certain occasions, a power which a monarch possesses at all times,—because the senate en-joyed some of the powers belonging to a council of nobles in an aristocracy,—and because the people had much of the power belonging to the people in a democracy,—decides that the Roman government was mixed of monarchy, aristocracy, and democracy. In a nearly similar manner Aristotle prescribes the manner in which a constitution is to be compounded of oligarchical and democratical institutions; adding, that the mixture is then most perfect, when it is doubtful whether the government should be called an oligarchy or democracy, and may with propriety be said to be either. Aristotle has, in the passage in question, expressed his doctrines with his usual perspicuity and precision; so that the purport of his reasoning, and the origin of his phraseology, may both be plainly discerned : but if he had adhered to his own definition of the three forms of government, formed on the numbers of the ruling body,* he never could have conceived the existence of a doubt as to the name by which a government should be distinguished.

It is evident that this theory of mixed governments, proceeding on the character of the institutions of a state, abandons the division of governments by the numbers of the governors, which it nevertheless presupposes; for the institutions which form the test of the mixture

* Politics, b. 3. ch. 7. (p. 346. B. ed. Duval.) ἀναγκὴ εἶναι κύριον ἢ ἕνα ἢ ὀλίγους ἢ τοὺς πολλούς. " One, or a few, or the majority, *must of necessity* be sovereign."

are themselves characterized by the names of
the simple forms of government, defined by the
numbers of the sovereign body, in which they
commonly prevail.   All, therefore, that need be
further remarked on this part of the subject is,
that the division of governments into monarchies,
aristocracies, and democracies, and the division
into simple and mixed governments, are cross-
divisions, founded on distinct principles; the
principle of classification for the latter division
being the presence or absence, in a combined
form, of certain practices, laws, and institutions,
which are assumed to be characteristic of monarchy, aristocracy, or democracy, as determined
by the distribution of the sovereign power.
Consequently, these two divisions are perfectly
consistent with each other; and a constitution
may be, at the same time, an aristocracy, for
example, in respect of the number of the governors, and a mixed government in respect of
its laws and institutions.

2. A government is sometimes called mixed,
when, by a change in the relations of the persons composing the sovereign body, or by lodging
the entire sovereignty in a part of that body
instead of the whole, the government would
become monarchical, aristocratical, or democratical. The train of thought by which some
persons are led to take this view of mixed governments, appears to proceed as follows. When

people see, in any state, a power which, if all
other powers were abolished, would make a
state either monarchical, aristocratical, or democratical (in the proper sense of those terms),
they call that power the monarchy, the aristocracy, or the democracy; and if there are two
or three such powers in a state, then they say
that it has a mixed government. Thus, in
England, if the King was alone sovereign, and
the Houses of Lords and Commons were abolished, the government would be a monarchy;
if the King and Commons were abolished, and
only the Lords remained, the government would
be an aristocracy; if only the House of Commons remained, then, according to the common
acceptation of democracy, the government would
be democratical. But as all these powers co-
exist at one and the same time, the government is said to be mixed. This is the manner
in which Blackstone treats the English constitution in the passage cited above : he considers
what would be the effect if the whole sovereign
power was lodged in each one of the three
branches, to the exclusion of the others; and he
then pronounces that the government is mixed.
Persons who try a mixed government by this
touchstone are, equally with those who use the
criterion of institutions, debarred from using the
classification of governments by the numbers of
the rulers, as opposed to mixed governments :

for even they must admit that these two divisions are quite consistent with each other, and that a government may be, at the same time, an aristocracy, for example, in respect of the numbers of its governors, and a mixed government in respect of the construction of its sovereign body. On the principle adopted by Blackstone, all governments of more than one, or republics, must be mixed governments; for, in every republic, if the chief magistrate was sovereign, it would be a monarchy: and therefore, whether it is an aristocratic or democratic republic, its government must equally be mixed. Thus, if the first Archon or General at Athens, the Doge of Venice, or the Stadtholder of the United Provinces, had been sovereign, Athens, Venice, and the United Provinces, would have been monarchies. So the government of the United States of America is mixed, because, if the President was sovereign, it would be a monarchy; if the Senate, an aristocracy; if the House of Representatives, a democracy. This mode of considering mixed governments proceeds, in great measure, from an unperceived ambiguity of the words aristocracy and democracy, which mean either a form of government, or a class of persons in a state; and of the word monarchy, which, properly signifying the sovereignty of one, is sometimes synonymous with royalty, the form of government, or the royal power in a state.

Hence it is thought, that because there is in a state, monarchy (meaning the King), and an aristocracy and a democracy (meaning classes of of persons), therefore the constitution is compounded of the three forms of government so called. This transition from the one signification to the other may be conveniently illustrated by the following extract from Mr. Mill's Essay on Government. Speaking of the union of monarchy, aristocracy, and democracy,* in the same state, he says: " As a part of this doctrine of the mixture of the simple forms of government, it may be proper to inquire, whether an union may not be possible of two of them? Three varieties of this union may be conceived; the union of the monarchy with aristocracy, or the union of either with democracy. Let us first suppose that monarchy is united with aristocracy (*i. e.* the forms of government). *Their* power (*i. e.* the power of the King and the aristocratic class, not of the forms of government called monarchy and aristocracy,) is equal or not equal. If it is not equal,"† &c. And he proceeds to examine a question wholly different from that proposed, viz. whether two powers in a state can

---

* See Mr. Mill's definition of these three forms of government, above, p. 56.

† This confusion of the different senses of monarchy, aristocracy, and democracy, is well illustrated by Mr. Bentham's exposition of Blackstone's sophisms, Fragment on Government, p. 88.

be equal; and moreover equal, not in legal power, but in moral influence. A trace of the same mode of reasoning may likewise be plainly discerned in the following passage from a recent article in the Edinburgh Review, on the subject of Mr. Mill's Essay on Government. " Mr. Mill (it is there said) tells us that it is a mistake to imagine that the English government is mixed. He holds, we believe . . . . that it is purely aristocratical. There certainly is *an aristocracy* in England, and we are afraid that *their* power is greater than it ought to be," &c. The Reviewer proceeds to shew that the aristocratic class are restrained from abusing their power by certain moral motives; whence he infers that the English government is mixed.* But even if the class of persons in England, called the aristocracy, had greater powers than they really possess, it would not follow that the English government is an aristocracy. The French aristocracy were a powerful class under the old French *régime,* but the government was not the less a monarchy. So likewise there was usually a powerful aristocracy of nobles or rich men in the Greek and Italian democracies, if it had not been exterminated or expelled in the fierce dissensions and massacres which so often took place in those ill-constructed and ill-administered

* Edinburgh Review, vol. 50. p. 108.

commonwealths.   In like manner, Mr. Mill's
elaborate argument that monarchy cannot be
mixed with aristocracy, is founded on the merest
verbal confusion.   If monarchy means the government of one, of course it cannot be mixed
with a government of more than one; if it means
royalty, it can plainly be combined with aristocracy: indeed, in most kingly governments,
both of ancient and modern times, the King has
only been the head of the governing body.

3. A third manner of viewing mixed governments, is to make them consist, not in the
arrangement or relations of the sovereign body,
nor in the political institutions of the state, but
in the moral influence exercised by different
individuals and classes in the community.   This
notion of a mixed government is contained in
the sentiments which Dionysius puts in the
mouth of Manius Valerius, when addressing the
Senate on an extension of the political rights of
the plebeians: whence we may infer that, in the
age of Augustus, the praise of a mixed government was one of the commonplaces of the
Greek rhetoricians.   " That the Roman state
(he says) will not be either an unmixed oligarchy
or an unmixed democracy, but a constitution
compounded of both these forms, is to us sena-
tors a signal advantage.   Either of these governments, when existing singly, is most prone to
run into violence and lawlessness.   But when

they are mixed in even proportion, any party in the state which may aim at change, and seek to unsettle the existing order of things, is restrained by the party of more moderate disposition, and less inclined to deviate from their accustomed habits."* It is in this light also that Cicero considers the subject in his Treatise *De Republica.* " All (he says) who have the power of life and death over the people are despots; although they prefer being called Kings, in imitation of the title of Jupiter. Again, when certain persons either from their wealth, their family, or other means, obtain the command of public affairs, they are in truth a mere faction, though they are called by the name of nobles. And if the people have the chief power, and all things are governed by their will, this state is called liberty, but is in fact licentiousness. When, however, there is a mutual fear of one man for another man, and of one class for another class, then, as no one relies on his own strength, a sort of compact is formed between the people and the nobles; whence arises that excellent form of polity, a mixed constitution."† A similar view of mixed governments is taken by Sir

---

* Ant. Rom. b. 7. ch. 55.

† " Sed quum alius alium timet, et homo hominem, et ordo ordinem, tum quia nemo sibi confidit, quasi pactio fit inter populum et potentes : ex quo exsistit id, quod Scipio laudabat, conjunctum civitatis genus." — De Rep. lib. 3. c. 14.

J. Mackintosh, in his Discourse on the Law of
Nature and Nations; who considers the mixture of
a government to consist in the mutual influence
exercised by different bodies and persons in the
state : his objections to the goodness of the
simple forms of government are, however, partly
founded on an assumption that the sovereign
power can limit itself, and partly on a confusion
of supreme, with despotic, or rather tyrannical,
authority. His opinions on this subject are contained in the following passage : " The privileges
of a powerful nobility, of opulent mercantile
communities, of great judicial corporations, have
in some monarchies approached more near to a
control on the sovereign. Means have been
devised, with more or less wisdom, to temper
the despotism of an aristocracy over their subjects, and in democracies to protect the minority
against the majority, and the whole people
against the tyranny of demagogues. But in
these unmixed forms of government, as the right
of legislation is vested in one individual or in
one order, it is obvious that *the legislative power
may shake off all the restraints which the laws have
imposed on it. All such governments, therefore,
tend towards despotism;* and the securities which
they admit against misgovernment are extremely
feeble and precarious." * And, after some further

* P. 61.

remarks, he adds, " that no institution so detestable as an absolutely unbalanced government perhaps ever existed ; that the simple governments are mere creatures of the imagination of theorists, who have transformed names used for the convenience of arrangement into real polities ; that, as constitutions of government approach more nearly to that unmixed and uncontrolled simplicity, they become despotic; and as they recede further from that simplicity, they become free."* The substance of these opinions, viz. that the mixture of a government depends on the reciprocal influence of different classes and individuals in the community, and that the simple forms of government are component parts of real constitutions, which the mind may consider apart from the rest, but which never occur in an elementary shape, is repeated, though with greater detail, in an article in the Edinburgh Review already mentioned. " Wherever a King or an oligarchy refrains from the last extremity of rapacity and tyranny, through fear of the resistance of the people, there the constitution, *whatever it may be called,* is in some measure democratical . . . . Wherever a numerical minority, by means of superior wealth or intelligence, of political concert, or of military discipline, exercises a greater influence on the

* P. 65.

society than any other equal number of persons; there, *whatever the form of government may be called,* a mixture of aristocracy does in fact exist. And wherever a single man, from whatever cause, is so necessary to the community, or to any portion of it, that he possesses more power than any other man, there is a mixture of monarchy. This (the Reviewer proceeds to say) is the philosophical classification of governments; and if we use this classification, we shall find, not only that there are mixed governments, but that *all governments are, and must always be, mixed.*" *

According to the doctrine contained in the two passages last quoted, a mixed government is not determined either by the formation of the governing body, or by the nature of the laws and institutions; but by the reciprocal moral influence of different persons and orders in the society. The doctrine of Cicero appears, indeed, to differ from that of the Edinburgh Review, inasmuch as he admits the existence of simple forms of government: but he admits it only in words, for his conclusion is incompatible with their existence; it not being conceivable that there should be any state, in which a moral influence of individuals and classes of men upon each other, or upon the governing power, does

* Edinburgh Review, vol. 50, p. 109.

not exist. On this principle, therefore all governments must be mixed. According to the doctrine of the Edinburgh Review, the French
government under Napoleon was a monarchy,
not because Napoleon was emperor and alone
possessed the sovereign power, but because he
had more power than any other man in the
state ; it was likewise an aristocracy, because a
numerical minority, viz. the army, exercised a
greater influence on society than any other equal
number of persons; it was a democracy, because
neither the emperor nor the army could venture
to the last extremity of rapacity and tyranny :
on the contrary, Napoleon thought it prudent to
render his dominion popular with his subjects,
and indeed by various arts actually succeeded in
so doing. The Reviewer, therefore, very justly
adds that, according to these definitions, every
government must be mixed ; and, he might
have added, mixed not of any two, but of
all the three forms. It follows necessarily,
from his explanation, that there are no simple
governments, that all governments are mixed,
and that all governments are at the same time
monarchies, aristocracies, and democracies ;
which of course implies that they are at the
same time monarchies and republics. To call
this a classification of governments is therefore
not less an abuse of language, than to call the

offence of one man a conspiracy ; it is, in effect, a denial of all classification, an abolition of all distinction between different classes of governments, which are thus joined together in one undistinguished heap. No government can differ from another in being a monarchy, an aristocracy, or a democracy, inasmuch as those names are common to all governments. There is no doubt that this system effectually removes the ambiguity, and explains the distinctions of the terms in question, by destroying both their signification and their difference; but whether the political vocabulary would be benefited by discarding as senseless those much used and much abused words without an attempt to turn them to some purpose, whether science would be advanced by this summary method of cutting, rather than of unloosing the knot, is very questionable. The weapons of political reasoning may be blunt and shapeless, and of uncertain employment: but is it not more advisable to sharpen and repair them, and to ascertain their uses, than to reject them, in the lump, as worthless lumber ?

No classification of governments can be serviceable which turns on moral influences, and not on the construction of the sovereign body, or some permanent attribute of the established constitution. The one principle affords a precise and definite ground of distinction, about which no two persons can disagree. The other depends on an uncertain opinion as to the comparative moral and political influence of certain persons and parties in the state, an influence which may be exercised in the most various ways, and is liable to fluctuate from year to year, and almost from day to day. And, after all, the system of the Edinburgh Reviewer assumes the very doctrine which it denies : for why does he say that a state is monarchical when one person in it has great influence ? Simply because a state governed by one person, who thus necessarily has great influence in it, is properly called a monarchy. Why is a state aristocratical when a minority have great influence ? For no other reason than that in a state where the few govern, or an aristocracy, the few possess great influence. Why is a state democratical where the people have sufficient moral influence to save themselves from being cruelly oppressed ? Because a state where the many govern, and thus enjoy a power similar to this influence, only greater in degree, is properly called a democracy.

Before the subject of mixed governments is dismissed, it will be necessary to advert to a topic usually connected with it ; the existence of mutual checks and counterpoises in a constitution supposed to be compounded of the three simple forms of government, or (as it is termed) *the balance of powers.** This question, which has been often discussed with much eagerness and little advantage, turns entirely on a confusion of moral influence and legal power. Legally, there can be no competition between different powers in the same state, as the sovereign power is supreme and undivided; nor can any other power, according to law, enter into competition with it. But the acts of the persons composing the sovereign body may be influenced by the wishes, interests, and proceedings, as well of each other, as of other persons and classes in the community. So that although a legal balance of powers is impossible, a moral balance must always exist.

Besides the division of governments into monarchies and republics, or into monarchies, aristocracies, and democracies, and into pure and mixed, there need only be noticed that into *national* and *federal* governments, which proceeds on a principle different from any other classification. A *federal* government is when an union is formed between several states, by the terms of which some part of the sovereignty is lodged in persons whose powers extend over all the states, and the remainder is lodged

* See Paley, Moral and Political Philosophy, b. 6. ch. 7.

separately in persons whose powers are confined to each particular state. A *national* government is when the sovereign power, by whomsoever exercised, extends over the whole country, without any territorial distinctions.*

---

* *Theocracy* is defined by Johnson to be a " government immediately superintended by God." In this sense, it is applied by many writers to the Jewish state. Thus Blackstone speaks of " the theocratic establishments of the children of Israel in Palestine" (1 Com. 191). Sometimes, however, it is used to signify a government of priests, a sacerdotal aristocracy. Hence the governments of Ancient Egypt, Modern Rome, &c. have been termed theocracies. See Heeren, Ideen, vol. 2. part 2. p. 430—5. ed. 4.

XI.

PEOPLE.—COMMUNITY.

THE word People sometimes signifies the whole nation, or society, the *populus*,* including all persons in the state from the highest to the lowest, whether governors or subjects, noble or ignoble, rich or poor, young or old, male or female. In this sense Blackstone divides the *people* into aliens and natural-born subjects, and into the clergy and laity.

Sometimes it signifies the whole nation with the exception of the persons composing the government ; or the governed as opposed to governors. Thus we say that the government is supported by the people, is hated by the people, &c. In this sense it is used by Blackstone, when he makes the people of England include the whole society except the supreme

---

* That is, as *populus* was used in the later ages of the Roman commonwealth ; for in early times, as Niebuhr has shewn, it denoted only the patrician order as opposed to the plebeian. See his History of Rome, vol. 1, p. 365. Engl. transl.

magistrates, or the king and the two houses of Parliament.*

Sometimes it signifies the party opposed to the aristocratic party of the day, or the *popular party*. Thus, at the beginning of the French revolution, the *tiers état*, or all who did not belong to the *noblesse* or clergy, formed the people, or popular party; at a later period, when the state of parties had greatly changed, the poor, as opposed to the rich and respectable, were the people, or popular party. †

---

* Blackstone uses the word People in a fluctuating manner, and his divisions into which it enters will not bear examination. He divides magistrates into two kinds,—" supreme, or those in whom the sovereign power of the state resides," which he explains to be the King and Parliament; and " subordinate, or those who act in an inferior secondary sphere," 1 Com. 338. He afterwards says, that the people is the whole nation, inclusive of the subordinate, but exclusive of the supreme magistrates, *ib.* 366. Yet, he proceeds to divide the people into aliens and natural-born subjects, and into clergy and laity, *ib.* 376 : according to which, a peer or a member of the House of Commons could not be a natural-born subject or a layman, an English bishop could not be a clergyman, inasmuch as they belong to the sovereign legislature.

† " Even in the time of Aristotle (says Niebuhr, Hist. of Rome, vol. 1, p. 516,) this word (viz. δῆμος) has assumed a variety of senses, and denotes, in democracies, the nation and assembly of the people as opposed to the magistrates, in oligarchies the commonalty; while popular usage employs it for the needy and common folk : " that is to say, in democracies, δῆμος signified the whole nation except the magistrates ; in oligarchies, the whole nation except the sovereign body : in popular usage, the poor.

The same appears to be the case in England at this time : all measures tending to increase the power of persons of affluence and good education are now considered anti-popular ; all measures tending to increase the power of the poor are now considered popular. " It cannot be denied, (says a writer in a late number of the Edinburgh Review,) that it is for the immediate interest of the *people* to plunder the *rich.*" * In the same manner, those persons who espouse the cause of the anti-aristocratic party are called " friends of the people." The anti-aristocratic party appears to have obtained the appellation of the popular party, or the people, from being the most numerous, or containing a majority of the *whole* people ; and not because the measures which it recommends, and the principles by which it is guided, are most conducive to the welfare of the community. It may indeed *happen* that such is the case, but the name does not seem to have been derived from this circumstance.

Community is synonymous with the first sense of people, and is a collective name both for all the persons exercising the sovereignty of an independent state, and those owing obedience to them.

It may, however, be remarked, that, in using

* Vol. 49, p. 180.

the words *people* and *community* in their widest
political sense, we usually mean all the members
of the society except women and children, that
is, only the adult males. If this meaning is not
given to the terms in question, there never was
such a government as a democracy, or a government of the many; all states which were not
monarchies must have been aristocracies; for,
even at Athens, where every male citizen above
the age of twenty * had a voice in the supreme
legislative assembly, the number of females, old
and young, and of males under twenty, probably
more than quadrupled that of the male governors; so that, after excluding half a million of
slaves, the Athenian democracy was in fact
wielded by an inconsiderable minority even of
the free population.†

It has been already stated that Mr. Mill, in
his Essay on Government, defines a democracy
to be a government in which " the community
undertakes the protection of itself, and of its
members," or, " a government of the many."
He afterwards says, that " whenever the powers

---

* The common age at which persons were permitted in
the Greek states to take a part in public affairs, appears to
have been *thirty;* in Athens it was otherwise. See Clinton's
Fasti Hellenici, part 1. p. 386, note ᵗ. The same writer
states, that according to the census of Great Britain in
1821, the males above the age of twenty were 4,897, in
20,160 persons, *i. e.* somewhat less than a fourth.

† See above in DEMOCRACY.

of government are placed in any hands other
than those of the community, whether those of
one man, of a few, or of several, those principles
of human nature which imply that government
is at all necessary, imply that those persons will
make use of them to defeat the very end for
which government exists:" in other words, that
a democracy is the only good form of government. But as he considers that an assembly of
all the members of a community would be too
numerous for the transaction of business, he
would have the community choose representatives, to form the sovereign body. The question, therefore, next arises, who are to compose
the electing body, and whether any *part* of the
community has an interest the same as the
whole community? This question he answers
by saying that " one thing is pretty clear, that
all those individuals whose interests are indis-
putably included in those of other individuals,
may be struck off without inconvenience. In
this light may be viewed all children up to a
certain age, whose interests are involved in those
of their parents. In this light also women may
be regarded, the interest of almost all of whom
is involved either in that of their fathers or in
that of their husbands." The electoral body
would thus consist, according to Mr. Mill, of
" the aggregate males of an age to be regarded
as *sui juris,* who may be regarded as the

natural* representatives of the whole population."
By the community governing itself, therefore,
Mr. Mill means the adult males voting for the
election of representatives, or members of the
supreme body; that is to say, he considers the
sovereign body and the electoral body as together forming the governing body: unless indeed
he intends to exclude those who share in the
sovereign power from the governing body; but
on this point his language is somewhat perplexed.
If it is not assumed that the electors, being a
majority of the adult males, compose the governing body, then he proves that the only good
form of government is an aristocracy, after
having said that "the unfitness of an aristocracy †

---

* What is here meant by natural, does not very clearly
appear: probably it is used as nearly the contrary of *artificial*, that which is independent of human institution or
contrivance. See below in NATURE.

† This again causes some perplexity: for he defines an
aristocratical government to be when " the powers of government are held by any number of persons intermediate
between a single person and the majority." By majority,
therefore, we must understand not a majority of the whole
society, but a majority of the adult males; and by *powers of
government*, not sovereign power (as is commonly understood by that expression), but the power of electing persons
who are to wield the sovereign power. Thus, if a nation
consisted of 2,000,000 persons, out of whom 500,000 were
adult males, and the sovereign body consisted of 500 persons: then, if 250,001 adult males voted for the election of
members of the sovereign body, the government would be a
democracy; if 249,999, it would be an aristocracy.

(*i. e.* the class) to be intrusted with the powers of government rests on demonstration :" for the representative assembly, and the persons possessing the sovereign executive power must necessarily be a very insignificant minority of the whole population. It is however an unquestionable, though perhaps not uncommon, abuse of language, to describe the electoral body as possessed of the governing power, which properly belongs only to the sovereign body ; as the constituent is thus confounded with the representative, and incorrect notions of the nature of representation and sovereign power are suggested by the obscurity and vagueness of the language. On this confusion more will be said under the word REPRESENTATION.

It will be observed that, in the preceding extract, Mr. Mill, in order to strike off the women and children, assumes, and does not prove, that their interest is identical with that of the adult males. Commonly, however, this deduction is made, not only without proof, but even without mention, and is tacitly assumed as a matter of universal agreement.

On this exception of women and children from the whole community, when considered with reference to its government,—an assumption made by all writers on political science,—the true theory of government may (as it appears) be founded: inasmuch as they are thus unanimously set aside from the question, not on account of their poverty, not on account of their depravity, not on account of the smallness of their numbers (for they always form the largest portion of the society), not on account of their interest being hostile to that of the smaller number of adult males (for it is asserted that their interests are identical); but on account of their incapacity for ruling, the inferiority of their intellects, and their general ignorance of political questions and political science.* All classes of the community are more fitted for governing in proportion as they differ from women and children, and the less fitted as they resemble them, in these respects.†

* It must be observed, that when Mr. Mill excludes from his body of electors all women, on the ground that their interests are involved in the interests either of their husbands or fathers, he does not *account for* this exception; for his statement might be exactly reversed, and the electoral body might be made to consist only of adult women, on the ground that the interests of their husbands and fathers were involved in *their* interest. His argument goes no further than this: interest is the only thing to be considered in the formation of an electoral body: the interest of husbands and wives, fathers and daughters is identical; therefore, it is superfluous to give a vote to women, when they would be, as it were, the duplicates of their husbands and fathers. But, by parity of reasoning, if the electoral body consisted only of adult females, then the interest of the males would be equally secured, because it would be involved in that of their wives, daughters, and mothers.

† In this sense Cicero says: " In dissensione civili, quum boni plus quam mali valent, expendendos cives, non nume-

If *interest* alone was to be regarded as a qualification for rulers, women and children would have the strongest claim to an enjoyment of political rights: as being the weakest, and therefore most exposed to violence, as being the most simple, and therefore most subject to fraud, they have the greatest interest in good government.

If, on the other hand, *knowledge* alone were regarded, without a desire to promote the interests of the community, rulers might unintentionally, through indifference, or intentionally, through ill-will or selfishness, omit to adopt the measures which they thought best fitted to benefit the state.

The problem of government is to reconcile these two elements, and to combine the advantages derivable from knowledge with the motive afforded by interest.

This subject is of too great importance to be pursued further in this place; but I may be allowed to remark, that, on examination, it will probably be found that in the early periods of a nation's history, when the mass of the population was immersed in darkness and ignorance, greater weight was attached to the knowledge and wisdom of the governors, and their moral character, than to any other qualification;

randos puto" (De Rep. lib. 6.): a remark as applicable to times of domestic concord, as of civil war.

whence the expressions *witena-gemot, prud-hommes, boni homines, probi homines, buonuomini,* &c. in the middle ages; nor was it till experience had shewn that good education is no guarantee against the abuse of political power, and it was perceived how the most grievous oppressions had arisen from the interests of the rulers being opposed to the interests of their subjects, that the theory was imagined, that if the interests,—that is, the wishes—of the majority of any nation could be ascertained and carried into effect, such nation would infallibly be well governed. As, in the former theory, it was forgotten that knowledge without interest is not sufficient; so in this, it was not perceived that interest without knowledge is not sufficient; and that, though a man always wishes well to himself, yet in his actions, from ignorance or passion, he frequently pursues that very course which is the least fitted to ensure his own happiness. Each theory embraces, and each omits, an essential condition of the problem.

XII.

REPRESENTATION.—REPRESENTATIVE.— REPRESENTATIVE GOVERNMENT.

OF the several definitions of the word *representation* given by Johnson in his Dictionary, that which most nearly approaches its political meanings, is "the act of supporting a vicarious character." *To represent,* he likewise lays it down, is "to fill the place of another by a vicarious character; to personate, as the parliament *represents* the people." *Vicarious* he defines to be "deputed; delegated; acting in the place of another."

Representation, as is expressed by these definitions, in its primary political sense, means the standing in another's place; holding another's proxy; being the organ of his sentiments, and the instrument of conveying his wishes and determination. Thus an ambassador instructed to treat with a foreign power *represents* the king his master, or whatever power presides over the intercourse with foreign states. Thus, likewise, a person signing another's name under a power of attorney is his *representative.*

Representatives of this description were the deputies anciently chosen in England by the counties and boroughs to treat with the King concerning the amount of money required for the service of the state and the wants of the crown, which the several bodies, of whom they were the several organs, would agree to grant to the King. So completely was this transaction considered in the light of a bargain between two parties, that in early times the grant was made in the form of an indenture, each estate granting separately ; and the King's assent (as in the case of a common grantee) was presumed without being formally given.* This proceeding less resembled the making of a law, than a contract between an individual on the one part, and the committee of a company or a body corporate on the other part.† Frequently the representatives of the estate of the Commons, together with the other estates, required from the King a consideration, in the shape of some concession of his prerogative or sovereign power, for the subsidies which they granted to him ; and thus these persons appear as negociators treating with an independent power, from whom they

---

* Hallam's Middle Ages, vol. 2. p. 242. 4to. Constitutional History of England, vol. 2. p. 369. 4to.

† See a case in 13 Ed. 3. mentioned by Mr. Hallam, Middle Ages, vol. 2. p. 248, where the Commons could not grant a subsidy without first consulting their constituents.

K

require some sacrifice for their benefit, corresponding to the sacrifice which they make for his benefit. They granted subsidies for his immediate use and advantage, and not for the advantage of the whole community, of which they were members. In like manner, the deputies sent to the States-general of the United Provinces represented the provinces to which they respectively belonged, and acted upon the instructions which they received, without forming any independent opinion as to the tendency of a measure to promote the *common* good. *
They, like the deputies of the Commons' estate in England, and many German principalities,† were specially appointed to act in the interest of a particular class or part of the whole community.

Whether the name of a representative government, as applied to governments such as those of modern England, France, Bavaria, Holland, the United States, &c., was derived from an historical recollection of the times when, as in England, the deputies of the estates of the Clergy and the Commons were representatives

* See Sir William Temple's Observations on the United Provinces of the Netherlands, vol. 1. p. 64. 8vo ed.

† See Hüllmann's Ursprung der Stände in Deutschland, p. 653. ed. 2. Leo, in his Handbuch der Geschichte des Mittelalters, p. 767, remarks, that " the English Parliament had, in its origin, the very same character as the provincial assemblies of the estates in Germany (Landstände)."

in the original sense of the word, or from its analogy to strict and proper representation, seems to be uncertain; although the latter supposition is perhaps the more probable.

A representative government is when a certain portion of the community, generally consisting either of all the adult males or of a part of them, determined according to some qualification of property, residence, or other accident, have the right of voting at certain intervals of time for the election of particular members of the sovereign legislative body. This right of voting is properly a political right; nor does it bear any resemblance to the exercise of sovereignty. The possession of this right enables a voter to influence the formation of the sovereign body; but a voter never has any part of the governing power, nor does he wield a power which in any way resembles the authority of government, except that the decision of those who really wield that authority may be influenced by his vote. The moral duty incumbent on an elector is to vote for that candidate whose services as a member of the legislature are, in his judgment, most likely to prove beneficial to the state. His power, conferred by this right, is strictly limited, and is confined to one point, namely, the contributing to the choice of the supreme legislative body. There is no question of public policy,—no matter of legislation, in the decision of which he has directly any voice. At the times when the mass of electors are called on to exercise their franchises, (for example, after a dissolution of Parliament in this kingdom,) the legislative sovereignty is in abeyance, and no law can be made. But the power of a member of the legislature is by law unlimited, and may extend to any matter falling within the compass of legislation.

Indeed, no two things can be more clearly distinguished, than the powers of a member of a sovereign representative assembly, and the right of voting for his election. Yet they are perpetually confounded in popular discourse; as when a state is called a democracy, because a majority of its freemen have a vote for the election of representatives; for instance, the United States of America, the government of which, as has been already observed, is in strictness an aristocracy; and when the same term of universal suffrage is applied to the votes of the citizens in the ancient democracies, who were members of the supreme legislature, and the votes of electors in modern states, who are not. Nor is this confusion always confined to popular usage, but it occurs even in the most recent works of political philosophers. Thus, for example, Mr. Mill, in his Essay on Government, proposes the question—" Whether, between the two extremes of a very low pecuniary qualification, and a qualification so high as to constitute an *aristo-cracy of wealth*, there is any qualification which would remove the right of suffrage from the people of small, or of no property, and yet constitute an *elective body*, the interest of which would be identical with the interest of the community?" He then proceeds to say, that " it is not easy to find any satisfactory principle to guide us in our researches, and to tell us where we should fix. The qualification must either be such as to embrace the majority of the population (*i.e.* of the male adults), or something less than the majority. Suppose, in the first place, that it embraces the majority, the question is, whether the majority would have an interest in oppressing those who, upon this supposition, would be deprived of political power? If we reduce this calculation to its elements, we shall see that the interest which they would have, of this deplorable kind, though it would be something, would not be very great. Each man of the majority, *if the majority were constituted the governing body*, would have something less than the benefit of oppressing a single man. . . . . In that case the benefits of good government, accruing to all, might be expected to overbalance to the several members of such *an elective body* the benefits of misrule peculiar to themselves. Good government would, *therefore*, have a tolerable security. Suppose, in the second place, that the qualification did not admit a *body of electors* so large as the majority: in that case, taking again the calculation in its elements, we shall see that each man would have a benefit equal to that derived from the oppression of more than one man;* and that, in proportion as the *elective body* constituted a smaller and smaller minority, the benefit of misrule to the *elective body* would be increased, and bad government would be insured."†

Now, in these remarks, it is evident that the governing body and the electing body are confounded, and that a government is called an aristocracy of wealth, because the members of the *elective* body, not the members of the *sovereign* body (who, according to Mr. Mill's own definition,‡ give the name of aristocracy

---

* This argument is not conclusive, even if Mr. Mill's principles are admitted : for, in the first place, the elective body, not being the governing body, will not have the power to oppress directly ; and, in the second place, it does not follow, even if the electors are the majority, and have the power to oppress, that they will not oppress, because they have not an adult male apiece ; for they may be satisfied with oppressing women and children : which will much more than complete the required number.

† Supplement to Enc. Brit. vol. 4. pp. 500, 501.

‡ Above, p. 56. Having laid it down that " the unfitness of an aristocracy to be intrusted with the powers of government rests on demonstration," Mr. Mill, after all, makes his perfect state, (even according to his own definition as it appears,) an aristocracy ; *i. e.* a government, in which a small assembly, possessing the legislative sove-

to a state), are determined by wealth. This is merely a different form of the common error, that the sovereign power resides in the electors, who delegate it, by election, to their representatives, making them the instruments of their pleasure, and bearers of their commands. Thus Blackstone has the following passage on the election of members of the House of Commons:

" With regard to the elections of knights, citizens, and burgesses, we may observe, that herein consists the exercise of the democratical part of our constitution ; *for* in a democracy there can be no exercise of sovereignty but by suffrage, which is the declaration of the people's will. In all democracies therefore it is of the utmost importance to regulate by whom, and in what manner, the suffrages are to be given. And the Athenians were so justly jealous of this prerogative, that a stranger who interfered in the assemblies of the people was punished by their laws with death ;* because such a person was esteemed guilty of high treason, by usurping those rights of sovereignty to which he had no

reignty, is elected by the votes of all adult males. On the executive part of the government he says nothing.

* I know not whence Blackstone derived this statement, nor whether it rests on any authority. The usual course certainly was, that a foreigner, convicted of having exercised the rights of Athenian citizenship, merely forfeited those rights ; and, upon a second conviction, was sold for a slave. See Clinton, Fast. Hell. Part 1, p. 390, note.

title. In England, where the people do not debate in a collective body, but by representation, the exercise of this sovereignty consists in the choice of representatives." *

The suffrages exercised by the Athenian citizen and the English elector are, nevertheless, perfectly distinct in their nature : the one being a direct exercise of the supreme legislative power, on the passing of a decree or a law; the other being a vote which goes to determine the election of a person who is to possess a share of the supreme legislative power, and which is not, nor can ever be given, on any legislative question. " The proposition (says a writer in the Edinburgh Review,) which we would lay down as the corner-stone of the representative system, [is] that the people ought not to decide directly and finally on any public measures except the choice of their representatives. " † Whatever *ought* to be the case or not, it is certain that in this, or any other representative government, so long as those governments endure, the people, *i. e.* the electors, *cannot* by their votes decide directly and finally on any public measure : their power is confined

---

* 1 Com. 170; and again, p. 159 : " In so large a state as ours, it is very wisely contrived, that the people should do that by their representatives, which it is impracticable to perform in person."

† Vol. 20. p. 408.

to the choice of those who are to decide. The certainty of this fact is not at all impugned by such passages as the following :—

"Sovereignty (says Rousseau) cannot be alienated : it consists essentially in the general will; and will cannot be represented :—it is the same, or it is different ; there is no medium. The deputies of the people, therefore, neither are, nor can be, its representatives; they are only its delegates, *(commissaires;)* they cannot conclude any thing definitively. Every law that the people in person has not ratified, is null; it is not a law. The English people imagines that it is free, but it is much mistaken ; it is free only during the election of members of Parliament : as soon as they are elected, it is enslaved, it is nothing." *

These remarks, though mixed up with erroneous notions on the subject of liberty, chiefly proceed on the supposition that the electors of England are, between the sessions of Parliament, possessed of the sovereign power, which they surrender to their representatives : whereas, by the election of representatives, they enable the King at any moment to summon his Parliament, and so call the legislative sovereignty into existence.

Rousseau boldly rejects the doctrine that a member of the English House of Commons is

* Contrat Social, liv. 3. ch. 15.

permitted in any case to exercise an independent judgment;* while others maintain that he should be guided only by his views of the public interest, and not by the requisitions of his constituents. Between these two doctrines the following remarks are intended to steer a middle course : which, however, as they had not the advantage of studied composition and calm consideration, must not be scrutinized with critical minuteness.

" The fundamental principle of our constitution,—the great political discovery of modern times,—that, indeed, which enables a state to combine extent with liberty,—(is that) the system of representation consists altogether in the perfect delegation by the people of their rights, and the care of their interests, to those who are to deliberate and to act for them. It is not a delegation which shall make the representative a mere organ of the passing will, or momentary opinion, of his constituents . . . . According

---

* " A knight, citizen, or burgess of the House of Commons, cannot by any means make any proxy, *because* he is elected and trusted by multitudes of people," says Lord Coke, 4 Inst. 12. This reason is adopted by Blackstone, who however states it in a rather more objectionable form, " as he is himself but a proxy for a multitude of other people." 1 Com. 168. Such reasoning, however, is not only contradicted by the fact, but is directly at variance with Blackstone's own account of the powers of a member of the House of Commons, 1 Com. 159.

to the soundest views of representative legislation, there ought to be a *general* coincidence
between the conduct of the delegate and the
sentiments of the electors."*

However laudable the endeavour to mediate
between extreme opinions, yet, in this case, it
appears that there is no middle term, and that
one or the other must be true. Either a representative is a mere delegate, empowered only to
act according to the instructions of his constituents, and not concerned about the general
expediency or inexpediency (as it may seem to
him) of the course which he is pursuing; or
he is morally bound, no less than he is legally
able, to follow that line of conduct which he
considers most conducive to the public welfare.
Besides these two alternatives, there is no third:
a representative must be either a delegate or
a free agent; he must either follow the opinions
of others, or his own: nor is it possible to distinguish between cases in which he should be
his own master, and in which he should be the
servant of his constituents. There is no doubt
that, in all representative governments, the
sentiments of the representative will generally
coincide with those of his constituents, because

* The Lord Chancellor's Speech on Parl. Reform, Oct. 7,
1831, p. 71. See likewise, on this subject, some remarks
of Hume, in a note appended, in the early editions of his
Essays, to Part 1. Essay 4. Works, vol. 3. p. 36.

they will choose a person who holds their
opinions, and he will frequently be influenced by
the desire of insuring a subsequent return.
Nevertheless, according to the unquestionable
theory of representation, a representative is
neither an advocate to plead the cause of his
constituents, nor is he merely their organ,
obeying their instructions with just so much
discretion as a lawyer exercises on behalf of his
client: but he is a member of the sovereign
legislative body, acting by no delegated authority, entitled to form an independent judgment,
legally answerable to none for his conduct, but
bound by a moral obligation to consult and vote
for the good of the whole community. In all
cases of delegation, one party puts another in
his place; transferring to the delegate an authority which he is either unwilling or unable to
exercise for himself. Thus a man delegates to
his steward the management of his estate, to
a tutor the education of his children; arming
them with certain powers, which, for specific
purposes, he possesses in his capacities of proprietor and father. But no one can delegate
a power which he does not possess. If an
elector does not himself, under any circumstances, possess the power of making laws, he
cannot properly be said to delegate to another
the power of making laws. A representative
exercises this power by virtue of the votes of

his constituents, but not by a delegation from them.

The distinction between *real* and *virtual* representation appears to be founded on the same erroneous notion, that a representative is merely the delegate of his constituents: for a town or district is said to be *really* represented, when it returns a member to Parliament; to be *virtually* represented, when it does not return a member, but its interests are protected by those who *really* represent other places.*   Those who propose to remedy the evil of virtual representation by changing it into real representation, frequently support the change on false grounds: for it is not more expedient that a large town should be represented rather than a small town, because its interests will be watched by its own delegate; but because it is more likely to send a good representative to the national councils.

Lastly, it may be remarked that those who found the expediency of a representative government on the impossibility or inconvenience of assembling the whole community, acknowledging at the same time, that a nation must be well

* The idea of virtual representation appears to be expressed in the following passage: " The principle of representation, in its widest sense, can hardly be unknown to any government not purely democratical.   In almost every country, the sense of the whole is *understood* to be spoken by a part, and the decisions of a part are binding upon the whole."—Hallam's Middle Ages, vol. 2. p. 216.

governed if all public measures coincide with the supposed interest, or the wishes, of a majority of the community, should remember that there would be no difficulty in putting all important questions to the vote in primary assemblies, and polling the whole nation, without having recourse to the circuitous and uncertain process of representation. If representatives are to be considered as merely having the proxies of their constituents, and if they are returned merely to avoid the difficulty occasioned by numbers, surely it would be little less expeditious, and far more secure, to take the votes of the constituents in detail?

XIII.

RICH.—MIDDLE CLASS.—POOR.

THERE are two different ways in which classes
of things can be opposed to each other: viz. as
contraries, and as *extremes.* They are opposed
as contraries, when a class is logically divided in
such a manner that every individual of it, not
contained in the one member of the division, is
contained in the other; when the two species
are together equivalent to the whole genus to
which they belong. Thus true is contrary to
false, straight is contrary to crooked, odd is contrary to even, knowledge is contrary to ignorance; because all propositions which are not
true must be false, all lines which are not
straight must be crooked, all numbers which
are not odd must be even, and a person must
be ignorant of all things about which he has
no knowledge. On the other hand, things are
opposed as *extremes,* when they do not together
make up, or exhaust, the class or genus to which
they belong, but there is between them a middle
state, from which they are not precisely divided,
and into which they insensibly graduate at both

its extremities.   Instances of this class of opposites are old and young, tall and short, belief
and disbelief, love and hatred, hot and cold,
light and dark, &c.   For it does not follow that
because a man is not old, he is therefore young;
because he is not tall, he is therefore short;
because the mind does not believe, it therefore
disbelieves; because it does not love, it therefore
hates; because an object is not hot, it is therefore cold ; because it is not light, it is therefore
dark.   Between these several extremes there is
an intermediate state, which is respectively
called middle-aged, middle-sized, doubt, indifference, tepid or lukewarm, dusk or glimmering,
&c.   Such extremes are not the negative of each
other, nor are they divided by a clear and definite
line which can never be passed ; but they admit
of an imperceptible transition from one most
dissimilar state to another, and may be likened
to the opposite ends of a graduated scale,
between which there is an infinite number of
degrees, but no marked separation.   It is to
this kind of opposites that Mr. Herschel alludes,
in his Discourse on the Study of Natural Philosophy,* when he says that " there can be little
doubt that the solid, liquid, and aëriform states
of bodies, are merely stages in a progress of
gradual transition from one extreme to the

* § 252.   See also § 135 and 200.

other ; and that however strongly marked the distinctions between them may appear, they will ultimately turn out to be separated by no sudden or violent line of demarcation, but shade into each other by insensible gradations."

Among the many opposites which belong to the class of extremes, are the terms *rich* and *poor,* which denote two classes in the community, of which the members severally possess an amount of wealth greater or less than a certain fluctuating and uncertain quantity, which entitles its possessor to be called a person of moderate property, of middling fortune, neither poor nor rich ; or more commonly to be named a member of the middle ranks. In all societies which have advanced beyond a savage state, and have accumulated some stores of wealth, there necessarily exists this triple distinction of classes: for though all the members of a community may be equally poor, they cannot be equally rich. But although these classes must, except among the rudest savages, everywhere exist ; yet the *proportions* which they bear to one another in different states may be very various, and the three parts may be unequally developed by the peculiar circumstances of each community : for instance, in some states the middle class may be of small account, and the rich and poor together make up a large majority of the whole population; as, in countries where slavery prevails, the society is divided into rich and poor, with scarcely any intervening order: the same state of things also is described by Aristotle, as existing in many small Greek states where the opposite parties of rich and poor were, on account of the scantiness of the population, precisely distinguished; and by Thucydides * as originating in the bloody contests between the rich and poor, in which the middle ranks, who took no part in the struggle, were destroyed by both parties, as well because they would not join either side, as from a feeling of jealousy lest they should escape the common ruin.

However the pernicious institution of predial and domestic servitude, or an injudicious and unskilful arrangement of the sovereign power, may tend to obliterate the middle rank, and to destroy the connecting links between the rich and the poor, yet in all communities, settled in a fixed habitation, and restrained by a regular government, there must exist rudiments of all three classes; and the comparative historian may, like the comparative anatomist, discover throughout the various forms of civilized societies, traces of the corresponding orders which, though subject to disproportionate enlargement and contraction, sometimes swelled to an inordi-

* B. 3. ch. 82.

nate size, and sometimes shrivelled into insignificance, by the diseased action of the body
politic, may yet be clearly referred to one and
the same imaginary pattern.

The names of rich and poor are, however,
applied to different classes in the community,
not with reference to one particular standard,
but with reference to the condition of the society which they divide into the classes so
denominated. No man is absolutely rich, or
poor, or of middling fortune; but one man is
rich, and another is poor, as compared with a
third who is neither poor nor rich, but of moderate property. Accordingly, these terms as
much imply each other, and are as unintelligible without such a mutual reference, as master
and servant, husband and wife, debtor and cre-
ditor: nor can one man be called poor, without
supposing the existence of another who is called
rich; both names being applied to signify a
common relation to a certain middle point,
fixed according to the circumstances of each
particular case; as things are said to be high
and low, or long and short, as compared with
some arbitrary standard which varies according
to the nature of the object so characterised.
Hence it appears that the classes of rich and
poor in different states have *independently* no
resemblance to each other; they are only similar
in their *relative positions*. Thus a poor man

stands in the same relation to a rich man in England, as a poor man does to a rich man in France; but it does not therefore follow that either a poor or a rich man in France possesses absolutely the same average amount of wealth as a poor or a rich man in England. So, again, an Englishman and a Swiss might possess the same absolute amount of wealth, and the one be reckoned poor in England, and the other a person of middling property in Switzerland. In each state a certain rough average of wealth is struck, which may differ as much in different countries as the average duration of human life, or the average amount of knowledge: and all persons who possess about that amount of property are called the middle ranks; while those who exceed, and fall short of it, are respectively called the rich and poor. A poor man in one country is, therefore, no more in the same absolute condition as a poor man in another, than a degree of temperature, which might be called warm at the Pole, would be entitled to the same name under the Equator; or than the dealers in magic, who obtain the wonder and veneration of barbarians, would be respected for their wisdom by a civilized people.

It is to this mistaken notion, that poverty and riches are absolute, and not relative quantities,—that we may trace the error of supposing that the poor of a given country, because

they always retain the same name, are therefore
always in the same condition. That name is
applied to them, not because they enjoy a certain fixed amount of conveniences and necessaries ; but because the rich and the middle
class enjoy a *greater* amount of the same conveniences and necessaries. The class now called
poor in this kingdom hold the same place in the
community with regard to the other two ranks,
as the class described by Holinshed as living in
cottages without chimneys, sleeping on straw
pallets, under a covering of skins, with a log
under their heads for a bolster, and using only
wooden utensils : but in their actual situation
they resemble rather the middle class of the
time of Henry the Eighth ; although many
things are now reputed necessaries by the poor,
which were beyond the reach even of the middle
ranks in that age, and some, indeed, (such as the
glazing of windows,) would have been luxuries
unattainable to a British prince at a period long
posterior to the Christian era.

It likewise results from the preceding remarks
that the rich, and poor, and middling class, are
so named, not according to the aggregate wealth
of each class, but according to the separate
wealth possessed by each individual : so that
although the joint wealth of the rich in any
given state may be less than the joint wealth
of the middle class ; yet these two classes are

not the less entitled to their respective denominations. Thus, when it is said that the middle classes are the wealthiest order in the community,* it is not meant that they have *singly* the greatest wealth, (in which case they would not be called the middle class,) but that the sum of their wealth is greater than the sum of the wealth possessed by the rich. Nor even if it should happen in any country that the rich have together more wealth than any other class, yet they would not be called rich for that reason, but on account of their several possessions.

The class of persons having a smaller amount of wealth than those belonging to the middle rank, though commonly included under the single name of poor, are more properly subdivided into the *poor* strictly so called, and the

---

* " I speak now of the middle classes ... the most numerous, and far the most wealthy order in the community." The Lord Chancellor's Speech on Parliamentary Reform, 1831. p. 54. It is, however, very questionable, whether in this or in any other country, the middle classes are the most numerous order in the community. The line is of course indefinite, and may be differently drawn by different persons : but, according to the common acceptation of the word, the poor (including the paupers) are far more numerous than the middle class of this kingdom. The new population-returns will furnish some data for determining this question : but it is extremely improbable that the rich and middle classes together make up half the population of England. It seems to me likewise doubtful, whether the aggregate wealth of the rich is not in this country greater than the aggregate wealth of the middle classes.

paupers or *beggars*. In this sense the poor are those who, as compared with the rich and the middle class, severally enjoy a less quantity of decencies and necessaries, yet, on the whole, by means of constant labour and a frugal mode of living, are able to maintain a sufficiently comfortable existence : it is to this class that, in countries where slavery does not exist, those who are engaged in manual labour about manufactures, mining, and husbandry, for the most part belong. On the other hand, persons continually struggling with want, and threatened with the danger of starvation, or exposure to the weather from insufficiency of clothing or habitation, are called paupers or beggars. This distinction, precisely to the same effect as observed in our language, was pointed out many centuries ago by the comic poet Aristophanes, who, in one of his comedies, introduces a dialogue on the comparative merits of poverty and riches, between a man who had obtained the assistance of the God of Riches and a personification of Poverty in the shape of a female ; in which, after the former had described a person in a state of great penury and privation, and asked whether that is a picture of happiness, she replies, that " the state of a man who has nothing at all is not poverty, but beggary. A poor man is he who lives sparingly, and always keeps to his work ; who, while he has no superfluities, at the same time suffers no privations."*

Mr. Wilmot Horton, in his Inquiry into the Causes and Remedies of Pauperism,† proposes " to define the general term *poor*, as denoting those persons who possess nothing disposable, in exchange for which they can obtain the means of subsistence, other than their own labour." This is an attempt to give an absolute definition of poor, equally applicable to all countries, and without reference to the other wealthier classes in the community, or to any fixed amount of property. In truth, however, we call a person rich without any reference to the *manner* in which he gains his livelihood, so that the whole amount which he receives exceeds a certain amount, the possession of which characterises the middle rank ; and, in like manner, we say that a person belongs to the middle rank, so that his income, however acquired, exceeds that which is considered as characterising the poor. Thus a person may possess no capital or certain income, and may depend for subsistence entirely on his own labour : yet if the proceeds of that labour are very considerable, he may be called

---

* πτωχοῦ μὲν γὰρ βίος ὃν σὺ λέγεις ζῆν ἐστιν μηδὲν ἔχοντα.
τοῦ δὲ πένητος ζῆν φειδόμενον καὶ τοῖς ἔργοις προσέχοντα,
περιγίγνεσθαι δ' αὐτῷ μηδὲν, μὴ μέντοι μηδ' ἐπιλείπειν.

                                      Aristoph. Plut. 552.

† Fourth Series, p. 9.

rich; if they are of a moderate amount, he may be called a man of middling fortune. Many professional men, such as physicians, lawyers, soldiers, &c., are entirely dependent for their subsistence on their own exertions, and yet belong to the class of rich, or to the middle rank. It is true, that all poor persons have nothing but their own labour to give in exchange for the means of subsistence; but it is not true, that all persons who have nothing but their own labour to give in exchange for the means of subsistence, are poor. So entirely do we exclude from our consideration the manner in which a person is maintained, so that his maintenance be large, that the children of the rich are always reckoned in the class of rich during the lifetime of their parents, on whose charity they are, nevertheless, for the most part as completely dependent, as an English pauper on the parish-rate, or a street beggar on the compassion of passengers.

Mr. Wilmot Horton, in the passage just cited, proceeds to divide the poor into four classes: viz.—1. Labourers; 2. Helpless Poor; 3. Paupers; and 4. Beggars. *Labourers* he describes as those poor persons who are enabled to obtain by their labour the means of subsistence. This definition, however, combined with the foregoing general definition of poor, would include all persons, whose income, however considerable, depends on their personal exertions; and therefore would comprehend very many persons, who are not in common language, nor can with any propriety be denominated poor. The *helpless poor* are those persons who have no property, and are physically incapable of gaining the means of subsistence by their own labour. *Paupers* are those able-bodied poor who cannot get, in exchange for their labour, wages sufficient to procure the means of subsistence; while *beggars* are those who, being able to work, prefer to rely for their subsistence on the voluntary gifts of others. Of these four classes, the helpless poor and the beggars are identified in common language; as the latter term is not restricted to those who are *able* to work. Nor, except in countries where there is a compulsory provision for the indigent, can the classes of paupers and beggars be distinguished; as those who are not able to maintain themselves, and have not a legal right to be maintained at the public cost, must, if they are to live, be maintained by the free gifts of others: in other words, all paupers must be beggars. If, therefore, from this quadruple division, we exclude the labourers, who must be considered as a class of the whole community, not of the poor only,— and remark that in countries where the indigent are not maintained by a public tax, the other three classes, of helpless poor, paupers, and beggars, necessarily fall together,—there will remain the classification proposed above: viz. the poor in its general sense, being divided into the poor strictly so called, and the paupers or beggars; that is, those who by their labour or any other means receive a certain limited income, and those who derive a mean subsistence from the gratuities of others.

Fielding, in his interesting tract on *The Causes of the late Increase of Robbers*, had previously suggested a general definition of the poor, which is liable to the same objection as that just examined, inasmuch as it makes not the amount of income, but the mode of acquiring it, the test of poverty. " By the poor (he says) I understand such persons as have no estate of their own to support them without industry, nor any profession or trade by which, without industry, they may be capable of gaining a comfortable subsistence."* This definition would, obviously, exclude all persons belonging to the class of rich and the middle ranks, who have not a large or moderate income independent of their own exertions, or the charity of their relations.

The same author further divides the class of poor into—1. Such poor as are unable to work; 2. Such as are able and willing to work; 3. Such as are able to work, but not willing. The

* Inquiry into the Causes of the late Increase of Robbers, § 4.

division on which this strictly accurate classification is founded, viz. into those who are able, and
those who are unable to work, agrees with that
known to our law, of the able-bodied and impo-
tent poor.   It is scarcely necessary to remark,
that a beggar, and a pauper or a person receiving
an allowance from the poor-rate, may belong to
any one of these three classes.

It has been above remarked, in several places,
that a democracy is sometimes understood to
mean, not a government of the majority, but of
the poor ; that the aristocracy is sometimes
identified with the rich, and the people with the
poor ; that aristocratical measures are such as
favour the rich as distinguished from the poor,
and popular measures such as favour the poor
as distinguished from the rich.   These terms,
however, which properly refer respectively to
the classes of rich and poor *alone*, are occasionally applied, with an uncertain signification, as
denoting not the rich, but those who are not
poor, that is, the rich and the middle class ; not
the poor, but those who are not rich ; that is,
the poor and the middle class.   Important mistakes may be committed when the argument is
made to turn on this double meaning ; and
when that which is true of the rich or poor
alone, is inferred also to be true of the rich or
poor together with the middle class.   But such
terms are properly applied, when, although the

middle class may be allotted to either side, yet
the poor or the rich are the predominant consideration, and in proportion as a person is richer
or poorer, so much the greater is his gain or
loss. Thus, when a measure is said to be aristocratical or democratical, it may perhaps have
little influence on the middle class, but be of
such a character that it will greatly increase the
political power of the rich or of the poor. Thus
Aristotle, in saying that democracy is a government in which the poor rule,* meant not that
the rich or the middle class were *excluded* from
the government, that the poor were *alone* rulers;
but that the poor, as opposed to both those
orders, had a preponderating influence in the
constitution, and administered it according to
their own imagined interests.

A different view of this question is however
taken by a writer in the Westminster Review,
who has pointed out, with great distinctness, the
error of supposing that the community is divided
into rich and poor; or (as he expresses it) that
" rich and poor bisect the community :" but
nevertheless appears to be mistaken in some of
the inferences which he would derive from that
observation.

" Oligarchy, (he says,) according to the definition of Aristotle, has place when the wealthy

* See above, p. 85.

few possess the powers of government, and
employ them for their own ends, not for the
public good : democracy is when the poor many,
possessing the powers of government, use them
for their own interest, not for the public interest.
The philosopher seems to imagine that if the
wealthy, as a class, possess no distinct privileges,
the power of government must necessarily be in
the hands of the poor ; and that the poor have
an interest contrary to the public interest.   Now
the word *poor* is here employed in a double
sense ; signifying, at one time, the whole community excepting the rich ; at another time,
*that portion of the community which is in a state of
beggary and starvation.*   It is only in the latter
sense that the poor can ever be said to have an
interest distinct from the public interest : for the
whole community, excluding the rich, if this be
meant by the word *poor*, has obviously the same
interest as the whole community including the
rich.   According to this latter sense, since not
more than one man in a hundred can be called
rich,* ninety-nine hundredths of the community
are poor ; and the interest of ninety-nine hundredths of the community must always be the
same as the interest of the whole community. . . . . It is from this confusion of the

---

* This statement is probably not meant to be taken
strictly ; as the ratio of the rich to the other two ranks
must obviously be different in different countries.

meaning of the word *poor*, that the necessity, alleged in political reasonings, of a balance between conflicting interests, takes its rise. The rich have an interest distinct from the community; the poor are asserted to have an interest distinct from the community : consequently, in order to secure the interests of the community, you must pursue neither the interest of the rich, nor the interest of the poor, but a balance between the two. As an essential element of this balance, the rich are to possess certain political powers, apart and as a class : if they do not, all political powers will be in the hands of the poor, the interest of the poor alone will be consulted, the rich will have no protection against injury, and the interest of the community will be neglected.* The whole fallacy of this reasoning is at once seen, when the community, instead of being divided into rich and poor, are divided, as they ought to be, into rich and not rich ; *and when it is understood that the interest of the rich, as possessors of unresponsible power, is always at variance—the interest of those who are not rich always coincident—with that of the whole community."* †

---

* The argument here stated (whether ever advanced or not) is manifestly fallacious, for the first reason mentioned by the Reviewer. His second reason will be examined in the text.

† Westminister Review, vol. 5. pp. 291, 292.

On this passage it may in the first place be remarked, that the poor, in the sense in which that word was understood by Aristotle, are *not* persons in a state of beggary or starvation. Not to mention that in the Greek states the working classes were almost exclusively slaves, and that few of the citizens could be in a state of utter destitution, there is no doubt that the distinction above cited from Aristophanes was that received in the common language of Greece,* as a comic poet would naturally appeal to the prevailing sentiments and opinions of his hearers. Aristotle, therefore, by the word *poor,* in his definition of democracy, understood that portion of the community who are raised above absolute want, but are nevertheless more circumscribed in their means than the middle class. This, probably the most numerous portion of every society which has hitherto existed, has not in modern times as yet been often possessed of the powers of government; but in the Greek republics such a state of things was by no means rare; and it was when the sovereign power was wielded by a body, of which the rich

* The poor of Aristotle would indeed include the beggars of Aristophanes; but the beggars of Aristophanes would not include the poor of Aristotle. The Greek words are, πένης and πτωχός: the latter being derived from πτώσσειν, to *crouch,* or *cringe,* the action of a person humbly suing for a favour.

and the middle class were indeed members, but
in which they formed an insignificant minority,
and were unable to counterbalance the numbers
and power of the poor, that Aristotle called the
government a democracy. No charge can be
less well-founded than to impute to Aristotle a
confusion of the part of the community who are
not rich under the common name of poor, and a
neglect of the middle classes; when that philosopher enlarges elsewhere, with evident satisfaction, on the importance of the middle class
to the well-being of a state; on the benefits
arising from their number and influence, and
the evils caused by the frequent absence through
Greece of a numerous and respectable middle
order, whereby the rich and the poor were
brought into immediate contact, and easily
moved to acts of violence by reason of their
precise demarkation from each other. So far is
he from representing the community as divided
into the rich and poor, and giving the improper
name of poor to all who are not rich, that he
distinctly lays it down, that all states are divided
into three parts, the very rich, the very poor, and
those who are between them. And afterwards,
among other arguments to shew the importance
of the middle class, he says, that "Those communities admit of being well governed, in which
the middle classes are considerable; the best
state of things being when the middle classes

M

are more powerful than both the rich and the poor together; next to this, if they are more powerful than either of these orders separately: for, even in that case, their weight, being thrown into either scale, makes it preponderate, and so prevents either the rich or the poor from establishing a government for their own peculiar interest." * It is, therefore, certain, that Aristotle did not overlook the existence of a middle order in the state, but that in his definition of democracy he used the term poor in its proper sense, conceiving that class to have an interest distinct from that of the whole community.†

Further, it is necessary to advert to the sense in which the Westminster Reviewer states, that the rich and the poor separately have an interest distinct from the interest of the community; but that the interest of the poor, together with the

---

* Polit. b. 4. c. 11. There is much more to the same effect, both in this and the following chapter : and Aristotle quotes with approbation the verse of Phocylides,

πολλὰ μέσοισιν ἄριστα, μέσος θέλω ἐν πόλει εἶναι.

The new edition of Hume's Works contains a short Essay *on the Middle Station of Life*, suppressed in the later collections of his Essays. It contains some good remarks, but is altogether of little merit. vol. 4. p. 550.

† The middle class was supposed to have the chief interest in establishing a government mixed of aristocracy and democracy, as being neither the aristocratic nor the democratic class, *i. e.* neither the poor nor the rich, which explains the sense in which Aristotle understands a mixed government.—See Plutarch, Solon, ch. 13. Above, p. 94.

middle class, is identical with the interest of the whole community.   For this purpose, it should be observed that the word *interest* bears two very distinct senses : 1. That which, to competent and dispassionate judges, appears expedient, upon an enlarged and prospective view of all the circumstances of the case ; the facts being considered, not as constituting an individual case, but as a specimen of an entire class; and, 2. That which the person or persons may *think* expedient, or desire, without any regard being had to its *real* effect, as estimated by the best means within the reach of human wisdom.   Now, it is only in the latter of these senses, that different classes of the community can be said to have opposite interests : for one of the greatest and most valuable discoveries of political science has been, that oppression and unequal privileges are, on the whole, for long periods of time and large bodies of men, almost as hurtful to the classes for whose imagined benefit the distinction is made, as to those whom it obviously and directly injures.   Thus the interest of the manufacturers and agriculturists, of the rich and poor, are ultimately and in substance the same, though the members of each party conceive them to be at variance, and most frequently act upon that supposition.   Thus the rich have in many countries thought that they were benefited by keeping the manual labourers in a state of personal servitude ; and that they would be impoverished by the manumission of their slaves : whereas they would inevitably have been benefited by the additional wealth and knowledge, and the increased security of government and property, which the whole community, and they not the least, would have derived from that change. In the same narrow sense of the word interest, the Edinburgh Review remarks, that " it cannot be denied that it is for the immediate interest of the people (*i. e.* the poor) to plunder the rich."* For the poor, as a class, have ever entertained a feeling of hostility to the institution of property, conceiving that it is a contrivance established for the rich and against themselves, enabling others to live on the produce of *their* labour. It is chiefly to this mistaken but most prevailing opinion, and the measures to which it has given rise, that Aristotle alludes when he says that democracy is a government in which the poor govern for their own, and not for the public good.† It was a common practice in Greece and its colonies, for citizens who had fought their way to the rights of citizenship, or were impoverished by

* Above, p. 120.
† His opinions on this subject are expressed very fully in his Rhetoric to Alexander, ch. 3, where he points out the dangers to be feared, and the mode of guarding against them.

any accidental cause, for example, by a loss of territory, to demand a new division of all the land, and an equal partition of it among the citizens. To this practice (not to be confounded with the agrarian laws of the Romans, which were partitions of *unappropriated* public land,) Aristotle alludes in many passages of his Politics; * and such divisions were made or proposed in different states, on several occasions.†
Of the same nature was the abolition of all claims of debt, and sometimes even a forced repayment of the interest already received by the lenders; ‡ which measures, indeed, could only be proposed after an open conflict between the rich and poor. It is in the Greek states that the most striking examples of the collision of the poor and rich, and the confliction of their supposed interests, are to be found, on account of the insignificance of the middle class in those communities, and the direct share which the poor had in the enactment and administration of the laws, by means of their admission to the legislative and judicial assemblies of the citizens, and the appointment of public officers by lot. Thus it was not only at times of popular commotions, but during the regular course of the government, that the rich were unfairly and

* B. 5. ch. 8; b. 6. ch. 3, and ch. 5.
† Müller's Dorians, vol. 2. pp. 165, 169, 190.
‡ Plutarch. Quæst. Græc. 18.

harshly dealt with. So, at Athens, the practice
of multiplying occasions for the confiscation of
property, and of willingly entertaining accusations which, if supported, would entail that
punishment, was very prevalent : * in the same
manner, and for the same motives, that grounds
for accusations of treason were, in more recent
times, diligently sought after by the European
princes. So Aristophanes describes the poor
of Attica as being anxious for war,—the rich
and the farmers as adverse to it ; † because the
poor would receive a share of the spoil, if there
was any (and the Greeks always considered war
in the light of an extensive plundering expedi-
tion), while the rich would sustain the loss, if
the war was unsuccessful, and the cultivators
were liable to have their lands ravaged by the
victorious enemy. At Megara, too, the leaders
of the popular party (*i. e.* the poor) on one occasion banished so many of the rich, for the sake
of confiscating their property, that the numbers
of the exiles became sufficiently large to enable
them to return and engage with the people,
whom they overcame, and then established an
oligarchy ; ‡ making (as Aristotle has remarked)

---

* Boeckh's Economy of Athens, vol. 2. p. 127.

† ναῦς δὴ καθέλκειν τῷ πένητι μὲν δοκεῖ,
  τοῖς πλουσίοις δὲ καὶ γεωργοῖς οὐ δοκεῖ.

                            Aristoph. Eccl. 297.

‡ Aristot. Pol. b. 5. ch. 5.

their preponderance in the government the
prize of their victory. Isocrates describes the
Argives, during the short intervals of war, as
destroying the most opulent citizens, and re-
joicing at their ruin more than others would
rejoice at the death of an enemy.* These instances (which are only a few out of a large
number) may serve to put in a clear view the
hostile spirit which often exists between the
poor and the rich, and which has not hitherto
been powerfully developed, or been attended
with important effects in most modern states,
for reasons which cannot here be investigated.
But that the class of poor have almost constantly acted in opposition to the interests of
the rich, and that the class of rich have frequently acted inopposition to the interests of
the poor, is not more certain than that their
real, and permanent, and general interests, are
in perfect unison with each other.

Now the assertion of the Westminster Reviewer, that the interest of those who are not
rich is always coincident with the interest of
the whole community, is true, if we take interest in its largest sense, to signify that which
is ultimately beneficial to the community: but
in that sense, neither is the essential interest of
the rich or poor, *separately*, distinct from the

* Philipp. p. 92. D.

interest of the community. But if, in a proper democracy, *i. e.* a government in which a majority of the adult male population partake of the sovereign power, the poor (who, in every country, are, and always must be, more numerous than the rich and the middle rank taken together) were to propose, and by their numbers carry, that the property of the rich should be divided in equal shares among all the members of the community, then the interest of the rich would not coincide with the supposed interest of the *whole* community ; for they are members of the community, and would conceive themselves injured. If the interest of the community means the *real* interest of all and every of the members composing it ; the interest not only of any two classes together, but of every class by itself, must coincide with the interest of the community. If the interest of the community means not the *real*, but the *supposed* interest of all and every of its members, then the supposed interest of any number of persons less than the whole, is not coincident with the interest of the whole community.

This difference in the significations of the word interest may be illustrated by a verse of an ancient poet, which occurs in a collection of maxims made by Lord Bacon :

" Cum vitia prosint, peccat qui recte facit."

Of which the following translation is given:—
" If vices were upon the whole matter profitable, the virtuous man would be the sinner." *
In other words, ' if it were for the general and
permanent interest of mankind to commit vice,
the virtuous man would be the sinner.' In this
sense, all vice is contrary to a man's interest; that
is, his true interest is to act virtuously.   But it
is often said that a man preferred his duty to
his interest,—that his right moral judgment was
perverted by his interest, &c.; in which cases
interest means, not that which is, on the whole,
beneficial to mankind; but that which the individual desires, or what, to the majority, would
be an immediate gratification.

Even if the subject could be properly discussed at length in this place, it would be needless to attempt, after the excellent dissertation
of Dr. Arnold,† to trace the manner in which
the division of political interests, in the early
periods of national development being commonly into the nobles and the rich, when the
rich are the *popular* party,—is changed at a later
epoch into that of the rich and poor, when the
rich become the *anti-popular* party. Thus much
however it may be proper to observe, that at no
time do the poor consider their interest as identical with the interest of the rich; but that,

* Bacon's Works, vol. 1. p. 418. ed. Montagu.
† See his edition of Thucydides, Appendix 1.

when the rich are excluded from political power
and privileges, on the ground of their not belonging to certain families, this is the prominent
grievance of the day: and while this lasts, the
other division of interests, though it equally
exists, is not brought into light, nor does it
become the point of separation between the
contending parties. So long as the rich are the
excluded party, claiming to be admitted to equal
rights, the discontents of the poor remain un-
heeded, or are enlisted in the cause of the rich.
This first contest, therefore, is of a purely political character, and is chiefly carried on between
persons of property and education, who may
thus on both sides be expected neither to rejoice
in massacre and bloodshed for their own sake,
nor to be indifferent about the destruction of
property which takes place in all violent civil
wars. But when the struggle comes on between
the rich and poor, or (as Dr. Arnold has expressed it*) between property and numbers, the
contest is not so much for political privileges, as
for the equalization of wealth; not so much for
setting up the low, as for putting down the high:
no hopes of accommodation can be entertained,
because the claims of the attacking party are as
unreasonable as their end is unattainable. Add
to this, that when the rich are the discontented

---

* See his edition of Thucydides, pp. 633, 634.

party, being, even in a state of political disability, somewhat accustomed to rule, they are less likely to make a grievous abuse of power than those who come into possession of it for the first time, full of hatred and envy against their opponents who have lived in luxury while they perhaps have been pinched by want, and determined to retaliate on them for their former superiority of condition.　To this inferior moral state of the poor when contending against the rich, as compared with that of the rich when contending against the nobles, the greater bloodiness and atrocity of the former contest is to be attributed : it is, in its nature, a war of extermination, directed to an inaccessible object ; nor is it to be expected that the flame of such a conflict will be extinguished, till it has consumed all the materials which feed it.　Hence, it is no matter for surprise that Dr. Arnold should remark, that he knows no instance in which the struggle between property and numbers has, after having come to a crisis, terminated favourably.　Indeed it is difficult to understand how a contest could have a favourable issue, of which the object is to abolish a distinction not factitious or arbitrary, but necessarily existing in all communities in which a right of property exists, and of which all the members are not on the same level of barbarism.　In the ancient states, this political crisis was followed by every form of evil—native despotism, foreign despotism, invasion, unprincipled oligarchies, unprincipled democracies, national poverty and decline. Whether the same crisis, which seems impending in some modern states, will be averted by the prudence of the rich, the numbers, wealth, and respectability of the middle class, the diffusion of knowledge among the poor, and, above all, by the extension of the rights of citizenship to the whole population, is a problem which time alone can resolve.

XIV.

NATURE.—NATURAL.—UNNATURAL.— STATE OF NATURE.

On account of the great number and diversity of significations belonging to the word *Nature,* and the difficulty of fixing them with clearness and precision, it will be desirable to examine all its principal meanings, without regard to their political bearing, as they mutually serve to explain and throw light on one another.

Nature is sometimes used as identical with God, or the Being which made the universe: as when we speak of the works of Nature; or when it is said that Nature makes nothing in vain. It is also employed by atheistical writers, in an indistinct sense, to denote some supposed power or motion which has affected existing matter, and presides over the world. This meaning may be discerned in the two following passages, which, though taken from Latin authors, may serve to exemplify the English usage, as they admit of literal translation into our language:

Horace, speaking of the gods of Epicurus, says—

> —— " Namque deos didici securum agere ævum,
> Nec si quid miri faciat Natura, deos id
> Tristes ex alto cœli demittere tecto."

Juvenal also has these verses :—

> " Sunt in fortunæ qui casibus omnia ponunt,
> Et nullo credunt mundum rectore moveri,
> Natura volvente vices et lucis et anni."

In both these passages Nature expresses an active supreme power, distinct from God.

Akin to this sense, is the use of Nature, not as a real being, but as a personification of the active powers of the universe, of the various causes always in operation around us. This usage of the word, which suits only with a figurative and poetical style, is sufficiently illustrated by the following passage from Shakspeare :—

> " Thou, Nature, art my goddess; to thy law
> My services are bound." *

Nature is also used to signify the material things created by God, the outward objects which strike the senses. Thus we speak of the order of Nature, the laws of Nature, the beauties of Nature, an observer of Nature. In this sense is to be understood Lord Bacon's work *on the*

---

* Lear, act 1. sc. 1.

Interpretation of Nature. In this sense too it occurs in the following passages of Pope, who makes great use of this word:

> " All are but parts of one stupendous whole,
> Whose body Nature is, and God the soul." *

> " Let ruling angels from their spheres be hurled,
> Being on being wreck'd, and world on world;
> Heaven's whole foundations to the centre nod,
> And Nature tremble to the throne of God."†

So likewise Sir Walter Scott:

> " Call it not vain: they do not err
> Who say that, when the poet dies,
> Mute Nature is his worshipper,
> And celebrates his obsequies."

Hence is derived the phrase natural philosophy, as opposed to mathematical and moral philosophy; natural philosophy being that philosophy which is concerned about objects that strike the senses, and do not refer to the qualities or conceptions of the human mind. The expression *exact sciences* as opposed to *moral sciences,* comprehends both natural and mathematical philosophy, and is a division founded, not on the quality of the subject matter, but on the greater or less certainty of the results.

Nature is likewise used to signify the qualities or attributes of any thing; that which any thing is, or the system, order, arrangement, or mutual

---

* Essay on Man, ep. 1. v. 267.   † Ibid. v. 254.

relations, of different things. Thus we speak of the nature of God, the nature of the human mind, the nature of the human body, the nature of society, the nature of government, the nature of an army, the nature of the air, the nature of the sun, &c. So Lucretius wrote a poem *on the Nature of Things*.

From this acceptation of the word are derived the expressions *good-nature* and *ill-nature*, as applied to mankind, in the sense of benevolent and malevolent disposition.

Hence also the phrase *human nature*, which appears to signify the sum total of the faculties, dispositions, and propensities of mankind; or the condition of the human race. Thus Dryden, paraphrasing Juvenal, speaks of

> " A soul, that can securely death defy,
> And count it Nature's privilege to die."

And Milton,

> ———— " O why did God,
> Creator wise, that peopled highest heaven
> With spirits masculine, create at last
> This novelty on earth, *this fair defect
> Of Nature*, and not fill the world at once
> With men, as angels, without feminine ?"

In this general sense, Nature includes all the constituent parts of the human mind and disposition, whether bad or good, all which are comprehended in the following passages of Shakspeare :

" His nature is too noble for the world." *

" How quickly nature breaks into revolt,
When gold becomes her object." †

" If the balance of our lives had not one scale of reason
to poise another of sensuality, the blood and baseness of our
natures would conduct us to most preposterous conclusions."‡

So likewise, in the Paradise Lost, the Angel
Michael addresses Adam in the following words:

———" Judge not what is best
By pleasure, though to nature seeming meet,
Created, as thou art, to nobler end
Holy and pure, conformity divine."

Hence nature is used to signify the disposition
which a man would have if he did not regulate
his passions and appetites, and educate his mind
by moral discipline. In this sense Lord Bacon
uses the word in his Essay on *Nature in Men:*
thus, " Nature is often hidden, sometimes over-
come, seldom extinguished." " A man's nature
runs either to herbs or weeds; therefore let
him seasonably water the one, and destroy the
other." Horace applies the same term to the
original good taste and feeling which a mistaken
system has been unable wholly to stifle:

" Naturam expellas furca: tamen usque recurret,
Et mala perrumpet furtim fastidia victrix."§

Sometimes, however, nature is taken in a

* Coriolanus, act 3. sc. 1.　　† 2 Hen. 4. act 4. sc. 4.
‡ Othello, act 1. sc. 3.　　§ Epist. l. 1. ep. 10. v. 24.

N

narrower sense, to express only the prevailing part of the human disposition, those moral principles which are found to actuate the majority of mankind in a civilized state of existence. In this sense we say, that parricide, incest, and other crimes, are contrary to our nature, are revolting to human nature, &c. So the author of the poem of *New Morality* speaks of

" Crimes by God and Nature loath'd."

The ordinary sense of *natural* has the same origin, signifying that which is agreeable to the nature of any thing. Thus a *natural death,* as opposed to a *violent* death, is a death which happens in the regular course of nature, and does not arise from any extraneous cause. In this sense, it is opposed to miraculous or supernatural, as, ' a miracle is a disturbance of the natural order of things.' As applied to mankind, it sometimes follows the general sense of *nature* just described; as, ' it is natural to men to be kind, to be cruel, to better their condition, to love their children,' &c.; so Johnson said, that " all men will naturally steal : " * sometimes, in the narrower sense, (when it becomes a laudatory term,) as when it is said that a man is wanting in natural love, that he violates natural decency, &c.

* Boswell's Life, vol. ii.

" The word *natural* (says Hume) is commonly taken in so many senses, and is of so loose a signification, that it seems vain to dispute whether justice be natural or not. If self-love, if benevolence, be natural to man ; if reason and forethought be also natural ; then may the same epithet be applied to justice, order, fidelity, property, society. Men's inclination, their necessities, lead them to combine ; their understanding and experience tell them that this combination is impossible, where each governs himself by no rule, and pays no regard to the possessions of others. And from these passions and reflections conjoined, as soon as we observe like passions and reflections in others, the sentiment of justice, throughout all ages, has infallibly and certainly had place, to some degree or other, in every individual of the human species. In so sagacious an animal, what necessarily arises from the exertion of his intellectual faculties may justly be esteemed natural."* In these remarks, Hume properly understands natural to mean that which is agreeable to man's nature, in the general sense above pointed out.

Unnatural is sometimes used to signify that which is inconsistent with the nature of any thing, and could not have happened without some extraordinary deviation from the usual

---

* See Hume's Essays, Appendix 3. Works, vol. 4. p. 391.

course of things. Thus we call an incident in a tale of fiction unnatural; and we speak of an unnatural birth, meaning a monstrous birth.

Unnatural is likewise used to signify that which is contrary to the good principles of human nature : as, an unnatural offence, an unnatural child; so in Hamlet the murder of the king is called an act " foul, strange, and unnatural." " The Irish (said Johnson) are in a most unnatural state; for we see there the minority prevailing over the majority."* Here by *unnatural state* Johnson must have meant a state which he considered as unfavourable to good government; for there is nothing monstrous or unusual in the smaller governing the larger number. The same person is reported to have " wondered that the phrase of *unnatural* rebellion should be so much used, for that all rebellion was natural to man."* If nature means only the good part of man's disposition, then rebellion (without sufficient cause) is unnatural; if nature means the whole of man's disposition, then rebellion is natural.

Nature, again, is opposed to art, or human institutions. In this sense, nature is a negative term, and means that which is *not* made or fashioned by man.

---

* Boswell's Life, vol. 2. p. 118.
† Boswell's Tour in the Hebrides, p. 403.

These usages, which are of frequent occurrence, will be sufficiently exemplified by the following passages:

> " All nature is but art unknown to thee ;
> All chance, direction which thou canst not see." *

> ——— " As nature's ties decay,
> As duty, love, and honour fail to sway,
> Fictitious† bonds, the bonds of wealth and law,
> Still gather strength, and force unwilling awe." ‡

" Agriculture (says Gibbon) is the foundation of manufactures: since the productions of nature are the materials of art." §

In like manner the proverb says, that " habit is a second nature ;" and Shakspeare, that " use almost can change the stamp of nature."

So likewise we say that " artificial flowers, or fruit, look as if they were natural:" by the latter word meaning that which is not the work of man's hands.

In a nearly similar sense, we speak of a natural manner, and an artificial manner; a natural voice, and an artificial voice; by *natural* understanding that which would be if man did not make it otherwise.

---

* Pope's Essay on Man, ep. 1. v. 289.

† Goldsmith probably either wrote, or intended to write, *factitious ;* for the bonds of wealth and law, although in a certain sense contrived and fabricated by man, or *factitious*, are by no means unreal and imaginary, or *fictitious*.

‡ Goldsmith's Traveller.

§ Decline and Fall, vol. 1. p. 70.

It appears that the use of *natural*, as opposed to *revealed*, is formed by an analogical application of this sense of nature : natural religion meaning a religion which may be derived from the exercise of our unaided reason, without a revelation from God.*

From the sense of nature as opposed to human institution or ordinance, has arisen the expression *natural child*, signifying a child born out of wedlock, as distinguished from one born after marriage, which is an institution of men.

In some of the writings of Mr. Bentham, the method of *natural* procedure in courts of justice is strongly recommended, and opposed to that of *technical* procedure. It is impossible to suppose that any mode of judicial procedure should be left to the discretion of the judge, guided by no rules. Mr. Bentham must evidently, by natural procedure, have meant procedure governed by certain rules, but by rules different from those commonly established. In this case,

---

* Natural as opposed to *spiritual*, (1 Cor. xv. 44, 46.) signifying the present state of man as opposed to his state after death, appears to be derived from *nature* in the sense of *human condition ;* so likewise in Hamlet, the ghost describes himself as,

> ——— " Confined to fast in fires,
> Till the foul crimes, done in my *days of nature*,
> Are burnt and purged away."

And Hamlet himself afterwards speaks of

> " Passing through nature to eternity."

natural seems to be a vague term of praise signifying that system which, to the writer, seems most expedient.

When, however, we use such expressions as " trade should be left to take its natural course," &c., we mean that trade should be left to take that course into which it would fall if subjected to no regulations or restrictions whatever.*

From a general view of the above examples, it follows that the various significations of nature fall into two classes : 1. It expresses a *positive* idea, as when it means essence, quality, disposition, &c.   2. It expresses a *negative* idea, as when it merely excludes art, or human regulation and contrivance.†   It is from the latter sense of nature, when it denotes the absence of human skill and institutions, connected with a mistaken

---

* " Natural may be opposed, either to what is *unusual, miraculous,* or *artificial.* In the two former senses, justice and property are undoubtedly natural. But, as they suppose reason, forethought, design, and a social union and confederacy among men, perhaps that epithet cannot strictly, in the last sense, be applied to them. Had men lived without society, property had never been known, and neither justice nor injustice had ever existed. But society among human creatures had been impossible without reason and forethought. Inferior animals that unite are guided by instinct, which supplies the place of reason. But all these disputes are merely verbal."—Hume's Essays, App. 3. Works, vol. 4. p. 392.

† " The idea of a natural society is a negative one. The idea of a political society is a positive one."—Bentham, Fragment on Government, p. 13.

belief as to the progress of society, that the famous political theory of the *state of nature* has been derived.* It has been imagined that a cultivation of the moral and intellectual faculties, and an advance in the arts and comforts of social life, have corrupted and debased mankind;† and that the ignorance and barbarism,

---

* The negative sense of this expression is well marked in the explanation of the corresponding French phrase, in the Dictionnaire de l'Académie. " On appelle *état de pure nature*, l'état des hommes sauvages, sans société, et sans lois. "

† It is singular that the doctrine of the possession of wealth being hostile to virtue, should occur in the writings of a person who has composed a treatise on Political Economy. " Prudence (says Mr. Mill, in his Essay on Government, p. 505, comparing the aristocratic body with the rest of the community, *i. e.* the rich with the middle class and the poor) is a more general characteristic of the people who are without the advantages of fortune, than of the people who have been thoroughly subject to their *corruptive operation*." A sentiment of this kind might naturally be expected in Goldsmith's Deserted Village, or in Mandeville's Fable of the Bees: but how is it consistent with a work, of which the object is to point out those circumstances which most favour the productiveness of industry, and the production, distribution, and accumulation of wealth ? It may, however, be said, that, in his work on Political Economy, Mr. Mill described the circumstances which are most favourable to the increase of wealth, in order that they might be avoided: that he shewed how industry may be encouraged, in order that the most effectual mode of repressing it might be perceived: that the knowledge of the best means of increasing wealth implies the knowledge of the best means of diminishing it. Thus his work on Political Economy, would be

prevalent at some early period of the world, were attended with an amount of virtue and happiness unknown in succeeding times. Hence the term, *a state of nature,* has been employed to designate a supposed state of primitive simplicity, before the introduction of the arts of civilization,* and the establishment of government and laws. The phrase itself and the theory connected with it have, in this country, been diffused chiefly by the writings and authority of Locke; though neither he nor any one else has ventured to fix on any time or country which furnishes an example of this form of society, if society it is to be called; and his state of nature is as pure an offspring of the imagination, as Plato's perfect republic, or Sir Thomas More's Utopia. As, however, Locke's account is somewhat diffuse and indistinct, I shall prefer giving Pope's description, in his Essay on Man, of the state of nature, and the change from that state to civilization and government, as being shorter and more explicit. If any one objects to taking an account of a political theory from a poet, let him produce

---

like a treatise on poisons; the object of which is not to recommend the use of the poisons, but to ascertain their antidotes.

* Hence, in familiar language, a *state of nature* is employed to mean a *state of nudity;* clothes being the work of men's hands.

one from a prose writer, which, when it is examined, will be found to be more prosaic or less inconsistent with reason and reality:

> " Nor think in nature's state they blindly trod ;
> The state of nature was the reign of God :
> Self-love and social at her birth began,
> Union the bond of all things, and of man.
> Pride then was not ; nor arts, that pride to aid ;
> Man walk'd with man, joint tenant of the shade :
> The same his table, and the same his bed ;
> No murder cloth'd him, and no murder fed.
> * * * * * * * *
> Ah, how unlike the man of times to come,
> Of half that live the butcher and the tomb ;
> Who, foe to nature, hears the general groan,
> Murders their species, and betrays his own."*

The poet then describes man

> " From Nature rising slow to Art,"

as addressed by the voice of Nature, which enjoins him to take instruction from the lower animals ; for example, to learn the art of building from the bee ; the art of ploughing from the mole ; of sailing from the nautilus, &c. Moreover, to imitate forms of government from the same original :—a republic from the ants ; a monarchy from the bees.

> " Great Nature spoke : observant man obey'd,
> Cities were built, societies were made."

The result of this account seems to be, that in the state of nature God ruled the world ; that is,

---

* Essay on Man, epist. 3. v. 146.

God alone ruled it,—there being no human rulers. Benevolence and self-love existed; but, notwithstanding the existence of self-love, all men lived in concord, and the feeling of pride was unknown. There were no arts or government: men lived with the beasts,* and subsisted exclusively on vegetable food. In the state of nature men killed neither beasts nor men. After some time, mankind learnt, by observing some of the lower animals, to imitate their ways; and having thus invented the arts of social life, upon the same model they formed societies under an established government.

Such is an outline of this puerile theory of the progress of society; untenable from its self-contradictions, even as a hypothesis, and distinctly refuted by facts: a theory which could only have arisen from the distempered imagination of some day-dreamer, and could only have been tolerated by a blind ignorance or wilful neglect of all history. Pictures of this description may delight the mind, when presented to it in an avowedly poetical and fabulous shape, as in the Greek legends of the golden age; but when introduced into a didactic poem, or a philosophical system of government, they shock the reason without amusing the fancy.

* This supposition implies a change in the nature of beasts, as well as of man: for beasts avoid man, and prey upon him, which have never been subject to his attacks.

To refute it in detail would be superfluous; nor indeed need any thing more be said, than that there is no record of such a state of existence, at any time, in any country. No one can doubt, that if a history is shewn to be utterly destitute of historical evidence, it must fall to the ground: yet Locke treats this objection as devoid of weight, and proposes to answer it, by observing that " all princes and rulers of independent governments, all through the world, are in a state of nature," and that members of different communities are, as towards each other, in a state of nature.* These statements are, in a certain sense, strictly true; but they afford no answer to the fatal objection which Locke treats so lightly. The question is, whether there ever was a number of men living together, not forming a society, or recognizing a common sovereign, or an established law of the state; but following a certain law of nature as plain or even plainer to be understood than the positive laws of commonwealths, of which each man is judge in his own cause, and which each has the power to execute for himself; yet never abusing this power, but using it always as calm reason and conscience dictate.† To this inquiry it is answered, that there is no account of such a state of existence, and therefore it is to be

* Locke on Government, b. 2. § 14.
† Ibid. § 13, 8.

rejected as a chimera. On the other hand, Locke replies, that sovereigns are subject to no law, and members of different states acknowledge no common law; and therefore there are persons living in a state of nature. But this reply does not touch the objection which it professes to remove: it is objected that there never was a collection of men living together peaceably before the establishment of a government, all acknowledging a certain law, which each man makes and executes for himself. This objection is not answered by saying that *after* the formation of societies, and the establishment of governments and laws, there are some persons in those societies not subject to the law, and persons in different states who acknowledge no common law. The doctrine of the state of nature may be readily admitted, if it is confined to persons living in civilized communities, and to a period posterior to the establishment of government.

The ancient errors respecting the innocence and virtue of savages, and their superiority over civilized man, have in late times been so generally exploded by the advancement of historical knowledge, more especially since the researches of modern travellers have disclosed the real habits and character of barbarous nations, that scarcely a person could, perhaps, be now found to defend such a theory of the progress of society as is advanced by Locke and Pope;

nevertheless, it is sometimes important that such groundless speculations should be set forth, so that their absurdity may appear, and the doctrines deduced from them be shewn to want a foundation. Many a person might be startled by imperfections dragged into the broad daylight, which would pass unobserved if suffered to remain hidden in their former obscurity. It might indeed have been expected, that when a theory was abandoned by common consent, and never mentioned but to be rejected, the practical deductions from it would have shared a like fate: that " when the brains are out, the man would die." Still we find traces of the belief in a state of nature lingering in many expressions of frequent occurrence, which had their origin in that delusion; and which only owe their currency to an ignorance of the impure source from whence they are derived. It is thus that a theory which, in its day, had a sufficient vogue to transfer its peculiar and technical expressions into common language, may continue, by that means, to influence our reasonings after it has fallen into deserved oblivion; and that its very obscurity may favour the circulation of the errors to which it gave birth.

No one has furnished a more efficacious antidote to the erroneous and mischievous notions respecting the virtues of savages, and the tendency of civilization to corrupt mankind, than

Archbishop Whately, in his lately published Lectures on Political Economy; whose discussion of this subject must afford delight and instruction, even to those who already are most firmly convinced of the principles which it establishes. It is on account of the excellence of this discussion, and the authority which it deservedly carries, that it becomes the more necessary for me to advert to the explanation there given of the expression—" *a state of nature*," as it disagrees with that suggested in the preceding pages.

" There is no good reason (he says) for calling the condition of the rudest savages a state of nature : on the contrary, such language is as much at variance with sound philosophy, as the dreams of those who imagine this state to resemble the golden age of the poets are with well-ascertained facts. The peaceful life and gentle disposition,—the freedom from oppression,—the exemption from selfishness and from evil passions,—and the simplicity of character of savages,—have no existence but in the fictions of poets and the fancies of vain speculators : nor can their mode of life be called, with any propriety, the natural state of man. A plant would not be said to be in its natural state, which was growing in a soil or climate that precluded it from putting forth the flowers and the fruit for which its organization was destined. No one who saw the pine grow near the boundary of perpetual snow on the Alps, stunted to the height of two or three feet, and struggling to exist amidst rocks and glaciers, would describe that as the natural state of a tree, which, in a more genial soil and climate a little lower down, was found capable of rising to the height of fifty or sixty yards. In like manner, the natural state of man must, according to all fair analogy, be reckoned not that in which his intellectual and moral growth are, as it were, stunted and permanently repressed; but one in which his original endowments are, I do not say brought to perfection, but enabled to exercise themselves and to expand, like the flowers of a plant; and especially, in which that characteristic of our species, the tendency towards progressive improvement, is permitted to come into play." *

If *nature* is taken to mean the whole compound of the moral and intellectual faculties and disposition of man, and if *natural* signifies that which is agreeable to the nature of any thing, then it is natural to man to improve his external condition, to regulate his passions, and to cultivate his mental powers; in other words, to

* Whately's Introductory Lectures on Political Economy, pp. 137, 138. The sentiments expressed in the latter part of this passage coincide exactly with the definition of nature given by Aristotle: οἷον γὰρ ἕκαστόν ἐστι τῆς γενέσεως τελεσθείσης, ταύτην φαμὲν τὴν φύσιν εἶναι ἑκάστου : " that which any thing is, when arrived at a state of completion or perfection, I call its nature."—Politics, b. 1. ch. 2.

advance in civilization : and to this course of things he has a natural tendency, in the same way that wealth has a natural tendency to increase at a faster rate than population. But although his *tendency* is to move in this direction, it is not the less *natural, i. e.* consonant with his nature, for him to recede instead of advance in the career of improvement, in the same way that population sometimes increases faster than wealth: as is witnessed by the mighty revolutions that have reduced to misery, ignorance, and barbarism, countries once the seat of gigantic empires, and the home of every art and science ; which have converted the palaces of kings, the sites of vast cities, and the territories of powerful and active commonwealths, into wastes scarcely tilled by a few slaves, or occasionally visited by a roving tribe of barbarians: such instances of national decline and degradation are unhappily too frequent to be called unnatural, or to be considered as monstrous deviations from the ordinary course of human affairs. Although the opinions of those philosophers who conceived that all human affairs revolve in a cycle, and must, after a regular succession of changes, end where they began, are not less mistaken than that doctrine which compares the life of a state with the life of an individual, and teaches that its forces will be impaired by long existence, as a man is enfeebled by old age : yet it is impossible, with some modern historians, to consider the state of mankind as one of perpetual progression, or to flatter ourselves that every retrograde movement will only be a voluntary retreat, by which society collects all its powers in order to enable it to take a more vigorous spring in advance.

In this general sense, therefore, it is *natural* to man to recede, as well as to advance, in civilization ; though his *tendency* is towards improvement. He might, therefore, be in a *natural state,* whether in his original barbarism, or having made some progress in the ascent of civilization, or having again relapsed into his former rudeness. But being in a *natural state* appears to be by no means synonymous with being in a *state of nature,* as Dr. Whately's argument assumes. In the one phrase *nature* signifies that which any thing is, the essence or constitution of any thing; in the other, it expresses the absence of art or human regulation. A state of nature is (if I may for once make use of such a word) a state of *inartificialness.* Men are supposed to be in a state of nature when there are no arts, luxuries, or refinements whatever ; nor any established government and laws. From this state of original simplicity and separateness they emerged into a state of civilization, by learning the useful arts from some of the lower animals, according to Pope; and by forming a government on the basis of the social compact, according to Locke and many other writers. This expression, however, does not imply that it is more natural to man (or more consonant to his nature) to be savage than to be educated; more than the expression a *natural child* implies that it is more natural to mankind to permit a community of women than to establish the institution of marriage : it is a mere negative term to express the non-existence of certain contrivances and ordinances of men. Nevertheless, it is highly probable that the very mistaken notion of a state of nature being more natural to man than a state of arts and government, may be suggested or confirmed by the doubtful form of the expression in question.

The *law of nature* has not been so favourite an expression with modern political writers, as *natural rights;* but has been chiefly used by writers on ethics and jurisprudence. It is a phrase of great antiquity, being used both by the Greek philosophers and the Roman lawyers, and is of a date long anterior to the theory of the state of nature, with which it had originally no connexion. By the moderns, however, the law of nature has often been made an integral part of that theory ; in whose writings (for instance, in those of Locke) it usually signifies, not laws enacted by a legislature, but moral rules, which are binding on men independently of law; and, according to the above hypothesis, were the only rules by which the conduct of men was guided in the state of nature: and which, though unwritten and unascertained, either by common agreement or by the command of a governor, were yet more intelligible and fixed than the established laws of a civilized state.

XV.

LIBERTY.—FREEDOM.—FREE.

LIBERTY and FREEDOM,* as well as *Nature,* have both a positive and a negative sense; and these senses require to be accurately distinguished, in order to avoid the confusions and mistakes which they have so often occasioned.

1. Liberty, in the positive sense, signifies rights, the enjoyment of which is beneficial to the possessor of them. Thus we speak of the liberty of a British subject, meaning certain rights which a British subject may exercise, such as the right of suing out a writ of *habeas corpus* if he is imprisoned without reason.† So it is

* Crabb, (Dict. of Synonyms,) in *Freedom*, says, that " freedom is personal and private ; liberty is public." There is no ground for this distinction: and in the remarks in the text, both words are intended, where only either the Saxon or the Norman form is expressed.

† According to Blackstone, the " spirit of liberty is so deeply implanted in our constitution, and rooted even in our very soil, that a slave or a negro, the moment he lands in England, falls under the protection of the laws, and so far becomes a free man." 1 Com. 127. Upon which passage, Mr. Christian remarks, that " it is not to the soil or to the

said, that " a man has a liberty to use his own
property as he wills, so that he injures not
others ;" for example, that he may ride his
own horse, till his own land, fell his own trees,
&c. ; that is to say, the law annexes these rights
to the right of property, and guarantees the
proprietor against the disturbance of them. In
like manner, we speak of giving one the freedom
of a borough or corporation, *i. e.* conferring on
him the rights and privileges which belong to
the members of such a body. *Liberties,* in the
plural number, when employed with a political
reference, is always equivalent with *rights.**

A second positive sense of liberty, is when it
is used to signify the possession of certain rights
by one part over another part of the community.
In this sense it is opposed to *slavery* or *servitude.*
A freeman is he who is not a slave. In communities where there is a class of slaves, liberty
is a distinction, and the freemen compose a pri-
vileged order in the state.

In a nearly similar sense, Sir James Mackintosh, in his Discourse on the Study of the
Law of Nature and Nations, defines liberty as

air of England that negroes are indebted for their liberty,
but to the efficacy of the writ of *habeas corpus,* which can
only be executed by the sheriff in an English county."

* " The rights, or, as they are frequently termed, the
liberties of Englishmen."—Blackstone, 1 Com. 140. And
see Hale's Analysis of the Law, § 13.

consisting in *security against wrong ;* * *i. e.* in the enjoyment of the protection of the sovereign against a breach of law; in other words, in the possession of legal rights. Hence he properly infers, that " liberty is the object of all government:" for all government must have for its end, the investing of all the members of the community with certain legal rights. But there is likewise an ulterior end, or a standard whereby these rights are to be judged; viz. their tendency to produce the well-being of the society.

It is sometimes imagined that all laws are a restraint on liberty; and that liberties, such as that of moving a man's body, or tilling his own field, are fragments of original natural liberty, which have been left untouched by the encroachments of the legislature, and which man would enjoy without the existence of a government. " Political or civil liberty, (says Blackstone,) which is that of a member of society, is no other than natural liberty, so far restrained by human laws (and no further) as is necessary and expedient for the general advantage of the public."†
In this view, liberty is made to seem independent of law, and all law as an abridgment of liberty. There is, indeed, no doubt that a wandering savage, who has occupied a plot of ground, possesses the power of using his limbs, and cultivating

* P. 59. † 1 Com. 125.

his land : but to suppose that these liberties are, under a settled government, only spared by the legislature, and not created and secured by it, betrays a complete misapprehension of the nature of legal rights, and the acts of a sovereign body. Under an established government, no absence of law can be beneficial; because every act which may be done by man must be either permitted or prohibited by the legislature. What the law does not forbid, it sanctions ;* and will protect those who do it from obstruction. If a legal prohibition to do an act were removed, without a legal permission to do the same act being granted, the repeal of the prohibition would be nugatory; for although the law would not prevent any one from doing the act hitherto prohibited, it would not secure him against the interruption of others. The absence of a disabling law, without the presence of an enabling law, would be of no avail, as the act of the subject would be neither legal nor illegal; it would lie without the pale of the civil jurisdiction; and might would be the only right, as in an unsocial state. All acts of persons living under an established government, must be either lawful or unlawful ; if they are unlawful, the law

* " What the law does not enjoin, it forbids," ἃ μὴ κελεύει, ἀπαγορεύει, says Aristotle, Ethics, b. 5, ch. 11, but not quite correctly, for the law *permits* many things which it does not prohibit.

prohibits them from being done; if lawful, the law
authorizes them to be done, and guarantees the
enjoyment of the right or liberty which it confers.
Therefore, in a state of society, all liberty arises
from the existence, and is secured by the protection, of law. The liberty of speaking, or of
moving, is as much a right conferred by law, as
the right of suing on a bill of exchange, or of
arresting a debtor; for without law there would
be no security for its enjoyment.*

2. In its negative sense, liberty or freedom
signifies not the enjoyment of a beneficial right,
but the exemption from a painful duty, or the
absence of unnecessary or hurtful restraint; as
the *freedom of trade—liberty of the press—free
discussion*. In this sense, liberty is opposed to
oppression or *tyranny;* of which more will be

---

* " Men (says Sir J. Mackintosh) are more free under
every government, even the most imperfect, than they would
be if it were possible for them to exist without any government at all : they are more secure from wrong, more undisturbed in the exercise of their natural powers, and therefore
more free . . . than if they were altogether unprotected against
injury from each other."—Discourse on the Law of Nature
and Nations, p. 59. If liberty consists in security against
wrong, not only are men living under a government *more*
free, *more* secure, and *more* undisturbed, than men living
without a government, but without a government there is
absolutely *no* security, and therefore no liberty. Security
is derived from the protection of a third party besides the
injured person and the wrong-doer, which in a savage state,
by the hypothesis, does not exist.

said when we come to the subject of FREE GOVERNMENTS.

Persons who speak of liberty in general, of the blessings of liberty, of the cause of liberty, may be understood to use this word to denote an immunity or exemption from certain restrictions which they consider as pernicious to society.*

Liberty is likewise used to signify *independence of a foreign power; i. e.* an absence of foreign dominion. In its first negative sense, it refers to the relations of the members of a state, as towards each other: in the second, to the relation of the whole state to another state. In the first, the exemption is from oppressive power; in the second, from *all* power, whether oppressive or inoppressive. Thus, according to Sir William Temple, " a free nation is that which has never been conquered, or thereby entered into any conditions of subjection."† So likewise Gibbon, in speaking of the first deliverance of Britain from the Roman yoke, says, that " the restoration of British freedom was not exempt from tumult and faction."‡ In like manner we

---

* " Every one (says Montesquieu, treating of the different significations of this word) has given the name of *liberty* to the government which agrees with his habits, or inclinations."—Esprit des Lois, b. 11. ch. 2.

† On the Original and Nature of Government, Works, vol. 2. p. 87.

‡ Decline and Fall, ch. 31.

speak of the *free towns* of Germany and Italy, meaning those towns which were independent of external control, and administered their own government. It is true that these cities enjoyed what is termed a free government; but the exemption from external dominion, and not from domestic tyranny, appears to have been the origin of their name. This too is very frequently the sense of ἐλεύθερος and ἐλευθερία in the Greek writers;* and with good reason, as the evils of foreign dictation and dominion were more severely felt in the states of Greece than the evils of native tyranny.

A state may be free in the second sense, without being free in the first sense; *i. e.* it may be independent, without having a free government: nor is the converse by any means impossible, as we know from the example of the kingdom of Poland, as regulated at the Congress of Vienna, which was an attempt to reconcile freedom with dependence,† *i. e.* to establish a commonwealth with a foreign prince at the head of it; and from the government of Hungary, which still exists.

Another negative signification of liberty is when it denotes the absence of imprisonment, in the sense of *being at large*. Thus we say

* See Wachsmuth, Hellenische Alterthumskunde, vol. 1, part 2. p. 447.
† See Malchus, Statistik, § 99.

that a captive has regained his liberty, when he escapes from the place of his confinement.

Liberty, therefore, may mean both the possession of rights and immunity from duties ;* in both of which senses it appears to be taken

---

* Blackstone divides rights into absolute and negative; and absolute rights he defines to be " such as would belong to persons merely in a state of nature, and which every man is entitled to enjoy, whether out of society or in it."—1 Com. 123. He then says, that " the absolute rights of man are usually summed in one general appellation, and denominated the *natural liberty* of mankind. This natural liberty consists properly in a power of acting as one thinks fit, *without any restraint or control,* unless by the law of nature."—Ibid. 125. Thus far it appears, that absolute rights are not positive rights conferred by a legislature, but a mere absence of legal restraint, or *natural liberty.* Afterwards, he lays it down, that " the absolute rights of every Englishman, taken in a political and extensive sense, are usually called their liberties :" and proceeds to explain how these "rights and liberties" exist by virtue of certain acts of Parliament.—Ibid. 127. Here, then, *liberties* are positive rights conferred by the legislature, having no connexion with *natural liberty.* Finally he says that " the rights themselves, thus defined by these several statutes, consist in a number of private immunities; which will] appear, from what has been premised, to be indeed no other, than *either* that residuum of natural liberty which is not required by the laws of society to be sacrificed to public convenience, *or else* those civil privileges which society hath engaged to provide, in lieu of the natural liberties so given up by individuals."—Ibid. 129. At length, we find that these " absolute rights" may be either the immunity from certain legal duties, or the possession of certain legal rights, or perhaps both at the same time. It is, perhaps, difficult to conceive greater confusion and obscurity of thought, than is displayed in this laboured discussion.

by those who make liberty the end of government; *i. e.* they make it consist in the enjoyment of all beneficial rights, and the absence
of all pernicious duties. From this explanation,
however, it is at once seen, that liberty cannot
be the ultimate end of government, as there
must be some measure by which the expediency
and inexpediency of these several rights and
duties is to be estimated. Persons who employ
this phraseology are perhaps liable to be misled,
by considering only the negative side of liberty,
into an opinion that the removal of *all* restrictions is desirable, and that the goodness of a
government is to be estimated by the absence
of regulation. This opinion is supported by the
often quoted sentence of Tacitus, "that the
most degenerate states have the greatest number
of laws;" "In corruptissimâ republicâ plurimæ
leges;"—a position not only not true, but the
very reverse of the truth, as the progress of
civilization is to multiply enactments, in order to
suit the extended relations and the more refined
and diversified forms of property introduced by
the improvement of society. It is such an absence of restrictions, abolished merely for the sake
of promoting liberty, without any regard to the
public good, that is termed *licentiousness*, (when
that word has a political sense,) and sometimes,
improperly, *anarchy*, which word, though properly
it means an absence or privation of government,

is often (as will be shewn below) used figuratively to express an insufficiency of restraint.

The theory of *natural liberty* is an endeavour to reconcile the advantages of a social, with the immunities of a savage life. According to this doctrine, man, in a civil state, is supposed to possess some of the freedom from legal restraint which exists in a state of nature, yet, at the same time, to be entitled to the protection of the government.* This theory, therefore, involves a self-contradiction. A man cannot claim an exemption in right of his civilized condition, while he refuses a burden in right of his savage condition. He cannot deny the existence of legal duties, while he asserts the existence of legal rights. He cannot call for the assistance of the sovereign power, given only upon a condition which he repudiates. If a man objects to being imprisoned for debt, on the ground that it is an infringement of his natural liberty, in the same breath he demands the aid of the law against a person wrongfully imprisoning him. If he will not obey the law which orders him to prison, how can he appeal to the law for protection against those who force him to it ? " How can any man claim, (as Burke has justly inquired,) under the conventions of civil society, rights which do not so

---

* See Blackstone, 1 Com. 125.

much as suppose its existence,—rights which are absolutely repugnant to it?"*

Generally, however, the phrase in question, on account of the vagueness and uncertainty of both the words which compose it, conveys no precise notion; and Locke's position,—that men are naturally free,—may be considered no less unmeaning and insignificant than the opposite position of his adversary Filmer, that men are *not* naturally free. The argument by which the latter writer establishes his assertion; viz. that men are born in subjection to their parents, and, being under their authority, are not by nature free,† is founded on the customary confusion of law and morality; for though a child, in a savage state, owes a moral duty to his parents, he is bound to them by no legal obligation.

The idea of natural liberty in a savage state is, an exemption from the duties imposed by government, and an entire command of a man's actions, so far as he is not hindered by superior force. The idea of natural liberty in a social state, as already explained, is derived from the doctrine of the *social compact*, as delivered by Locke, Rousseau, and others. This theory teaches that mankind, when in the state of nature, made a compact by which the whole

---

* On the French Revolution, p. 88.
† Locke on Government, b. 2. § 6.

surrendered to a part of the community their
natural rights and natural liberty, on condition
of being well governed; and if this condition
is not fulfilled, (of the fulfilment of which they
themselves are the only judges,) they may at
once resume their natural rights and natural
liberty.* After the conclusive objections of
Hume,† Paley,‡ and Whately,§ to this theory,
and after the remarks already made on Rousseau's explanation of sovereignty, on the meaning
of legal rights, and on the state of nature, it
would be unnecessary to examine this subject
in detail; nor indeed does this historical account
of the origin of all governments require any
other answer than that " it is a mere fiction,—
the supposition of a thing which never had any
existence." ‖

It may perhaps seem extraordinary that so
acute and sagacious a writer as Locke should,
in laying the foundations of his theory of government, have preferred to reality and truth

---

* Hobbes's state is formed by a compact, but made between subject and subject, and not between subject and
sovereign: the condition being that, if you will surrender
your right of self-government, I will surrender mine.—Leviathan, p. 2. ch. 17.

† Essay on the Original Contract, part 2. essay 12.

‡ Moral and Political Philosophy, b. 6. ch. 3.

§ Bampton Lectures, pp. 238—297.

‖ Edinburgh Review, vol. 17. p. 424. See also Sir J.
Mackintosh on the Law of Nature and Nations, p. 57.

his own 'exsufflicate and blown surmises' about
a state of things which he must have known to
be purely imaginary.* But he had doubtless
made up his mind as to the conclusion to be
proved; and people are accustomed to be satisfied with very slight evidence for the assertions
which they make in accounting for a position
which they consider as unquestionable. "This
is not the first instance in the world (as Mr.
Bentham has remarked in relation to another
subject,) where the conclusion has supported
the premises instead of the premises the conclusion."†

The same easy faith in accepting a doctrine,
which, *if true*, would account for the subject to
be explained, may be discerned in Aristotle's
definition of a law,—that it is determined by
the common agreement of the state;‡—and
Cicero's definition of a state,—that it rests on

---

* " Were one (says Hume) to choose a period of time
when the people's consent was the least regarded in public
transactions, it would be precisely on the establishment of a
new government. In a settled constitution, their inclinations are often consulted; but during the fury of revolutions,
conquests, and public convulsions, military force or political
craft usually decides the controversy."—Essay on the Original Contract.

† Principles of Morals and Legislation, vol. 2. p. 278.

‡ Rhet. ad Alex. c. 1. λόγος ὡρισμένος καθ' ὁμολογίαν
κοινὴν πόλεως, μηνύων πῶς δεῖ πράττειν ἕκαστα. Compare
Athenæus, lib. 11. p. 508. A.

a *consensus juris ;* * or that the law is established
by general consent : for although it is true
that legal duties, imposed by the sovereign, are
binding in the same way as duties to which a
party becomes liable by entering into a contract,
and that many of the attributes of law are explicable on the hypothesis of a covenant ; yet
it is certain that no such covenant ever exists ;
nor if it had existed, could a contract be of any
value which there is no third party to enforce.

According to the *historical* theory of the social
compact, the existing government of a state was
settled by agreement of the whole community
at an original convention ; and that agreement
having once been actually made, its reciprocal
obligations are transmitted through all the succeeding generations of rulers and subjects, every
new person becoming (as it were) the member
of an old partnership upon ascertained conditions. Now as this account is liable to the
fatal objection that no such agreement ever was
made, and therefore could not be perpetuated,
another theory has been devised, which may be
termed the *fictitious* theory of the social compact; which declares that, although no compact
that obedience to governors is conditional on
their governing well was in fact ever made, yet
it is *implied,* and may be assumed to exist,

* De Rep. lib. 1. c. 25.

though it never did exist.* This doctrine will require a closer examination, on account of the proneness of mankind to acquiesce in any explanation of a position which they wish to see established; and to be satisfied with fiction where truth is not to be had.

In common language, a thing is said to be implied, when it follows from another by a certain inference. Thus, the making of a bargain implies two parties to it; a servant implies a master; a husband implies a wife; the power of writing implies the power of reading; &c. In all these instances the existence of the thing implied is a necessary condition for the existence of the thing which affords the implication, and, therefore, the one cannot happen without the other having preceded it. In the language of the English law, implication has a different meaning, and is nearly equivalent with *fiction*. Where a thing is presumed to exist under circumstances in which it might probably exist, though it has not existed, or (what comes to the same) is not proved to have existed, there is said to be an implication of law as to its existence. Thus, in many cases, a contract is

---

* " The original contract of society, which though perhaps in no instance it has ever been formally expressed at the first institution of a state, *yet in nature and reason must always be understood and implied* in the very act of associating together."—Blackstone, 1 Com. 47.

implied where no contract was made ; a promise to pay is implied where no promise to pay was made ; the meaning being that the legal consequences are the same as if such contract and promise had been really made, and their existence may be assumed in argument without proof. It is thus evident that neither on the common nor on the legal explanation of implication can the assumption of the social contract be supported. It cannot be inferred from the existence of government, as all must admit that governments *may* exist without a previous convention. Nor can it be considered as a legal fiction; for a legal fiction is a supposition avowedly false, but treated as if it were true, for the imagined convenience of administering the law. A legal fiction without the sanction of law is a mere absurdity; and, therefore, it cannot be pretended that the social compact, which serves as the foundation of all law, derives its own force from the existence of law.

How far a belief in the doctrine of the social compact still exists, may be uncertain ; but it is not uncertain that the popular notions as to the natural liberty and equality of mankind have their origin in this political system, and that they are frequently entertained by those who are ignorant of the polluted source to which these expressions may be traced. The confusion of the exercise of sovereign power with tyranny, or of the coercion of government with oppressive restraint, has further contributed to foster these erroneous conceptions : for thus, not only does it appear that man in a civilized state may, if he pleases, consider himself as a savage in respect of his legal obligations, but the very act of governing is represented as tyranny and misrule. Hence it is that Rousseau can describe the English people as only being free during the election of members of parliament ; and as soon as these are elected, relapsing again into a state of slavery. Reasoners of this description should at least be consistent, and, as they cannot serve two masters, should cleave alone to the mammon of barbarism ; never lifting up their eyes to the arts of civilization and the institutions of government ; but imitating those, who

" Led their wild desires to woods and caves,
    And thought that all but savages were slaves."

If, therefore, the statement of the doctrine of the social contract enables us to deduce the pedigree of these vulgar errors, and to shew, not only that such opinions are false, but also to track them to their fountain-head, it may point out to some persons the startling character of the assumptions on which their belief must be founded ; who may thus, when the *connexion* of the theory and its results is made evident to their minds, cease to resemble those

weak-minded enthusiasts, who continue to practise the superstitious observances enjoined by
a creed which they have abandoned, and to
worship the idols which they acknowledge to
be mere wood and stone.

XVI.

FREE GOVERNMENT.—ARBITRARY GOVERNMENT.—TYRANNY.—DESPOTISM.— ANARCHY.

A FREE government is not a government in which liberty prevails, or in which there is an absence of inconvenient restraints and oppression on the part of the sovereign power; but a government in which there is a plurality of rulers, and fixed laws respected by the administrative authority. A free government is thus opposed to an arbitrary or despotic government, such as the Roman, French, or Austrian empires. In this sense, Hume* opposes free states to absolute monarchies, and Rousseau speaks of " the difference between *free* and *monarchical* states;"† *i. e.* between states where the

---

* " The provinces of absolute monarchies are always better treated than those of free states." Parc 1. essay 3.

† Contrat Social, liv. 3. ch. 8. According to Sir James Mackintosh, " as general security is enjoyed in very different degrees under different governments, those which guard it most perfectly, are by way of eminence called *free*. Such governments attain most completely the end which is common to all governments. A free constitution of government,

sovereignty belongs to one, and where it belongs to several. Substantially, therefore, the division of states into free and arbitrary governments, coincides with the division into republics and monarchies, in the strict use of those terms. It may be observed, that a state is not the less a free government because it contains a class of slaves; in the same way that a constitution is called democratic, in respect of the freemen or citizens alone, without any consideration being had of the number of the slave population.

It is a common mistake to suppose that *liberty* can only be enjoyed under a *free* government; and that in despotisms the people are subject to the absolute rule of a master, from which in free countries they are exempt: whereas in all governments the sovereign power must reside somewhere; and, wherever it resides, must be absolute. Thus, even Cicero says, that " in a monarchy the people do not enjoy liberty; which consists not in having a just master, but in having no master at all;"* a condition

and a good constitution of government, are therefore different expressions for the same idea."—On the Law of Nature and Nations, p. 60. However, one who thought with Hobbes that absolute monarchy is the best form of government, would probably not call *that* a free constitution. On the difference between free and despotic governments, see likewise Bentham's Fragment on Government, p. 113.

* " Desunt omnino ei populo multa, qui sub rege est, in primisque libertas ; quæ non in eo est, ut justo utamur

altogether incompatible with the existence of a government, and the exercise of sovereign authority.

Arbitrary or *absolute* monarchy is opposed to *limited* monarchy;* and this is properly a division, not of *monarchies*, but of *kingdoms* or governments of which a King is chief, founded on the numbers of a sovereign body. In a state where the prince is *alone* sovereign, it is said that the monarchy is absolute or arbitrary ; in a state where he is only part of the sovereign body, it is said that the monarchy is limited.

Tyranny is properly opposed to mild inoppressive rule, and has no relation to the numbers of the governing power. Thus Burke says, that "free governments have committed more flagrant acts of tyranny than the most perfect despotic governments which we have ever known." So likewise Sir Walter Raleigh, in his History of the World,

---

domino, sed ut nullo."—De Rep. l. 2. c. 23. The *kingdom* of which Cicero here speaks is governed " *unius* perpetua potestate," that is to say, it is a pure monarchy.

* Sometimes *a free monarchy* is used as equivalent to a *limited monarchy :* in the following passage, however, from one of Lord Bacon's Tracts, it occurs in a directly opposite sense. " It is impossible an elective monarchy should be so free and absolute as an hereditary, no more than it is possible for a father to have so full power and interest in an adoptive son as in a natural."—*Of a war with Spain*, vol. 5. p. 239. Here *free* means *unchecked*, *unlimited*, as Tacitus says, " Nec regibus *libera* aut infinita potestas." (Germ. 7), and *natural son* means *own child*.

remarks, that " that which we properly call tyranny is a violent form of government, not respecting the good of the subject, but only the pleasure of the commander. I purposely forbear to say (he continues) that it is the unjust rule of one over many; for very truly doth Cleon, in Thucydides, tell the Athenians, that their dominion over their subjects was none other than a mere tyranny; though it were so that they themselves were a great city, and a popular estate."* The following passages from the same author, will also serve to shew that tyranny is opposed to lenient or moderate rule, and may be exercised by many no less than one: " Now concerning the tyranny wherewith a city or state oppresseth her subjects, it may appear some ways to be more moderate than that of one man; but in many things it is more intolerable."† Again: " Many tyrants have been changed into worthy Kings, and many have ill used their ill-gotten dominion, which, becoming hereditary to their posterity, hath grown into the most excellent form of government, even a lawful monarchy. But they that live under a tyrannical city have no such hope: their mistress is immortal, and will not slacken the reins, until they be pulled out of her hands, and her own mouth receive the bridle of a more mightier

---

* B. 5. ch. 2. p. 812.   † Ibid. p. 813.

charioteer."* And afterwards : " The moderate
use of sovereign power being so effectual in
assuring the people unto their lords, and consequently in the establishment or enlargement of
dominion; it may seem strange that the practice
of tyranny, whose effects are contrary, hath been
so common in all ages."† The following passage of Locke, though less precise in its language,
clearly points out that tyranny is common both
to monarchies and republics : " It is a mistake
(he says) to think this fault (viz. tyranny) is
proper only to monarchies; other forms of
government are liable to it as well as that : for
wherever the power that is put in any hands for
the government of the people, and the preserva-
tion of their properties, is applied to other ends,
and made use of to impoverish, harass, or
subdue them to the arbitrary and irregular commands of those that have it; there it presently
becomes tyranny, whether those that thus use it
are one or many."‡

Tyranny, however, being the *abuse* of sovereign
power, is sometimes confounded with the *mere
exercise* of it, and sometimes with the exercise of
it *by one person,* or despotism. Thus, according to a writer in the Edinburgh Review, " the
difference between a *free* government and a

---

* B. 5. ch. 2. p. 813.   † Ibid. p. 817.
‡ On Government, b. 2. § 201.

tyrannical one, consists entirely in the different proportions of the people that are influenced by their opinion, or subjugated by force."* " Solon (says Mr. Mitford, in his History of Greece,) carefully providing for the responsibility of ministers, committed *absolute sovereignty* immediately to the multitude, who could be responsible to none. . . . . He intended, indeed, that the councils of the Areopagus and of the four hundred, should balance the authority of the popular assembly ; . . . . but against *sovereign power* committed immediately to the people at large, no balance could avail. Interested demagogues inciting, restraint was soon overborne, and so the Athenian government became . . . . a *tyranny* in the hands of the people."† Of the numerous errors contained in this passage, our present purpose only requires us to notice the confusion of *sovereign* with *tyrannical* power ; which may be likewise discerned in the following extract from one of Mr. Canning's speeches : " All power is, or ought to be, accompanied with responsibility. Tyranny is irresponsible

* Vol. 6. p. 145. A division of governments into free and arbitrary, stated in another volume of the same review, coincides with that into monarchies and republics, *stricto sensu.* " All civilized governments may be divided into *free* and *arbitrary ;* or, more accurately for our present purpose, into the government of England and other European governments" (written in 1807). vol. 10. p. 11.

† Vol. 5. p. 11.

power. The definition is equally true, whether the power be lodged in one or many; whether in a despot exempted by the form of government from the control of law, or a mob whose numbers put them beyond the reach of law. Idle, therefore, and absurd to talk of freedom where a mob domineers!"* If by power, at the outset of this passage, sovereign power is meant, sovereign power not only ought not, but cannot, be subject to responsibility. The succeeding argument appears to stand thus: because tyranny is irresponsible power, and because the dominion of the mob is irresponsible power, the dominion of the mob is tyranny. Such reasoning, however, is obviously unsound. If, instead of saying that tyranny is irresponsible power, Mr. Canning had said that irresponsible power is tyranny, he would have saved his argument, but at the cost of one of his premises; for all *sovereign* power, whether tyrannically used or not, is irresponsible. Nor (as has been already stated) is tyranny merely irresponsible power, but irresponsible power exercised in an oppressive and hurtful manner. Thus the power of the English Parliament is irresponsible, but not tyrannical. The power of Trajan, or Louis the Sixteenth, was irresponsible, but not tyrannical. The power of the republics of Athens and Carthage over their allies, of the

* Canning's Speeches, vol. 6. p. 379.

Emperor Napoleon over his subjects, was irresponsible, and also tyrannical. Tyranny having no reference to the number of the governors, sovereign power may be wielded as tyrannically by ten thousand as by ten, and by ten as one.

It thus differs essentially from *despotism*, which is the sovereign rule of one person. Despotism, however, is sometimes used incorrectly in the modern sense of tyranny, (for with the ancient sense of tyranny its proper meaning nearly coincides,) to signify the oppressive government of any number. Thus Mr. Mitford says, that an "irregular tax, not unknown where single despots have ruled, with the improper name of free gift, was frequently exacted by the despotic democracy of Athens."* And again : " Despotic governments, whether the power be in the hands of one or of a multitude, will have a near resemblance of character. . . . .We find, indeed, many marks of resemblance between the Turkish despotism and the Athenian democracy."† A "despotic democracy," and "a despotic government of a multitude," are, properly, contradictions in terms : but this abuse of language enables Mr. Mitford to insinuate (without proving) that, because the Athenian democracy has some points in common with the

---

* History of Greece, vol. 5. p. 19.
† Ibid. p. 21.

despotism of Turkey, it is therefore a *tyrannical* government.

According to Montesquieu, there are three kinds of governments; the republican, the monarchical, and the despotic. Republican government is when the whole or a part of the people has the sovereign power; monarchical, when a single person governs, but by fixed and established laws; while despotic government is when one person, without laws and rules, decides every thing by his will and his caprices.* Montesquieu here makes two kinds of monarchical government; one in which the prince rules according to fixed law; the other in which he rules according to the fancy of the moment. The same quality had been before pointed out by Aristotle, as characteristic of the government called by the Greeks τυραννίς, which word is most accurately rendered by *despotism;* but he extends the distinction further by applying it

---

* Esprit des Lois, liv. 2. ch. 1. See above, p. 56. Malchus, in his *Statistik und Staatenkunde,* § 96, divides the governments of the European states into — 1. Autocracies. 2. Limited monarchies. 3. Republics, which are subdivided into aristocracies and democracies. This division does not agree with that of Montesquieu, whose class of republics properly comprehends limited monarchies : but it coincides exactly with that of Hume, who discusses the question, " Whether the British government inclines more to absolute monarchy or to a republic," being itself a limited monarchy. Essays, part 1. essay 7.

to some oligarchies where a small number govern without established laws ; and to some democracies where the people do not suffer fixed laws to be administered by the regular authorities, but carry on the government by means of decrees in each particular case.* The difficulty under which this principle of division labours is, that in all governments, whatever seems good to the sovereign is law, whether it be a general rule enacted for the guidance of the executive power in all cases arising after its enactment, or a special decision passed on the occasion, when the necessity occurs. There is no doubt that the difference between these two classes of governments is immense ; inasmuch as one of the chief benefits of law is that it furnishes all persons in the community with a fixed rule whereby to guide their conduct. Perfect justice (if such a thing were possible), administered by a tribunal without reference to previous decisions or statute law, would be far less advantageous than an imperfect system administered according to known rules. But that the distinction between a legal monarchy

---

* " Another kind of oligarchy (he says) is when the son succeeds the father, and not the law but the rulers govern. This, among oligarchies, corresponds to despotism (τυραννίς) among monarchies, and the worst kind of democracy among democracies." — Politics, b. 4. ch. 5. The democracy in which no fixed laws exist, is described in the preceding chapter.

and a despotism is, that in the latter all things
are decided at the moment by the will of the
prince, cannot be admitted; because the will
of the prince, whether exercised in the form of
a permanent statute or of a temporary ordinance,
is equally law. The same may be said of oligarchies and democracies, in which the executive
is merged in the legislative power. Montesquieu's object doubtless was, to make a distinction between the French monarchy of his own
time, and the violent and tyrannical monarchies
of which there have been too many examples;
but the point of distinction which he has chosen
depends rather on the character and disposition
of the reigning prince, and the mode of his administration, than on any essential attribute of
the form of government.

Anarchy properly expresses an absence of all
government; an entire cessation of the exercise
of sovereign power. Improperly, it is used to
signify a feebleness or supineness of the sovereign, in consequence of which the subjects are
not sufficiently restrained or coerced. The following passage from the Edinburgh Review ably
describes the manner in which unfair arguments are founded on this ambiguity,— a description which applies with equal force to the
use made of the ambiguity of other political
terms. After saying that the question of political change had been stated as if despotism or

anarchy were the only alternatives, the writer thus proceeds—

" The instrument with which a great part of the delusion is wrought is—the grand instrument of delusion—ambiguity of language. *Despotism* is a pretty definite term; it is, where the sovereign is subject to little or no regular control of his power, and has scarcely anything to dread but from the chance of resistance in the body of the people. *Anarchy* is one of the most vague and ambiguous words in language. It means, in the way in which it is used by the friends of despotism, the utter dissolution of all government, and also every intermediate stage of government between that and absolute power. They paint as strongly as possible, and it is impossible they can paint too strongly, the evils to which the dissolution of government gives birth. This they call anarchy; and this term, with all the terrors which it brings, they endeavour to associate with every form of government but the baleful one to which it is the tendency of their endeavours to chain or to reduce mankind." *

* Edinburgh Review, vol. 17. p. 427.

XVII.

POWER.—AUTHORITY.—FORCE.

THE word *power*, when used in a political sense, appears to signify the possession of the means of influencing the will of another, either by persuasion or threats; or of constraining his person by the application of physical force. Thus ministers or party-leaders possess power, because they may influence the conduct of many persons by the promise of favours or the threat of injury : so it has been remarked, that knowledge and wealth confer power. Sovereign rulers and parents may forcibly constrain their subjects and children, when the motive arising from the fear of pain does not suffice to determine the will.

In civilized societies, power, which, in default of the desired influence on the will, is supported by the sovereign, and by the application of the physical strength at his command, is called *authority*. In other words, authority is power sanctioned and supported by the law. Thus we speak of the authority of government ; the authority of an officer over his soldiers ; of a father over his children, &c.*

Sometimes, however, *power* is used as synonimous with *authority*. For example, every person who takes the oath of supremacy declares his belief " that no foreign prince, prelate, person, state, or potentate, hath any jurisdiction, *power*, superiority, preeminence, or authority, ecclesiastical or spiritual, within this realm."† Now, it is clear, that the Pope, in his character of head of the Roman Catholic church, exercises power, in the ordinary sense of that word, within these realms, although it is not a power protected by the law, or authority.

When it is said that the power of rulers differs from the power of a band of conspirators only in degree,‡ the proposition is true as to the compulsive sanction, which in both cases is brute

* " By authority (says Hobbes, part 2. ch. 16) is always understood a right of doing any act : " that is, if we assume that sovereigns have rights.

† See also in 10 Geo. 4. c. 7. s. 2, the oath administered to Roman Catholics ; where the terms are slightly varied, and (what is singular) the word *power* is retained, while the word *authority* has been rejected. For, according to the common acceptation of these terms, the Pope has *power*, but not *authority*, in this kingdom.

‡ " The power of rulers is not, as superficial observers sometimes seem to think, a thing *sui generis*. It is exactly similar in kind, though generally superior in amount, to that of any set of conspirators who plot to overthrow it."—Edinburgh Review, vol. 50. p. 111.

force ; but the moral effect of the exercise of sovereignty, the means of influencing the wills of subjects without resorting to extremities, although these are fully as important as its physical force, are not taken into the account. It is true that all governments have been founded by force, and are maintained by force, but its influence in states where it is least used is commonly overlooked, for the following reasons, which may be applied to many subjects besides that in question.

The effects or consequences of any law, institution, or system, may be of two kinds, positive or negative : positive, when they cause a certain event to occur; negative, when they prevent it from occurring. Thus the positive effect of education is to make a man know many things of which he would otherwise be ignorant : its negative effect is to prevent him from committing many crimes, and falling into many errors, of which he would otherwise be guilty.* Now it is a very common error, in judging of political measures, especially of institutions in actual existence, to overlook this latter kind of negative effects, and not to give them sufficient

* This latter kind of effect is quaintly expressed by Polonius in the well-known lines :—

――――― " Now remains
That we find out the cause of this effect ;
Or, rather say, the cause of this defect ;
For this effect defective comes by cause."

weight. For this reason, institutions meant only to have a negative effect are sometimes thought unnecessary or hurtful, when in fact they are completely successful. For example, it is settled that in all questions litigated in courts of law, (with some exceptions which need not here be specified,) the presumption is in favour of the defendant and against the plaintiff or claimant. This presumption is established in order to prevent unfounded claims being brought forward, or innocent persons being harassed with vexatious actions; and because it *has* this negative effect, and plaintiffs, *therefore,* are generally on the right side, Mr. Bentham concludes that the rule is inexpedient, and that the presumption ought to be in favour of the defendant.* If a penal system was completely efficacious, there would be no crime; when, probably, some one would discover that punishments are superfluous, and would propose to abolish them. The same oversight is not unfrequently committed as to the operation of force on government. We are told that government must be founded on the national will, and can only exist with the consent of the people. No one doubts that it is desirable that the government should be beloved by the people; and that the people will, in general, know how to appreciate a good

* See Bentham on Evidence, by Dumont, b. 6. ch. 2.

government; but that all governments subsist by force, and that force ultimately is the sole check on wrong-doers, is equally certain. The existence and administration of a criminal law are necessary to the existence of a state; and no criminal law can be carried into effect without the means of applying physical constraint to those who infringe it. Nevertheless, the knowledge that force may, if necessary, be applied, induces offenders to submit without resistance. The fear of coercion renders the use of coercion unnecessary. The criminal walks willingly to the gaol and the scaffold, well knowing that if he does not go with his will he will be forced to go against it. The cases, therefore, in which force is *actually* applied are not many; and as the effect of the law authorising the use of force is to render its use unnecessary, it has been thought that force is of little benefit in civilized societies, and might be banished from the resources of government, although it is in fact the keystone on which all government must ultimately rest.* " In the community of nations, (it has been remarked,) the first appeal is to physical force. In communities of men, forms of government serve to put off the appeal, and

* " The power of the sovereign is nothing else than the power—the actual force of muscle or of mind—which a certain part of his subjects choose to lend for carrying his orders into effect."—Ed. Rev. vol. 20. p. 326.

often render it unnecessary. But it is still open to the oppressed or the ambitious. " *   Not only, however, is it open to the oppressed or ambitious against the government, but it is indispensable to the government against the oppressed or ambitious. Superior force is as necessary in order to punish a criminal as it is to repel an invading army or quell domestic sedition.

* Ed. Rev. vol. 50. p. 111.

XVIII.

PUBLIC.—PRIVATE.—POLITICAL.—CIVIL.— MUNICIPAL.

Public, as opposed to *private*, is that which has no immediate relation to any specified person or persons, but may directly concern any member or members of the community, without distinction. Thus the acts of a magistrate, or a member of a legislative assembly, done by them in those capacities, are called public ; the acts done by the same persons towards their family or friends, or in their dealings with strangers for their own peculiar purposes, are called private. So a theatre, or a place of amusement, is said to be public, not because it is actually visited by every member of the community, but because it is open to all indifferently ; and any person may, if he desires, enter it. The same remark applies to public houses, public inns, public meetings, &c. The publication of a book is the exposing of it to sale in such a manner that it may be procured by any person who desires to purchase it : it would be equally published, if not a single copy was sold. In the language of our law, public appear to be distinguished from private acts of parliament, on the ground that the one class directly affects the whole community, the other some definite person or persons.

Political signifies that which relates to a state, or a society of persons comprising several families, and united for the purpose of government. Hence man is called a political animal, as having a tendency to form a communion more extensive than a family; that is, an union of parents and children, together with their slaves or servants. *Social* has a wider signification than *political;* for man would be a social animal, if he merely lived in families: but, in order to be a political animal, he must form collections of families, or states.* In like manner, political science is that science which treats of the government of sovereign communities : political questions are those questions which relate to this matter : a politician is a person who occupies himself about such questions, &c. Hence, political economy is that science which is concerned about the economy of a state, which examines the same subject matter in respect of a political

* See Locke on Government, b. 2. § 77. To the "public relations of magistrates and people," Blackstone opposes " the private economical (*i. e.* family) relations" of master and servant, husband and wife, parent and child, guardian and ward, 1 Com. 422. On the distinction between families and states, see Niebuhr, History of Rome, vol. 1. p. 264. Eng. tran.

community, which domestic economy examines
in respect of a family. Originally, the words economy and economical were employed exclusively
(according to their etymology) to signify the
management of a family; and, in this sense,
they are constantly used by Xenophon, whose
Œconomics have no connexion with political,
and are confined alone to private management.
The same remark applies to the first book of the
Œconomics attributed to Aristotle; and it is
one of the many marks by which we are
enabled to discover that the second book of
those Œconomics is the work of a later writer
than the first: for in this treatise the word
economy has reached its modern acceptation,
and is applied to national, as well as domestic
finance. The Œconomics of Cicero, though
written at a more recent period, retained the
ancient use of the word, and were confined
within the original limits of the science, as being
chiefly derived from those of Xenophon.* The
analogy by which the word economy has been

---

* Οἰκονομία was rightly explained by Cicero to mean not
the management of a house, but of a man's entire property :
" non gubernationem villæ, sed dispensationem universæ
domus." (Vol. 4. part 2. p. 472. ed. Orelli): οἶκος, in
the language of the Athenians, being different from οἰκία,
and signifying not *house*, but *estate and effects* generally.
Cicero's treatise contained three books; the first, on the
domestic duties of the mother; the second, on the duties of
the father abroad; the third, on agriculture (ibid. p. 476).

transferred from the affairs of a family to those
of a state, to signify the regulation of its income
and expenditure, and the general arrangement
of public finance, seems perfectly unobjectionable : nor can I perceive why the term Political
Economy should not be considered as an appropriate and convenient name for this important
department of political science.   The term
Catallactics, which has been proposed as a
substitute for it,* even if its derivation were
correct,† would not be sufficiently comprehensive, if we understand an exchange to bear its
common meaning of a voluntary or uncon-
strained dealing between two parties.   For
although the payment of taxes may be ultimately resolved into an exchange, yet taxes
are levied from a man without his consent,
and by virtue of the sovereign authority.   The
science of exchanges would not, therefore, properly include the doctrine of taxation, which has
always been correctly considered as belonging
to the province of Political Economy.

Much importance has been attached by many
political writers to the distribution of rights and
wrongs into certain classes, determined by their
public or private character.   Thus Blackstone

---

* Whately's Lectures on Political Economy, p. 6.

† The word καταλλακτικὸς never has any reference to
exchanges, but means *reconciling* or *forgiving.*   In Aristot.
Rhet. b. 1. ch. 9. § 31, it has the sense of *practicable.*

says, that " wrongs are divisible into, first, *private wrongs*, which, being an infringement merely of particular rights, concern individuals only, and are called civil injuries ; and secondly, *public wrongs*, which, being a breach of general and public rights, affect the whole community, and are called crimes and misdemeanours." * This division is correct, though the reasons here given for it are untenable. A crime is called a public wrong, and a civil injury is called a private wrong, not because one respects the community, the other an individual; but because one offence is prosecuted by a public magistrate, and the offending party is punished for the benefit of the community ;—the other is prosecuted by the party wronged, and the offending party is compelled to make him compensation for the harm which he has sustained. The same act may be a crime in one country and a civil wrong in another, although its effects on individuals or the whole community are necessarily identical. Thus, according to the Mosaic law, adultery was punished by the death of both offenders, and was a crime: in England it is only a civil injury, for which the husband has a remedy against the adulterer by suing him for a pecuniary compensation, and against the adulteress by suing her for a divorce. If adultery was made a crime in this

* 1 Com. 122.

country, its effects, as towards individuals or the whole community, would of course be unaltered, although its legal complexion would be changed.

In like manner, political rights are not distinguished from private rights by their *tendency*,— for all rights either tend, or are supposed to tend, to the public good,—but by the *purpose for which they are exercised.* A private right is a right exercised for the immediate and peculiar benefit of the individual who possesses it : a political right is a right exercised not for the immediate or peculiar benefit of any individual, but for the good of the whole community. Thus the right of property may tend equally to the public good with the right of voting for the election of members of a representative body; but the one is exercised for the direct and separate benefit of the proprietor, though indirectly it tends to the benefit of the community ; the other is not exercised for the direct and immediate benefit of the voter, though ultimately it may tend to his good.

From a comparison of the remarks made in a former place on the subject of vested rights,*

* Above, p. 24. Since the remarks here referred to were printed, it has been suggested to me that the phrase *vested rights* is in fact devoid of meaning ; that it is never applied generally to any class of rights ; but that, when certain rights are attached, it is used as a specious and delusive

it results that no *political* rights can belong to
the class of *vested* rights, which must necessarily

phrase, by persons who think that those rights ought to be
preserved, *vested* having merely an intensive force, and
being equivalent to *sacred* or *inviolable*. According to this
interpretation, the use of the particular word *vested* would
be explained by supposing, that those who invented or
employ this expression, have wished to represent, that a
right so *vested* or lodged cannot be *divested* or taken away
by the legislature. If this explanation is correct, the phrase
vested rights would be a mere absurdity, and would belong
to the same class of expressions as natural, indefeasible, inalienable, indestructible, &c. rights, examined above, p. 23.
Now, there is no doubt, that the phrase *vested rights* is often
used in a dishonest manner, merely for the sake of raising
prejudice, and creating a vague and unfounded alarm, by persons who attach to it no definite meaning. But, if it were
laid down that all political expressions, which are sometimes,
or even frequently used in a senseless manner, are therefore
in their origin unmeaning and absurd, the political vocabulary would be contracted within very narrow limits. I am
very far from feeling confident that the explanation which I
have just mentioned may not be correct, and that the explanation which I have proposed may not be wrong: but, on
considering the peculiar kind of rights to which, when they
are called in question, the term *vested* is *usually* applied, it
seems to me probable, that the notion and epithet of *vested*,
as applied to rights, have been derived from the *investment
of capital*: that, when a man has invested his capital in a
certain manner, with a reasonable assurance of the permanency of a law, the right of property which by this investment he has acquired is called a vested right; and it is
considered as conferring on him a moral claim upon the
legislature for such a delay or compensation, as will enable
him either to withdraw his capital, or to reimburse himself
for his loss. If this view of the subject is correct, *vested
rights* would be an admissible phrase, signifying a limited

be rights of property, for the peculiar advantage of their possessors.

Civil is sometimes used in nearly the same sense as *political,* as when we speak of civil society, civil liberty; and, in fact, these two are the corresponding words of the Latin and Greek languages, *civilis* standing in the same relation to *civitas* as πολιτικὸς to πόλις. Civil, however, has, in our language, obtained two additional meanings; 1. When, as a division of laymen, it is opposed to *military* and *naval;* civil service, for example, being any service, not ecclesiastical, which is not concerned with the army or navy:* and, 2. When it is opposed to *criminal, i. e.* civil and criminal law,—a distinction which has just been explained.

Municipal is commonly used in reference to a corporate town, or some body politic subordinate

and definite class of rights: if the other view is correct, *vested rights* would be a dishonest and deceitful expression, improperly applicable to all rights, but properly applicable to none.

* Blackstone first divides the people into the clergy and laity (1 Com. 376); and the laity "into three distinct states, the civil, the military, and the maritime" (Ibid. 396). He then proceeds to say, that "the civil state consists of the nobility and the commonalty." Now, as a nobleman or a commoner may be either a clerk, a soldier, or a sailor, it is quite clear that either the division is incorrect, or the last statement is false. Blackstone indeed admits this inaccuracy: but he should have *avoided* his error, as well as *confessed* it.

to the sovereign; in which sense we speak
of municipal institutions, regulations, &c. The
municipia of the Romans were provincial cities,
which retained certain privileges and exemptions,
and possessed an independent subordinate jurisdiction and authority. Blackstone, however, has
perverted this term and made it synonymous
with civil or national; for which perversion he
assigns a most singular reason, viz. that he calls
the law of a state municipal law in compliance
with common speech, and then proceeds to say,
that in common speech it has *not* that meaning.
" I call it municipal law (he says) in compliance
with common speech; for though, strictly, that
expression denotes the particular customs of
one single *municipium*, or free town, yet it may,
with sufficient propriety, be applied to any one
state or nation which is governed by the same
laws and customs." *

* 1 Com. 44. See Bentham on Morals and Legislation,
vol. 2. p. 263, n.

XIX.

PROPERTY.—POSSESSION.—ESTATE.— ESTATES OF PARLIAMENT.

It does not fall within the scope of the present inquiries to investigate the legal meaning and incidents of property and possession: but, for the sake of many political questions, it is desirable to give a general outline of the notions conveyed by these two terms, and of the distinction between them.

Without, then, attending to the peculiarities of any one legal system, possession may be described as the actual use or occupation of any thing for a man's own convenience, pleasure, or profit. Thus a man is possessed of the clothes which he wears, of the house which he inhabits, of the goods in his premises, of the horses which he rides or drives, of the farm which he cultivates, &c.

Property, or the right of property, is the right of ownership of any object, without regard to the actual use of it; and it implies the right of obtaining possession, at some time or other·

Thus a man has a property in a field or house which he lets, in a book which he lends, &c.

Property and possession may, of course, coincide; but there may be possession without property, and property without possession.*

Each of the words, property and possession, (which, it may be observed, are often used as synonymous,) bears a double meaning; inasmuch as both signify the right itself, and the object of the right. Thus, in such expressions as the security of property, infringement of property, the right itself is meant; but when we speak of trespassing on another man's property, division of property, &c., it is the *object* of the right which we mean.

The word estate is liable to a similar ambiguity. Thus a freehold estate, an estate tail, an estate for life, &c., mean certain rights; but when we speak of a large estate, the boundaries of an estate, the map of an estate, we mean a portion of land, the object of the right.

It may be here useful to remark that the word estate is often used by English writers, in reference to the constitution of their own country, with a meaning which better deserves the name of a blunder arising from ignorance, than an ambiguity caused by the imperfection of language. " The Court of Parliament (says Lord

* See Blackstone, 3 Com. 176, 177.

R 2

Coke) consisteth of the King's Majesty, sitting there in his royal politic capacity, and of the three estates of the realm."* " The constituent parts of a Parliament (says Blackstone) are the King's Majesty, sitting there in his royal political capacity, and the three estates of the realm ;— the lords spiritual, the lords temporal (who sit together with the King in one house), and the commons, who sit by themselves in another. And the King and these three estates together form the great corporation, or body politic, of the kingdom."† Those persons who are acquainted with the history, either of this or any European kingdom, both during and after the middle ages, might reasonably think it superfluous to quote passages from well-known authors to establish a well-known fact. Nevertheless, many writers of high reputation have confounded the three estates of the English realm with the three powers or branches of the constitution or sovereign legislature, and have thought that the King is an estate. For example, we find even in Paley, such a passage as the following : " By the balance of interest, which accompanies and gives efficacy to the balance of power, is meant this ; that the respective interests of *the three estates of the empire* are so disposed and adjusted, that whichever of the three shall attempt any

* 4 Inst. 1. † 1 Com. 153.

encroachment, the other will unite in resisting it. If the *King* should endeavour to extend his authority by contracting the power and privileges of the *Commons,* the *House of Lords* would see their own dignity endangered," &c.[*] So it is said, in the Preface to Lord Clarendon's History, that " the true interest of this kingdom is supported *non tam fama, quam sua vi ;* its own weight still keeps it steady against all the storms that can be brought to beat upon it, either from the ignorance of strangers to our constitution, or the violence of any that project to themselves wild notions of appealing to the people out of Parliament, *as it were to a fourth estate of the realm :*"[†] where it is evidently meant that the people out of Parliament are a fourth power, in addition to the King, Lords, and Commons. Two of the propositions condemned in the celebrated Oxford decree, passed in 1683, are, that " the sovereignty of England is in the three estates, viz. King, Lords, and Commons ; " and that " the King has but a coordinate power, and may be overruled by the other two : "[†] doctrines manifestly false, as the King, Lords, and Commons, are not the three estates of the realm ; nor, if they were, could the King be overruled, either in an executive or legislative capacity, by

[*] Moral and Political Philosophy, b. 6. ch. 7.
[†] P. 11. ed. 1826.
[‡] See Wilkin's Concilia, vol. 4. p. 611.

the Lords and Commons. Yet several writers appear to have thought that these positions were improperly condemned; imagining, probably, that the language of this decree implied that the sovereignty did not reside in the three branches of Parliament, but in the King alone.*

* See, for example, Lingard's History of England, vol. 13. p. 341. Edinburgh Review, vol. 41. p. 27.

XX.

COMMUNITY OF GOODS.

COMMUNITY of Goods * may mean that no
right of possession or property whatever is
sanctioned by the legislature or protected by
the executive; in which case, not only all land
and all products of agricultural and manufacturing industry would be the prey of the first
taker, but even things in possession could not
be retained, and a man might be stripped of the
clothes on his body, or turned out of the house
which he inhabited, by any stronger man. If
goods were common to this extent, possession
could only be maintained, and would frequently
be acquired, by superior force. When men live
after this manner, their state is so miserable,
insecure, comfortless, and degraded, that, perhaps, its adoption has never been seriously recommended by any political guide.

It may likewise mean, that the legislature
recognises no right of *property*, but recognises

* By the word *goods*, I here mean all things which may
become the objects of property, whether movable or im-
movable.

the right of *possession*. In this case, a man's clothes, food, implements, and money, the house in which he resides, his beasts of burden, &c. would be protected by the law, as well as land in his occupation; but no *property* in land or other things could exist; nor could any one let lands or houses, lend money on interest, deliver goods on credit or to be conveyed by a carrier from place to place; or, in short, part with any thing out of the immediate occupation or possession of himself, his servants or his agents, if, indeed, a man would be permitted by law to occupy or possess any thing by means of another person. The inconveniences of such a state of things to the rich are obvious, but it does not appear that they would in any degree be balanced by countervailing advantages to the poor. A perfect community of goods would effectually put an end to inequality of wealth by making all equally poor: but a limited community of goods, admitting possession and excluding property, would not prevent inequality of wealth, and would press with greater hardship on the poor than on the rich, inasmuch as it would prevent the existence of credit, by which those who are occasionally exposed to want, profit more than those who perpetually have the enjoyment of superfluities. Under such a law, theft would be a crime and punishable as such, as all goods would necessarily be in the possession of *some* person; and there might be large capitalists employing large numbers of workmen. There would be profits of stock and wages of labour, but no interest of money, or rent of land.

The reason why the inequality of wealth presses severely on the poor, and gives the rich and the middle classes an advantage at every turn of the market, is, that, in disagreements about the rate of wages, the latter can refuse to continue their workmen, and, being able without material inconvenience to live for a short time on their capital, can hold out against the demands for an increased payment; whereas the poor, having little or no capital to fall back upon, are soon compelled to come into the terms of their employers. The same is the case with persons who live, not on the profits of stock, but on the wages of labour, if their wealth, derived from other sources, is sufficient to maintain them for a considerable time without employment. Thus, although the legal profession has always of late years been greatly overstocked, the rate of payment has never varied. The numerous lawyers who, though they are perfectly competent to perform their duties, have never any legal business, prefer living on their own fortunes to offering to practise at a rate lower than that sanctioned by the opinion and usage of their profession. So, likewise, the fees of physicians, (if we except a reduction for the sake of convenience caused by a change in the value of the gold coin,) have not, like the wages of poor labourers, varied continually from time to time, but have remained the same for many years. But the wages of agricultural labourers are constantly varying, and are, by the working of competition, driven down to the lowest point. In this manner the competition of the poor is more powerful, and operates more to their disadvantage, than the competition of the rich and middle ranks, whether capitalists or labourers.

It does not, however, very clearly appear, in what way it is proposed to remedy the evils attributed to the inequality of wealth, by taking away the right of property, and retaining the right of possession. With regard to land, such a law would compel all persons to cultivate the whole of their own estates ; and thus, by preventing their division into farms and holdings of a manageable size, would increase the difficulties of agriculture, and raise the price of provisions. In manufactures, as the whole concern is in the immediate occupation of the capitalist, no change would be produced, except the impossibility of giving or receiving credit, of the manufacturer selling goods without instant payment, or of borrowing money in any pressure of mercantile distress or alarm. All that branch of internal and external commerce which consists in carrying the goods of the manufacturer to the

market of the consumer, would be at once destroyed, if possession conferred entire dominion
over commodities, and the merchant would, as
in ancient times, be compelled to sail in the
same ship with his own merchandises.*

Aristotle, in combating Plato's arguments in
favour of a community of goods, says, that at
first sight, people are captivated by the plausible and benevolent appearance of that scheme,
especially when it is urged that such a community would put an end to litigation, perjury,
and disputes concerning property; which latter
argument Aristotle answers by saying, that
these evils arise, not from the institution of
property, but from the depravity of mankind.†
Doubtless they do; but it is not the less true,
that, if there was no property there would be no
disputes about property. The true answer is, that

---

* Mr. Millar, in the following passage, considers the existence of the right of possession without the right of property
as a mark of a barbarous state of society. " Among barbarians in all parts of the world (he says) persons who belong
to the same family are understood to enjoy a community of
goods, and to be all jointly subjected to the same obligations. In those early ages, when men are in a great measure
strangers to commerce, or the alienation of commodities,
the right of *property* is hardly distinguished from the privilege of *using* or *possessing*; and those persons who have
acquired the joint possession of any subject, are apt to be
regarded as the joint proprietors of it."—Historical View of
the English Government, vol. 1. p. 190.

† Politics, b. 2. ch. 5. p. 317. D.

litigation, or the power of calling in the assistance of the law to relieve a party harmed, has
been invented as a remedy for the evils caused
by the forcible or fraudulent abstraction of that
which is in the possession of others, and has
been produced by their labour. The lawsuit is
not the *cause* but the *remedy* of an evil which
would otherwise be remediless. A lawsuit may
be an evil, but the administration of justice has
been established on the express ground that it is
an evil far less than those which it redresses or
prevents. In like manner, it might with perfect
truth be said, that a community of goods would
extinguish the crimes of stealing, forging, de-
frauding, &c., in the same manner that a community of women, as proposed by Plato, would
put an end to adultery and illicit concubinage.
Nevertheless, although the world would be relieved of the names of these vices, it would
equally suffer from the mischiefs which they
produce. Society would not the less be injured
by the rights of universal plunder of goods and
promiscuous intercourse with women, because
those acts were not called by certain names
which signify the breaches of the rules meant
to repress them. If a revenue system was
wisely organized, the name of smuggling would
be unknown, but the evil itself, as well as its
name, would be banished. Not so under a
system of community of goods and women :

there would be the insecurity of property, and debasement of female character, with the consequent evils of indolence, ignorance, improvidence, and neglect of children : only those who caused these evils would not be called thieves and adulterers.

The modern advocates of a community of goods have, so far as I am acquainted with their writings, dealt much in vague and general assertions of the benefits to be derived from the equality of wealth, and the evils arising from its inequality, and have given florid descriptions of a state of universal harmony and concord, which they would represent as the natural result of their system.   But they have altogether omitted to make any detailed statement of the extent to which they would carry their community ; nor have they shewn, either that the existence of government and civilization is compatible with an absence of the right of possession, or that an abolition of the right of property while the right of possession remained, would produce an equality of wealth: unless indeed, by an equality of wealth, they mean an equality of poverty.   Instead of aiming at the conviction of competent judges by solid reasoning, they have often indulged in passionate declamation, or dogmatic assertion ; faithfully copying the wildness, the absurdity, and the fanciful reveries of their great leader, though without a particle of the varied and beautiful imagery and captivating rhetoric, which, in spite of all its incoherence and all its folly, will, to the end of time, make even the most sober-minded recur with delight to the Republic of Plato.

INDEX.

SCIENTIFIC DIVISION OF GOVERNMENTS.

(See page 52.)

GOVERNMENTS.

Where one is Sovereign.

Monarchy.

Where several are Sovereign.

Republic,
or
Commonwealth.

Where a Majority of the adult Males
are Sovereign.

Democracy.

Where a Minority of the adult Males
are Sovereign.

Aristocracy.

POPULAR DIVISION OF GOVERNMENTS.

(*See* Malchus, Statistik, § 96.)

GOVERNMENTS.

Where an Emperor, King, Prince, or Duke, is Head of the State.

Empire, Kingdom, Principality, Duchy; (Commonly called *Monarchy*.)

Where an Emperor, King, Prince, or Duke, is not Head of the State.

Republic.

Where such Head of the State is alone Sovereign. *Autocracy; Arbitrary* or *Absolute Monarchy*.

Where he is not alone Sovereign. *Limited Monarchy*.

Where a Majority of the adult Males have a direct legal Influence on the Formation of the Sovereign Body. *Democracy*.

Where they have not. *Aristocracy*.

INDEX.

A.

AMBIGUITIES, innocent, 10.

ANARCHY, 225.

ARISTOCRACY, the form of government, 52, 53, 54 ; defined, 79, 123 ; its meanings as the name of a class, 79, 156 ; its meanings confounded, 104, 106, 107, 134.

ARISTOPHANES, his distinction between poverty and beggary, 151, 160.

ARISTOTLE, his δικαιώματα πόλεων, 12 ; on tyrannical democracies, 38 ; on the power of the majority of a nation, 48 ; his division of governments, 53 ; definition of democracy, 85, 157, 164 ; his account of mixed governments, 93 ; examined, 102 ; his remarks on the middle class, 161 ; his definition of nature, 192 ; on the province of law, 200 ; his definition of law, 209 ; on governing without laws, 223 ; the Œconomics attributed to, 235 ; on community of goods, 251.

ARNOLD, Dr. on the enmity of the rich and poor, 169.

AUTHORITY, 227.

B.

BALANCE OF POWERS, 89, 97, 115.

BEGGARS, 151.

BENTHAM, Mr. on the meanings of *law*, 15 ; objects to calling the Athenian state a democracy, 87 ; on legal presumptions, 230.

T

D.

D'ALEMBERT on mixed governments, 91.

DEMOCRACY, 52, 53, 54 ; defined, 84 ; improperly applied to governments where the right of suffrage is extensive, 84.

Δῆμος, 119.

DESPOTISM, 53, 54 ; its meaning, 222, 226.

DIONYSIUS on mixed governments, 108.

E.

ECONOMY, 235.

EDINBURGH REVIEW, on hereditary royalty, 71 ; on mixed government, 111 ; confounds aristocracy the government, with aristocracy the class, 107 ; its classification of governments, 113 ; on the meaning of the word people, 120 ; on free governments, 219 ; on anarchy, 225 ; on force in government, 228, 231.

EFFECTS, positive and negative, 229.

ELECTORAL, confounded with sovereign body, 123, 132, 136.

Ἐλευθερία, 203.

ESTATE, 243.

ESTATES OF THE REALM, 243.

EXTREMES defined, 143.

F.

FAMILY, 234.

FEDERAL GOVERNMENT, 116.

FIELDING, his definition and division of the poor, 155.

FILMER, Sir Robert, on natural liberty, 207.

FORCE, its use in government, 228.

FREE GOVERNMENTS, 215 ; co-extensive with republics, 216 : free monarchy, 217 ; towns, 203.

FREEDOM,—see LIBERTY.

G.

GENTLEMAN, its meanings, 80.

GIBBON, his definition of monarchy, 62.

GOVERNMENT, its meanings, 1—3 ; mixed, 58, 89 ; federal and national, 116 ; problem of, stated, 126 ; free, 215.

FINIS.

R. CLAY, PRINTER, BREAD-STREET HILL.